THE OVERSEAS LIST

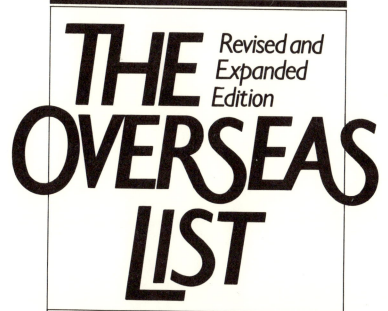

THE OVERSEAS LIST

Revised and Expanded Edition

Opportunities for Living and Working in Developing Countries

David M. Beckmann
Timothy J. Mitchell
Linda L. Powers

AUGSBURG Publishing House • Minneapolis

Preparation of this revised and expanded edition of *The Overseas List* was made possible by a grant from Church World Service. Royalties from the sale of this book will be used in the preparation of future editions or contributed to Church World Service.

THE OVERSEAS LIST—Revised and Expanded Edition
Opportunities for Living and Working in Developing Countries

Copyright © 1985 Augsburg Publishing House

Scripture quotations unless otherwise noted are from the Revised Standard Version of the Bible, copyright 1946, 1952, and 1971 by the Division of Christian Education of the National Council of Churches.

Library of Congress Cataloging-in-Publication Data

Beckmann, David M.
  THE OVERSEAS LIST.

  Bibliography: p.
  Includes indexes.
  1. Americans—Employment—Developing countries.
I. Mitchell, Timothy J., 1959–   II. Powers,
Linda L., 1961–   III. Title.
HF5549.5.E45B42   1985   331.7'02   85-22851
ISBN 0-8066-2181-8

Manufactured in the U.S.A.   APH 10-4865

       3   4   5   6   7   8   9   0   1   2   3   4   5   6   7   8   9

Contents

ONE

About This Book

- If you are thinking you might like to live and work in a developing country,

- If you would like to spend just a year or two abroad, or if you would consider a career that would involve frequent stays in Asia, Africa, or Latin America,

- If you are 20 years old and just starting out, or 40 and ready for a change, or 60 and wondering about volunteer work abroad after retirement,

this book is for you.

It is a comprehensive review of nearly all the ways that U.S. citizens come to live or travel in developing countries. It will be useful to those looking for a job or scholarship that would take them to the Third World, and it may provide insight and information to others who want to understand U.S. relations with the developing countries in more detail.

But we have written especially for Christians who are looking for opportunities for *service* among the many jobs and study programs listed. We have not presumed to omit any organization from our list because of doubts about the value of its work. Our purpose, however, is not just to recruit people for jobs in developing countries, but to recruit them for Christian service.

Karen Yamashita, a librarian at the Counseling Center of the University of California, Berkeley, wrote us about the first edition of *The Overseas List:*

The strength of *The Overseas List,* and the reason I recommend it to our clients, is in its particular orientation; the Christian approach to service, especially in developing countries, makes it unique in the international books genre. The thoughtful comments, with recommended background reading on various issues, are very helpful to a certain type of searcher for information. For a more general audience, I especially applaud your comprehensive indices. To divide references by occupation and country is unusual—and extremely gratifying for a reference librarian trying to quickly aid a patron.

We have included all sorts of ways people get to live and work in developing countries: short-term or lifelong, on subsistence wages or on high salary, in villages or in air-conditioned suburbs. Some are opportunities for people without much training to visit the Third World and perhaps be useful, while others require advanced degrees and a long-term commitment.

There are also a host of opportunities to live in the United States doing work related to developing countries—handling the foreign affairs of U.S. government and business, lobbying for change, teaching and learning about the Third World at U.S. universities or in U.S. churches, working with foreign students or refugees. Some stateside work may be more influential in the developing countries than the work of Americans living abroad. This book is focused, however, on opportunities involving residence or travel in developing countries.

By "developing countries" we mean most of Asia, Africa, and Latin America. The developing countries are extremely diverse economically and culturally, with perhaps only one characteristic in common: they are less affluent than the more industrialized nations. Sometimes the developing countries are referred to as the "Third World," a term coined during the 1950s to distinguish them from the two ideological blocs, capitalist and Communist, of industrialized countries.

This book is based on our own experience, extensive library research, interviews with professionals in specialized areas, and direct contact with virtually all the organizations listed to confirm that our information is correct and up to date.

We have given the most recent price information available to us in 1985 for many publications, fees, airfares, and the like, but prices are subject to frequent change. So *before you mail your check for a book, for example, confirm its current price with the publisher.*

The following general books on international opportunities may also be of use to you:

Casewit, Curtis W. *How to Get a Job Overseas*. New York: Arco Publishing, Inc., 1984. $6.95. Chatty, anecdotal, realistic, and readable.

Foreign Policy Association. *Guide to Careers in World Affairs*. New York: Foreign Policy Association, Inc., 1982. $4.95. Thinner and a bit dated. A good section on private nonprofit organizations.

Griffith, Susan. *Work Your Way Around the World*. Cincinnati: Writer's Digest Books, 1983. $10.95. How to travel on and on, stopping for a few weeks or months now and then to pick fruit, wait on tables, or care for children.

Kocher, Eric. *International Jobs: Where They Are, How to Get Them*. Menlo Park, Calif.: Addison-Wesley Publishing Company, 1984. $8.95. First-rate and well-organized, with good preliminary sections on academic preparation, job strategies and other such topics, as well as long lists of addresses. Particularly strong section on business, banking, and consulting.

Powell, James. *The Prentice-Hall Global Employment Guide*. Englewood Cliffs, N.J.: Prentice-Hall, Inc., 1983. $7.95. We call this book to your attention because, while widely marketed, it is not very thoroughly researched or useful. We don't recommend this one.

Sheehan, Gerard F. *Careers in International Affairs*. Washington, D.C.: Georgetown University, 1982. $10.00. Excellent and comprehensive, with a particularly strong section on research organizations. We recommend it above all the others. The 1982 edition was not very widely marketed, but you can get it by writing to the School of Foreign Service, ICC 487, Georgetown University, Washington, DC 20057. Sheehan is working on an updated version of the book.

You should also do your own original research. In the chapters that follow, we suggest many specialized references; if your local library doesn't have the books you need, order them from the publishers or through interlibrary loan. If you have access to a career-placement office, use it. Ferret out other sources of information, too, checking with friends or friends of friends for one-of-a-kind opportunities abroad. If you are a student, your school may have its own foreign-study scholarships and exchanges. If you are employed, your company (or a related company) may have work abroad for which you are especially qualified.

The job market is constantly changing, and your chances for landing a spot overseas are best when new opportunities are just opening up. To learn about them, you might keep your eyes open to newspapers and professional journals for job advertisements and articles about new contracts or programs that imply opportunities in developing countries. Seek out up-to-date information from knowledgeable people. Start a notebook of promising leads, including names and addresses of contacts and a running list of actions you plan to take in your search.

We don't recommend mass mailings to the many agencies we list. One reader of the first edition sent her resume to virtually all the private development agencies described in Chapter 3; she got back lots of form rejection letters, and many agencies didn't respond at all. This reader received more serious responses only when she wrote more careful letters to a select group of agencies and then followed up with telephone calls.

If you haven't worked abroad before

Many of our readers are people who have not lived in developing countries before.

If you are young and single and think you might someday like to spend a couple years in a developing country, do it now. As people grow older, it usually becomes more and more difficult for them to pull up roots. Also young people are usually adept at living on a low budget—roughing it. Finally, some volunteer and educational programs are specifically designed with young people in mind; when agencies hire people with advanced technical skills and experience, they often require that applicants have previous overseas experiences.

Some young people start out with unrealistic expectations, although few as unrealistic as those of this man who wrote us in response to the first edition of *The Overseas List:*

I am in search of an exciting summer experience abroad. I am 20 years old and a college freshman. I need loads of information on the subject and count heavily on you people to pull through in the clutch. I am particularly skilled in all types of athletics, mainly soccer, track and field (pole-vaulting), diving and gymnastics. My primary goal is to gain a memorable experience in a foreign country. I just need enough $ to survive while the trip across the waters is on me. Thanks a bunch.

The fact is that it's tough to get that first assignment abroad. We've also been in contact with an extremely well-qualified couple (he the chief financial officer of a large company, she an industrial engineer and MBA) who have been unable, despite thorough search, to find anyone willing to place them in a position of service abroad at subsistence wages.

The cost of sending people to a developing country and getting them settled makes any organization hesitant to give someone a first assignment abroad. This is especially true now, when many U.S.-based programs in developing countries and most of the developing countries themselves are in a period of heightened cost-consciousness. A person going to a developing country for the first time may have lots of energy and optimism to contribute but will usually have some difficulty getting oriented (especially if language is a problem). What's more, first-timers seldom want to commit themselves for more than a year or two, so they only begin to become truly effective shortly before they are ready to leave.

Most people find they gain much more than anyone else from the first year of their first stay in a developing country. For many people that year is one of the most stimulating, enriching experiences of their lives. But the intensive learning process that is likely to make the experience so meaningful to you must be counted as a training cost for any organization that wants you to get a job done for them.

So if this will be your first time abroad, you must either have some specialized skill that is much in demand, or someone must subsidize that first year—a scholarship program, for example, or perhaps an organization that is willing to invest in your potential to contribute to their work over a longer period. You may need to provide the "subsidy" yourself—by working for a lower salary than you could get at home, and perhaps by buying your own airline ticket too.

People who have not lived in a developing country before may find Chapter 2 of this book especially helpful. It talks about motives for going, including Christian motives. It also describes the economic difficulties that many developing countries are facing and how the job market for U.S. citizens who want to work in developing countries has tightened.

Chapter 3 is about private development agencies, like Church World Service or CARE. Most of the people who work for these agencies are experienced professionals, not inexperienced staff or short-term volunteers. If you haven't worked in a developing country before, and especially if you don't have much work experience in the United States, then your best chance is with one of the private development agencies that regularly use short-term volunteers (pp. 28-32 and the agencies marked with asterisks on pp. 35-60). An alternative to service abroad is working in the United States for one of the private organizations trying to influence public policy (pp. 63-68). Such organizations sometimes do more good for people in developing countries than agencies with programs abroad, but U.S.-based policy groups don't, of course, offer people who haven't been abroad before that invaluable direct exposure to a Third World situation.

Chapter 4 is about church missions. Many of the agencies listed in Chapter 3 are also church-related, but their main purpose is economic and social development. The missions listed in Chapter 4 are directly involved in evangelism and church building. They may also do development work, but usually on a smaller scale and in close connection with Christian preaching and teaching. Missionary agencies, too, rely primarily on experienced, long-term staff. But there are large programs for evangelical Protestant youth who want to spend a year, or even a summer, doing mission work abroad, and quite a few of the missionary agencies in other theological traditions also have programs for short-term volunteers. Protestant mission agencies that use short-term personnel are marked with asterisks in the list on pp. 79-89, and Roman Catholic agencies that send short-term personnel are listed on pp. 92-95. In addition, the churches are unique in the richness of their international person-to-person networks. As noted on p. 77, you may be able to use this network to get in touch with grass-roots church people in a developing country who would be willing to help you learn about their country and find useful work there.

All of Chapter 5, about opportunities for study in developing countries, will be of interest to people who are looking for their first stay abroad. Many opportunities for study abroad are expressly intended for students or other people who haven't had experience in developing countries before. Some of the best opportunities for living and working in developing countries are concocted by the traveler himself—perhaps drawing on a ready-made opportunity, but somehow giving it a special twist (pp. 110-13). Finally, tourism (p. 114) is an opportunity open to virtually everyone, and tourism can be considerably more worthwhile than the usual round of museums and beaches.

Chapter 6 includes many opportunities for teachers, including teachers who haven't been abroad before. One internationally prized skill that virtually all U.S. citizens have is the ability to speak English, and many people have earned their keep during their first stay in a developing country by teaching English (pp. 119-21).

International organizations (Chapter 7), the U.S. government (Chapter 8), and business (Chapter 9) generally require previous overseas experience of the people they hire to work abroad. But first-timers should find Chapters 7, 8, and 9 helpful in thinking about possible careers with an international dimension. Many people who eventually end up as U.S. Foreign Service officers or international consultants start with an initial short-term experience— study abroad, for example, or work for one of the private development agencies that use volunteers.

Within the U.S. government, the Peace Corps is still the main source of opportunities for people who haven't worked in developing countries before (pp. 152-53). International organizations and U.S. government agencies that work mainly with developing countries also hire a few interns, research assistants, and secretaries that have not had previous overseas experience (pp. 129-30, 132-38, 140-42, 147, 156-57), but these positions rarely involve travel.

Relatively few businesses recruit people for international work; most recruit people for the company in general, and, when international opportunities arise, they send veteran employees. The main opportunities abroad for relatively inexperienced people are in commercial banking, construction contracting, the travel business, and perhaps consulting. We've included special sections on those areas of business in Chapter 9 (pp. 183-94).

Chapter 10, about living in the Third World, is particularly useful for people who haven't already had the experience. The information about saving money on taxes and on airplane tickets is worthy of special note.

Chapter 11 offers reflections on service in developing countries from a Christian perspective. Whether on their first venture outside the United States or as veterans of many years in developing countries, U.S. Christians should make career decisions both prayerfully and intelligently.

Acknowledgments

A grant from Church World Service allowed Timothy Mitchell and Linda Powers to forego other work-study opportunities to work on *The Overseas List*. Church World Service also plans to help make the book widely available. Richard Butler is executive director of Church World Service, succeeding Paul McCleary who was executive director when this book project began. Bernard Confer shepherded the project for Church World Service and gave us the benefit of his long familiarity with work in developing countries. Church World Service is the disaster relief, refugee resettlement, and development agency of 31 U.S. Protestant and Orthodox churches of the National Council of Churches of Christ, U.S.A.

Bread for the World and Bread for the World Educational Fund provided essential support for preparation of the first edition of *The Overseas List*. Their help in promoting the first edition was crucial to its success, and we are delighted that they also plan to help publicize this revised and expanded edition. Bread for the World is a Christian citizen's movement devoted to influencing U.S. government policy to speed the end of hunger.

Elizabeth Anne Donnelly was David Beckmann's coauthor for the first edition. At that time, she was a volunteer staff member of Bread for the World. She has spent most of the intervening years as a Maryknoll lay missioner in Peru and is now a student at Harvard Divinity School.

John Maxwell Hamilton, an experienced foreign correspondent, drafted the section on journalism in Chapter 6 of this edition.

Alicia Saona typed the manuscript, plus hundreds of letters to organizations listed in this book.

We have also received assistance from many other people in compiling the information in this edition. The following people have been particularly helpful: Philip Farris, John Klein, James Phillips, Alexander Shakow, Tom Tsui, Mike Witt, and Alan Woods.

Janet and Andrew Beckmann genially tolerated this second intrusion of *The Overseas List* into the Beckmann family's private time.

David Beckmann is on the staff of The World Bank, but the opinions expressed in this book are his own, not necessarily those of The World Bank.

Why Go to a
Developing Country?

About 1% of the population of the United States—2¼ million Americans—were living abroad in 1983. About half of these people were living in developing countries.

Why are people living and traveling abroad in such large numbers? Perennial motives for travel are still important: adventure, profit, patriotism, curiosity, charity, and missionary zeal. But now travel is cheaper than ever before. A student can spend a year abroad more cheaply than a year at some colleges. Travel is also easier than ever before. A retired couple can travel to see wild game that only the most intrepid explorers could have seen a century ago. You can find someone who speaks English in nearly every country of the world, often in the most remote places.

Electronic communications have suddenly made all peoples of the world neighbors—squabbling neighbors, but neighbors nevertheless. We have a new awareness of common interest. We sense needs abroad with new urgency. We are caught up in an international mix of cultures unprecedented in history.

The United States has experienced an especially dramatic increase in global consciousness, travel, and power. At the end of the Second World War, the United States was clearly, for the first time, the most powerful nation in the world. In the generation since then, Americans have maintained a global presence—military bases, world-spanning operations in commerce and investment, an expansive diplomacy, and a far-flung network of missionaries and well-meaning volunteers.

Most U.S. citizens who leave home still go to a few, mostly affluent countries. About half the U.S. civilians residing abroad in 1983 were in only five countries (Canada, Germany, Britain, Italy, and Mexico), and another quarter were in another 10 relatively prosperous countries (France, Greece, Spain, Israel, Japan, Australia, Brazil, Colombia, the Philippines, and Saudi Arabia). The remaining quarter of the U.S. civilians abroad were scattered among another 126 countries. Among the U.S. civilians residing in the developing regions of the world, three-fifths were in Latin America and the Caribbean.

Over the last five years the number of U.S. civilians living in Europe has dropped significantly, mainly because recession reduced economic activity generally and then because the overvalued U.S. dollar makes it difficult for Americans to sell their wares. These factors also affected U.S. business in the developing countries, as did falling oil prices and the international debt crisis. Yet the number of U.S. civilians living in developing countries has, surprisingly, remained about constant over the last five years.

Vocation for Christians living abroad

The Third World is especially important to Christians because:

1. We believe that God is moving through history to free slaves and bless the needy. In our increasingly interdependent world, Christians must do what we can to assist the world's poor; if we do not try, we cannot rightly claim the name Christian. If the wealthier nations take advantage of the poor, God will surely visit us with violence and judgment. The gap between the world's rich and poor is a fundamental and potentially explosive moral issue—except for the threat of nuclear war, the most compelling moral issue of the generation.

2. We believe that God intends the unity of all people—not a unity of conformity enforced by self-righteous imperialism, but the unity of mutual acceptance among forgiven sinners. It is a unity foreshadowed in the church, which brings together people of all nations to share the unique gifts God has given to each.

3. We believe the Lord has called us to share the gospel with all nations. In our century the gospel is firmly planted almost everywhere. No longer do foreigners ''bring'' the gospel to Asia and

Africa. But it is crucial to the health of the church that Christians of all nations share their mutual experience in Christ and assist one another in mission. U.S. Christians abroad can offer distinctive insights and valuable encouragement to local churches, just as Christians from other countries can broaden and deepen our spiritual understanding when they visit or work in the United States.

It is not at all necessary to draw one's salary from the church to be engaged in Christian mission abroad. All Christians are called to share the gospel by word and deed in our daily lives and work. Lay Christians can influence people and institutions with which professional church workers have little contact. Lay witness is especially important in those developing countries where there are few local Christians and where professional church workers from abroad are not welcome. There would be almost no Christian presence in some Moslem countries, for example, but for the faithfully quiet witness of foreigners in secular occupations.

The complication for U.S. Christians abroad is that they represent not only their servant Lord, but also a powerful nation. They are likely to be employed in developing countries by relatively wealthy and potentially oppressive organizations. Could U.S. soldiers in Vietnam witness effectively to the love of Christ? Can U.S. business people in South Africa disassociate themselves from racism? Do sectarian missionaries who establish U.S. denominations in developing countries, rather than joining efforts with existing churches, further the cause of the gospel?

Christians need to be careful, not only about their personal morality, but about the morality of institutions they serve and the institutions' roles in the broader political context. The temptation is to wield U.S. power and wealth at others' expense. Christians should rather find ways to be of assistance to the very poor.

This book begins with the types of involvement in developing countries that would most obviously appeal to Christian motives: people-to-people development programs and missionary agencies (Chapters 3 and 4), opportunities to study and teach in developing countries (Chapters 5 and 6), and work for international organizations or the civilian aspects of the U.S. government (Chapters 7 and 8). But our very approximate estimate is that all these areas of work together account for something like a fourth of the U.S. citizens who are residents in the developing countries. The U.S. military (also Chapter 8) probably accounts for another fourth, and the rest, roughly half, are doing business in the developing countries (Chapter 9).

These estimates give us pause. It is no wonder that many people in developing countries see mainly the military and commercial sides of U.S. life.

On the other hand, people who want to work in the developing countries for religious or idealistic reasons should not restrict their field of vision too narrowly. Giveaway funds are scarce, so most people who limit themselves to looking for employment with churches or private development agencies never get beyond good intentions. Meanwhile, hundreds of thousands of Americans in developing countries, some of them Christians, are working in government or business. Too many of these people lack much awareness of the broader goals they might accomplish, and they tend to isolate themselves from local people. Many of them have important and useful work to do, but service-minded people might make better use of their opportunities.

In fact, some Christian missions are sectarian and hardhearted toward the poor, and some private development agencies are badly organized and self-serving. Many businesses, on the other hand, are genuinely helpful. Bata Shoe Company, for example, meets a basic need by producing shoes that poor Africans and Asians can afford. A Christian could certainly make his career in the Third World working for such a company.

The importance of perspective

The morality of virtually all aspects of U.S. presence in developing countries has been questioned. Many books and articles (listed in following chapters) critique or defend controversial aspects of the U.S. presence abroad—missionaries, voluntary agencies, foreign aid, the military, and multinational business.

A fundamental issue is whether the primary causes of poverty are among the poor (ignorance and technological backwardness) or whether the problem is oppression by the rich. People who believe the roots of poverty are among the poor tend to think that U.S.

"missionaries"—not only Christian evangelists, but technicians, business people, and volunteers — can help set things right. Those who view oppression as the root cause of poverty tend to see the United States as the kingpin in a worldwide oppressive order and U.S. citizens in the developing countries as crucial links in maintaining the system.

We think there is some truth in both views. The critical view of U.S. presence abroad makes most sense in Latin America. In Africa and South Asia the problem is absolute, grinding poverty and, especially in Africa, limited administrative and technological capacity to deal with it. In Latin America, on the other hand, there is a substantial, prosperous modern economy, but the masses are virtually excluded. They are somewhat better off materially than the poor in Africa or South Asia, and much more politicized. United States interests, which are extensive in Latin America, are sometimes allied with the status quo against the poor majority.

Christians thinking about serving in the Third World should read about Third World development. Thousands of books might be relevant, and newspapers are full of articles of interest. A few good introductions to development are listed below. They represent a variety of positions. Some suggest a positive evaluation of the role of people from the United States who work in developing countries. Others call U.S. presence in developing countries into serious question. All of them offer a general perspective.

Critchfield, Richard. *Villages*. Garden City, NY: Doubleday, 1983. A large proportion of the poor people in the world live in villages. Critchfield has dedicated much of his life to understanding villages, and this insightful book is based on extended stays and follow-up visits to villages in various regions of the Third World.

Feinberg, Richard E., and Valeriana Kallab, eds. *Adjustment Crisis in the Third World*. New Brunswick and London: Transaction Books, 1984. The economic traumas of the developing countries in the 1980s and implications for U.S. policy.

Meier, Gerald M. *Emerging from Poverty: The Economics That Really Matters*. New York and Oxford: Oxford University Press, 1984. A wide-ranging introduction to development economics. The successes and failures of Third World development. What economists have prescribed and problems they still need to tackle.

de Santa Ana, Julio. *Towards a Church of the Poor.* Geneva: World Council of Churches, 1979. A compelling, ecumenical statement on why and how the church can better join in the struggles of poor and oppressed people around the world.

Simon, Arthur. *Bread for the World.* Rev. ed. Ramsey, NJ: Paulist Press, 1984. An excellent analysis of hunger (worldwide and domestic) and its causes, with how-to advice on what Christians can do about it. Highly recommended.

World Bank. *World Development Report.* New York and London: Oxford University Press, annual. An authoritative review of current prospects and economic issues for developing countries.

Christians looking for opportunities to live and work in developing countries should be familiar with basic development issues so they can cull out unhelpful ''opportunities'' and, in whatever situation they find themselves abroad, act on the basis of informed and independent conscience. Also, when they return to the United States and are asked to share their opinions, the information they give will help shape public opinion. Such follow-up back home sometimes makes more of an impact than the work abroad. It provides another opportunity for Christian service and calls for a broad, informed perspective on world development.

A difficult period for developing countries

When President Kennedy established the Peace Corps in 1961, many developing countries were just beginning their national independence, and most developing countries were enjoying rapid economic and social progress. Nearly everywhere in the Third World, incomes, school attendance, and life expectancy were rising. The United States and other industrial nations were expanding their programs of development assistance, and the Peace Corps opened a way for inexperienced young Americans to help developing countries realize their soaring aspirations.

Today, in the wake of global economic turbulence, most developing countries are struggling to regain the growth rates of the 1960s and 1970s. The shining hopes of the independence era have been tarnished by a postindependence history replete with coups, internal conflict, and corruption. Although well-managed programs of development assistance have helped to raise incomes and reduce poverty, the task has proved more complex than some early supporters of foreign aid imagined, and economic progress has not guaranteed political stability or gratitude toward the donor countries.

Economic and social progress began to slow down in parts of the Third World in the mid-1970s as the global economy as a whole began to sputter. The global recession of the early 1980s was the most severe economic slump since the Depression of the 1930s, and, for the first time in decades, per-capita income in nearly all developing countries declined.

Even under optimistic assumptions, it will take some years before most developing countries recover the pace of progress they achieved in the 1970s. Nearly all the middle-income developing countries of Asia (Korea, for example) recovered relatively quickly from the global recession, and the giant low-income nations of Asia, notably China and India, are also achieving high growth rates. But the heavily indebted countries of Latin America will not fully recover from the debt crisis of 1982 and 1983 within the foreseeable future, and the bulk of sub-Saharan Africa is likely to suffer continuing economic decline and perhaps recurrent famine.

In some Latin American countries, the debt crisis pushed military dictators to cede power to democratic governments. Another political bright spot in the Third World is China, which is presently moving away from past policies of extreme state control and isolationism. But several other political trends among the developing countries are less auspicious, particularly for U.S. citizens abroad. Relentless economic decline in much of Africa has put almost unbearable pressure on fragile nations. The resurgence of Islam and other religions has raised religious tension in the Middle East and South Asia. More generally, the heightened East-West tensions of recent years, together with the continuing strength of Third World nationalism, tend to shadow the presence of U.S. citizens abroad with controversial political connotations.

At the same time, contributions of development assistance from the industrial countries, especially from the United States, have slowed down, and a greater proportion of aid is tied to the immediate political and commercial interests of the industrial countries. Since the U.S. government and other industrial-country governments also provide crucial financial backing for the United Nations and other international agencies, the cutback in government funding has tightened the job market for international development work generally. In the aftermath of the debt crisis, banks and businesses have cut back on their Third World investments too.

Americans who wanted to serve in a developing country in the 1960s were part of a trend. But if you want to serve in a developing country now, you are going against the trend, and job opportunities are harder to find.

In late 1984 and 1985, the mass media turned their attention to famine in Ethiopia and elsewhere in Africa. In response, private and government contributions to private development agencies went up sharply. The private agencies working in Africa have thus been able to expand their staff, and it just may be that public attention to famine in Africa will help to reverse the trend toward diminished U.S. assistance for Third World development.

THREE

Private Development Assistance

Many private agencies work to promote economic and social improvement in the developing countries. The strong U.S. tradition of private effort to help developing countries is historically rooted in the missionary movement and disaster-relief efforts of the 19th century. Some of the private development agencies listed in this chapter are religiously inspired or even affiliated with a particular church, but if they are listed in this chapter (rather than Chapter 4) their main focus is economic or social development, rather than religious teaching. Private development agencies are a diverse lot, each with its own distinctive objectives and methods.

This chapter begins with a summary table and is then divided into four sections according to four types of private development agencies:

- agencies that specialize in placing short-term volunteers,
- agencies that are administered mainly by long-term professional staff,
- private organizations that are trying to change public opinion and public policy in the United States, and
- foundations that make grants to organizations involved in Third World development.

The summary table below lists, alphabetically, all the agencies in the first two categories. They account for virtually all the overseas jobs. The table shows, at a glance, the personnel and financial data

24

we have for all these agencies. The last column indicates the page on which the agency is more fully described.

Private development agencies listed alphabetically

Organization	United States Domestic	Overseas	Staff Volun-teers	Total	Budget	Page
Accion International/AITEC	10	6		16	1,000,000	44
The Africa Fund	9			9	300,000	44
Africare	26	30		56	8,000,000	44
Agricultural Cooperative Development International	23	30		53	5,000,000	48
Agricultural Development Council, Inc.		20		20		46
Aid for International Medicine						51
American Dentists for Foreign Service	3	3		6	50,000	51
American Friends Service Committee	375	20		395	16,000,000	35
American Institute for Free Labor Development	51	19		70	10,000,000	57
American Jewish Joint Distribution Committee	12	20		32	40,000,000	35
American Near East Refugee Aid	8	5		13	1,500,000	44
Amigos de las Americas	9	150		159	1,000,000	28
Association for Voluntary Sterilization	75	42		117	10,000,000	55
Baptist World Aid	2			2	1,249,000	36
Pearl S. Buck Foundation, Inc.	35	146		181	3,014,000	47
CARE		175		175	242,359,000	42
Catholic Medical Mission Board	32		52	84	9,700,000	51
Catholic Relief Services	125	150		275	323,798,000	36
The Centre for Development of Population Activities	18			18	761,000	56
Christian Children's Fund, Inc.					47,400,000	47
Christian Foundation for Children		11		11		48
Christian Reformed World Relief Committee	20	55		75	6,942,000	36
Church World Service		45		45	40,000,000	36
CONCERN	5	1	20	26	300,000	28
Cooperative Housing Foundation	22	17		39	3,000,000	49
Cooperative League of the USA	37	13		50	4,100,000	49
Dental Health International	2				90,000	51
Direct Relief International	22		25	47	6,700,000	52
Dooley Foundation/INTERMED-USA	5	6		11	1,000,000	52
Ecumenical Development Cooperative Society	2	4				37

Ecumenical Youth Service Esperanca, Inc.	5	4		9	1,200,000	28 52
Family Planning International Assistance					20,000,000	56
Fellowship of Reconciliation	28	25		53	830,000	57
Food for the Hungry			69	69	9,000,000	37
Foster Parents Plan International	53	65		118	38,238,000	48
Foundation for the Peoples of the South Pacific	7	9		16	1,000,000	44
Goodwill Industries International Department	3			3	250,000	52
Habitat for Humanity				155	1,300,000	58
Heifer Project International	62	8		70	5,100,000	46
High/Scope Educational Research Foundation	80			80	600,000	50
Holt International Children's Services	45	600		645	4,000,000	48
Institute for International Development, Inc.						58
The Institute of Cultural Affairs	200	450		650	4,000,000	42
Interchurch Medical Assistance, Inc.	5			5	4,728,000	53
International Christian Youth Exchange						29
International Eye Foundation	10	15		25	4,000,000	53
International Executive Service Corps			500	500	10,000,000	29
International Human Assistance Programs, Inc.	14	18		32	4,000,000	42
International Institute of Rural Reconstruction	7	121		128	1,900,000	46
International Planned Parenthood Federation	40	42		82	52,000,000	56
International Rescue Committee					18,348,000	58
International Voluntary Services			24	24	1,500,000	29
Jubilee						37
Helen Keller International	23	9		32	2,494,000	53
Laubach Literacy International	2	103		105	259,000	50
The Lisle Fellowship, Inc.						30
Lutheran World Ministries			40	40		37
Lutheran World Relief	17	12		29	16,500,000	38
MAP International	70	3		73	15,119,000	53
The MEDEX Group	19	6		25	2,300,000	54
Mennonite Central Committee	96		525	621	25,000,000	38
Mennonite Economic Development Associates, Inc.	6	5		11	775,000	39
Near East Foundation		23		23	900,000	45

Operation Crossroads Africa						30
Opportunities Industrialization Centers					3,500,000	58
Option						54
Orthopedics Overseas, Inc.			20	20		54
Overseas Education Fund	20	15		35		43
Oxfam America	5	2		7	5,100,000	43
Pan American Development Foundation	25	5		30		45
Partners of the Americas						45
Partnership for Productivity International	17	140		157	4,500,000	43
Pathfinder Fund					7,000,000	57
People to People Health Foundation, Inc.	100	90		190	10,000,000	54
Planning Assistance, Inc.	14	5		19	670,000	59
Population Council	200			200		57
The Presiding Bishop's Fund for World Relief					4,890,000	39
Project Concern International					2,891,000	55
Salvation Army					8,500,000	39
Save the Children Federation, Inc.	60	63		123	40,000,000	47
Seva Foundation	8	1		9	500,000	55
Summer Institute of Linguistics				4730	41,500,000	39
Technoserve	25	93		118	3,400,000	46
Tolstoy Foundation, Inc.	97			97	338,000	59
Unitarian Universalist Service Committee	30			30	2,000,000	40
United Church Board for World Ministries	55	252		307		40
United Methodist Committee on Relief	6		1000	1006	13,000,000	40
VITA	35	7		42	3,700,000	59
Volunteers in Overseas Cooperative Assistance			45	45		30
U.S. Committee for UNICEF						47
World Concern	52	99		151	7,500,000	41
World Council of Credit Unions, Inc.	25	7		32		49
World Education, Inc.	8	21		29	1,000,000	50
World Rehabilitation Fund						55
World Relief	34	138	45	217	15,000,000	41
World Vision International		1875		1875	100,000,000	42
YMCA International Divison	9			9	4,221,000	60
YMCA World Ambassadors						31
Totals of Available Data	2545	5299	2365	15,086	1,307,814,000	

Volunteer-sending agencies

Volunteer work often provides one's first opportunity to live and work in the Third World. Most agencies prefer volunteers with practical skills and work experience, but there are also opportunities for promising but relatively inexperienced people.

The following private development agencies specialize in sending volunteers to developing countries. Annual income from a recent year, if available, is shown in parentheses at the end of each listing.

Amigos de las Americas (5618 Star Lane, Houston, TX 77057). Founded in 1965, Amigos has grown to more than 30 chapters throughout the United States and currently operates projects in Mexico, the Dominican Republic, Costa Rica, Venezuela, Ecuador, Peru, and Paraguay. Approximately 450 volunteers travel with Amigos each summer to assist in public-health programs such as immunizations, vision screening, dental hygiene, animal husbandry. Adult volunteers at local chapters recruit, offer training in Spanish and cultural awareness, and help the young people raise funds for the participation fee. The $1500 to $2000 fee includes airfare, room and board, supplies, and training. Must be at least 16 years old or have completed the sophomore year of high school. Nine domestic staff, approximately 150 overseas. ($1,000,000)

CONCERN (P.O. Box 1790, Santa Ana, CA 92702). Nondenominational, nongovernmental international hunger-relief and development organization founded in Ireland in 1968. Volunteers are professionals in the fields of health, engineering, and education who share their knowledge and skills with disadvantaged people and, by the end of their assignments, will have trained others to carry on and to build on what they have started. Qualifications: at least 21 years old; a degree or advanced degree in public health, nutrition, agriculture, engineering, or medicine; and fluency in Spanish for placement in Latin America. Overseas field experience preferred. CONCERN provides room, board, round-trip transportation, and a monthly stipend of $50 to volunteers. A repatriation allowance of $50 per month is placed in an account in the United States. Minimum commitments of one year. 5 domestic staff, 1 staff member, and 20 volunteer professionals overseas in Bangladesh, Ecuador, El Salvador, Honduras, Mexico, and Sierra Leone. ($300,000)

Ecumenical Youth Service (World Council of Churches, 150 route de Ferney, 1211 Geneva 20, Switzerland). Sponsors work camps in Africa, Asia, the Caribbean, and the Middle East. Usually involve discussion, reflection, and agricultural or other manual work. Last one to four weeks. Volunteers must be 18 to 30 years old, pay own travel expenses and insurance, and contribute about $3 a day toward living expenses. Camps are usually in July and August; due date for applications is different for each camp.

International Christian Youth Exchange (74 Trinity Place, Room 610-D, New York, NY 10006). Helps place students in secondary schools abroad, and also organizes community volunteer service internships (such as work in programs for disabled youths, day-care centers, environmental organizations, and drug-and-alcohol-abuse programs). National program committees in 26 countries of Central and South America, the Mediterranean region, and the Near East. Sponsored by most major denominations; no particular religious affiliation is required. Both the school program and community-service internships are one-year programs. Open to applicants aged 16-24. Cost of program is $3600, and college credit can be earned. December 15 application deadline.

International Executive Service Corps (8 Stanford Forum, P.O. Box 10005, Stanford, CT 06904-2005). Through short-term volunteer executives (mainly recently retired business people and technologists), IESC provides managerial and technical assistance to all types of industries and services, including food production and agricultural projects. Assigns nonsalaried executives to about 500 projects per year in 75 developing countries for two- to three-month periods. Volunteer executives must have combination of management and industry-specific skills and ability to communicate and to adapt to different cultures. Applicants and spouses subject to rigid screening prior to first assignment. No stipend, but travel and living expenses paid for both volunteer and spouse. More than 300 leading U.S. corporations and a number of foreign firms and governments contribute financially to IESC. IESC maintains a skills bank and makes assignments depending on demands for specific skills by specific clients. Has field offices in 28 developing countries, each headed by a country director (generally a retired U.S. business person with extensive international experience). 500 volunteers, 1153 registrants in skill bank. ($10,000,000)

International Voluntary Services (1424 16th St. N.W., Suite 504, Washington, DC 20036). Recruits specialist volunteer technicians to work in developing countries at request of governments and institutions. Primarily aims to support local institutions and groups that can effectively serve poor rural people, actively involving the poor in their own development toward self-reliance. Current project sites in Bolivia, Ecuador, Honduras, Bangladesh, Botswana, and Zimbabwe. Seeks volunteers with skills and experience related to rural development, agriculture, public health, and small business/cooperative development. Highly competitive (about 10 acceptances per 1000 applications). Volunteers normally serve two to three years. They receive $150 per month savings, plus housing, living allowance, insurance, and travel for themselves and up to four dependents. Presently 24 volunteers overseas. ($1,500,000)

The Lisle Fellowship, Inc. (c/o Rockland Community College, 145 College Road, Suffern, NY 10901). Pioneer educational program in intercultural understanding and global perspectives that offers students and other adults an experience living and learning in cross-cultural settings. Participants assigned to field placements with community social-service organizations. Currently six-week summer program offered in India. Fees range from $750 to $2000 and include room, board, and in-country travel, but not always travel to and from the program location. Financial assistance available to applicants with outstanding ability and experience. Academic credit available in cooperation with many institutions. Application for summer programs due May 1.

Operation Crossroads Africa (150 Fifth Ave., New York, NY 10011). Operates rural village-level projects in Africa. Project groups consist of 8 to 12 volunteers. Focuses on cross-cultural understanding through close contact with community-development process. Special projects include art and archaeology, rural health, agricultural development, and basic construction. Programs are normally for six to eight weeks during the summer. Academic credit can be earned if personnally arranged with an institution. Program locations include Botswana, Lesotho, Malawi, Zimbabwe. Open to qualified and highly motivated undergraduates, graduates, and teachers; about 80% of applicants are accepted. Application fee is $15. Applications are due end of March. Knowledge of French required for some assignments. Cost is $2750, and limited financial assistance is available.

Volunteers in Overseas Cooperative Assistance (1800 Massachusetts Ave. N.W., Washington, DC 20036). Formerly Volunteer Development Corps. Established by U.S. cooperatives to provide short-term services of technical experts in organization, management, and operation of cooperatives in developing countries. Recruits experienced, often retired, personnel with expertise in cooperative philosophy to serve as volunteers for periods of less than 90 days. Covers cost of transportation, food, lodging, immunization, passports and visas, while host agency provides for in-country travel, work space, and secretarial services. Recruits 38-50 per year.

YMCA World Ambassadors (YMCA of Michigan, 301 W. Lenawee St., Lansing, MI 48914). Study/service seminars held each summer in a number of countries, including Egypt, Ghana, Kenya, the Philippines, and some Latin American countries. Participants serve as volunteer leaders for ongoing YMCA programs and as members of an international team meeting definite social needs of a community. Participants responsible for own expenses. Program cost ranges from $1300 to $2000 exclusive of airfare. Provides assistance in personal fund raising. Six- to eight-week summer stay. Foreign language proficiency not required, and academic credit can be earned for participation. Designed especially for college students, but other adults welcome. May application date.

In addition, some of the private agencies that rely mainly on long-term professionals also use some volunteers; these agencies are marked with asterisks in the listing on pp. 35-60. Quite a few private agencies use doctors, dentists, and nurses on a volunteer basis; see especially the health agencies marked with asterisks on pp. 51-55.

Some of the missionary agencies, discussed in Chapter 4, use short-term staff (the agencies marked with asterisks on pp. 79-90 and also the agencies listed on pp. 92-95); and although the missionary agencies' main work is evangelism, they often assign volunteers to serve in schools, clinics, and small-scale programs of economic and social development. Some opportunities for nonformal educational (pp. 110-14) or for teaching English as a foreign language (pp. 119-22) may also be of interest to people looking for volunteer opportunities abroad. Finally, the largest and most celebrated volunteer-sending agency is the Peace Corps (pp. 152-53).

For further information on volunteer opportunities, check:

International Directory of Youth Internships: A Directory of Intern Volunteer Opportunities. Available from The Foreign Area Materials Center, 60 East 42nd St., Suite 1231, New York, NY 10017. $2.

International Directory for Youth Internships with the United Nations, Its Specialized Agencies, and Nongovernmental Organizations. See p. 130.

Volunteer: Comprehensive Guide to Voluntary Service Opportunities in the U.S. and Abroad. Published jointly by the Commission on Voluntary Service and Action and the Council on International Educational Exchange. Catalogs voluntary service organizations that are seeking full-time volunteers. Available from the Commission on Voluntary Service, 475 Riverside Drive, Room 1126, New York, NY 10115. $5.50, plus $1 for mailing or $2.50 for first-class mailing.

The Coordinating Committee for International Voluntary Service (c/o UNESCO, 1 rue Miollis, Paris 75015, France) is the most authoritative source of information on nongovernmental, volunteer service programs throughout the world. CCIVS represents more than 125 organizations involved in voluntary service and assists UNESCO with programs related to youth and international development. You can write CCIVS for a list of its publications and for information on long-term overseas service opportunities.

Volunteers often work in close contact with poor people. Some volunteers prove to be surprisingly productive, and nearly all contribute to the fund of goodwill among nations. But few people have the dedication to continue "living poor" for more than a few years, and volunteers sometimes have too little expertise—and too little money at their disposal—to make substantial changes. Thus, most people who continue in development work eventually graduate to salaried positions.

Private development agencies

For some former volunteers, a professional position in a private development agency is the answer. The staff of these agencies are often paid enough to maintain their families in average U.S. style, but perhaps not as much as they could earn in business or government. The projects of the private development agencies range in size from a few hundred dollars to a few million dollars, which is still much smaller than most of the projects financed by government-sponsored agencies. Their relatively small scale of operations often allows the staff of private agencies to remain in contact with the people they are trying to help.

Normally new staff are assigned to programs in the field. Personnel who stay for some time with a particular organization may eventually move into managerial positions in capital cities abroad or to headquarters in the United States. For others, career development may involve moving to another development agency, either private or official. A typical resume might show two years with one private agency in Cameroon, three years in Togo with another agency (maybe with one year in Lomé, the capital), then perhaps a position in Washington with the U.S. government's Agency for International Development (AID).

Most long-term positions in the private development agencies require advanced degrees in economics or other development-related fields, as well as substantial field experience. Some short-term consultancies are available for people with specialized expertise (hydraulic engineering, for example). The most well-known private development agencies are swamped with applications, mostly from people without the requisite qualifications. Our advice is to be realistic about your prospects, pick out those agencies with which you have the best chance, and then somehow draw attention to yourself (through a personal contact, for example, or at least a follow-up phone call).

Salaries vary widely among the private development agencies. A starting salary for a young field officer in CARE would approach that of an entrance-level U.S. government employee. Expenses are relatively low in many Third World posts, especially outside the large cities (see pp. 209-11). Thus, a job with CARE does not mean scrimping to get by. Highly technical personnel—a specialist in tropical fishery, for example, or a doctor—are paid more than generalist administrators in the field. Managers at an organization's headquarters usually receive the highest salaries, although they could usually earn more doing similar tasks in government or business.

The best review of the private development agencies is still John G. Sommer's *Beyond Charity: U.S. Voluntary Aid for a Changing Third World* (Washington, D.C.: Overseas Development Council, 1977). Each agency is different, and some are much more effective than others, but Sommer suggests the following generalizations about the characteristic strengths and weaknesses of private development agencies.

Because private development agencies are relatively small, they can be more effective than intergovernmental agencies in people-oriented programs of intercultural sharing, training, community organization, and consciousness raising. They pioneered in assisting the least advantaged directly, while the governmental and intergovernmental agencies were still concentrating on basic infrastructure and industry. Private development agencies can also keep their administrative costs down and respond more quickly and flexibly than larger bureaucracies.

On the other hand, most private development agencies have relatively small budgets, so their impact is limited. Some of them rely heavily on U.S. surplus food, the distribution of which, if not delicately handled, can depress agricultural prices and discourage local food production. There are also problems related to the pressures of relying on public contributions. From a fund-raising point of view, appeals for emergency relief and "tearful child" advertisements have characteristically been most successful. But except immediately after a disaster, outright grants of food or other goods are seldom effective in helping people overcome their poverty, and child sponsorship programs are expensive to administer. Some private agencies have been tempted to do what is popular among their U.S. donors rather than what will best help poor people, and fund-raising publicity sometimes only reinforces prejudices that Third World peoples are dependent and the United States their great benefactor.

Private development agencies' broad popular support within the United States gives them unique opportunities to educate the U.S. public about the Third World, and the better agencies have managed to educate their constituencies to support development as well as relief. Their publicity emphasizes initiative and leadership by people in the developing countries themselves, and their requests for funds take the "helping them to help themselves" approach. Several of the child sponsorship agencies are shifting from one-to-one sponsorship arrangements to community-development programs that help children in the context of their families and neighborhoods, and they have been able to educate many of their contributors to support this more developmental approach. Other private development agencies, Oxfam for example, go far beyond fund raising to inform their constituencies on issues of public policy that are related to global poverty.

Listed below are private development agencies that have significant numbers of staff living or traveling in developing countries. Organizations are listed alphabetically under the following headings:
Related to Church Groups
General Humanitarian

Serving Particular Regions
Agriculture
Children
Cooperatives
Education
Health
Population
Other Specialized Areas of Action

Jewish aid-to-Israel agencies are not included, because Israel is highly developed in comparison to Third World countries. The information was obtained from the agencies themselves. An annual budget figure is shown in parentheses at the end of each listing to give job seekers a sense of program size. Those agencies that use some volunteers in addition to their regular staff are marked with an asterisk.

Related to Church Groups

American Friends Service Committee (1501 Cherry St., Philadelphia, PA 19102). Quaker, pacifist humanitarian organization with programs of social change and relief that are focused on peace and social justice. Operates programs in Guinea-Bissau, Somalia, Mali, Zimbabwe, Laos, Kampuchea, Hong Kong, Chile, El Salvador, Honduras, Jordan, Israel, and Lebanon. Employment opportunities are few and very selective. Applicants must have considerable experience in a developing country, experience in program development, administrative and communication skills, and sometimes also language fluency (French, Spanish) and technical skills (in agriculture, for example). Academic degree per se rarely required. Overseas positions are not salaried, but are on a full maintenance basis. 375 domestic staff, 20 expatriate staff, and more than 100 local staff overseas. ($16,000,000)

American Jewish Joint Distribution Committee (60 E. 42nd St., Suite 1914, New York, NY 10165). The major American agency aiding Jewish communities overseas. Operates a broad range of health, welfare, rehabilitation, education, and cultural assistance programs in Israel and other Middle East countries, Europe, North Africa, Asia, and South America. Services include care of aged, support of voluntary programs for handicapped children, financial assistance to religious schools, and development of community-center programs. Overseas employment generally but not necessarily requires U.S. citizenship with experience in Jewish communal work. 12 domestic staff, 20 overseas. ($40,000,000)

Baptist World Aid (1628 16th St. N.W., Washington, DC 20009). A funding agency for the relief and development work of the Baptist World Alliance. Supports community development projects (such as food-for-work programs), small-scale economic development projects, primary and vocational schools, and disaster relief. Two domestic staff. Does not employ any overseas staff or volunteers, but works through its member bodies and thus saves on administrative costs. ($1,249,000)

* *Catholic Relief Services* (1011 First Ave., New York, NY 10022). Operates relief, welfare, and self-help programs in more than 75 countries to assist refugees, war victims, and other needy persons. While past emphasis had been on relief and refugee aid, nutrition and socioeconomic development have been increasingly stressed as the first steps toward self-sufficiency. Aid is strictly humanitarian, not linked to proselytizing. Job applicants must generally meet the following requirements: (1) bachelor's degree, preferably in social sciences; (2) proficiency in a foreign language, usually French or Spanish; (3) previous "hands-on" experience in a Third World country for one or two years; (4) Catholic background. Jobs involve management, program planning, and project analysis and design. Employees receive a base salary plus allowances and benefits. Has used only specialized volunteers in past, but is considering new programs that may use more volunteers. About 125 domestic staff, 150 overseas. ($323,798,000)

Christian Reformed World Relief Committee (2850 Kalamazoo Ave. S.E., Grand Rapids, MI 49560). Works through local Christian groups to enable them to reach out to the poor. Management and technical skills offered in literacy, agriculture, and health care. Bachelor's degree required, experience in development-related field preferred. Three-year contract. 20 domestic staff, including 4 in foreign program. 55 overseas in 16 countries of Asia, Africa, and Central America. ($6,942,000)

Church World Service (475 Riverside Drive, New York, NY 10115). Provides emergency relief, technical assistance, refugee resettlement, and interchurch aid. Emphasis on development involving local people and institutions through indigenous colleague agencies and community committees, some of which raise as much as 80% of the cost of their own programs. CWS is the disaster relief, refugee resettlement, and development agency of 31 U.S. Protestant and Orthodox churches of the National Council of Churches of Christ, U.S.A. CWS works cooperatively with the World Council of Churches and regional and national councils of churches around the world. CROP, the Community Hunger Appeal of CWS, provides food, seeds, tools, and other resources to support CWS self-help programs. CWS sponsors programs of disaster relief and rehabilitation, agriculture, nutrition and public health, education, functional literacy, planned parenthood, low-cost housing, social welfare, leadership development, medical aid, and community development in Africa, Asia, the Caribbean, Europe, Latin America, and the Middle East. Personnel serve two-year terms. Previous overseas experience expected, especially for representational positions. Currently 45 in the field. ($40,000,000)

Ecumenical Development Cooperative Society (475 Riverside Drive, New York, NY 10115). Organized in 1977 by the worldwide ecumenical Christian movement, EDCS has been called "the churches' World Bank." Provides an alternative investment channel for a portion of the funds that churches and Christians in the industrial countries now have invested in corporations and banks. Financed by loans and grants from denominations and through a $10 million public offering of the U.S. Conference for the World Council of Churches. EDCS makes low-interest long-term loans and provides technical and management assistance for projects of the poor that raise their incomes and promote social justice. Currently has over 165 member organizations and a paid-in share capital of over $8,000,000. Two U.S. domestic staff, four staff in Europe, Latin America, and Asia.

* *Food for the Hungry* (7729 East Greenway Road, Scottsdale, AZ 85260). Provides relief and development assistance, does research on appropriate technology, and provides education on world hunger. Combines development activities with evangelism. Presently 69 volunteers serving in four nations through its International Hunger Corps. ($9,000,000)

Jubilee (300 W. Apsley St., Philadelphia, PA 19144). A nonprofit organization committed to getting at the roots of justice and despair. Its motto is "justice rooted in discipleship." Jubilee publishes a monthly magazine, *The Other Side;* markets Third World handicrafts to help provide a livelihood for impoverished people; and produces educational literature about the effects of U.S. military and economic intervention in developing countries. Also directly involved in programs in the Philippines, Hong Kong, Chile, Thailand, South Africa, Honduras, Nicaragua, Peru, and elsewhere.

* *Lutheran World Ministries* (U.S.A. National Committee of the Lutheran World Federation, 360 Park Ave. S., New York, NY 10010). Provides financial support and recruits U.S. staff for Department of World Service of the Lutheran World Federation, which in turn channels aid to indigenous development efforts around the world and operates programs of relief and development in situations of special need, such as refugee resettlement and

natural disaster. LWM also operates the Lutheran World Ministries Volunteer Service (formerly World Brotherhood Exchange Volunteers), which matches volunteers with agencies abroad. This program is open to all volunteers and Third World agencies wishing to join in Christian service, but its strongest contacts are among Lutheran churches in Bangladesh, Nepal, India, Pakistan, Liberia, Zaire, Tanzania, Madagascar, and Papua New Guinea. Interested in all sorts of skilled people: health-care professionals, veterinarians, teachers, administrators, accountants, secretaries, librarians, maintenance mechanics, auto mechanics, carpenters and builders, farmers and agriculturalists, and others. Depending on position, length of service varies from two months to two years. Volunteers normally provide for all their own expenses, including transportation, and receive no stipend. They sometimes receive support from friends or churches in the United States, but are themselves responsible for recruiting assistance. For overseas terms of six months or more, some financial assistance may be available by application to the World Brotherhood Exchange Volunteer Support Fund. Host agencies normally provide housing and occasionally a living allowance. LWM publishes a quarterly newsposter on volunteer positions available. 35-45 volunteers serving overseas each year.

* *Lutheran World Relief* (360 Park Ave. S., New York, NY 10010). Supports and operates programs for disaster relief, refugee assistance, and social and economic development in Asia, Africa, and Latin America. Projects include small industry, well digging, land reclamation, forestation, construction of irrigation wells, reservoirs, roads, schools, community centers, and demonstration projects in nutrition and social work. Also supports medical-assistance and family-planning programs. Desires applicants with an undergraduate degree and two years previous overseas experience. Terms of service ordinarily for three years. LWR also offers a two-year volunteer program for young people in which most expenses are paid, including language training and a modest monthly stipend. 17 domestic staff, 12 overseas. ($16,500,000)

* *Mennonite Central Committee* (Akron, PA 17501). Cooperative relief and service agency of Mennonite and Brethren in Christ churches in North America. MCC originally experienced growth through offering alternative service opportunities for conscientious objectors during the Second World War. Places over 525 volunteers overseas in some 43 countries for three-year assignments in agricultural development, nutrition, economic and technical development, education, medical services, and social services. Emphasis on meeting both physical and spiritual needs, with local church as base of operation. Volunteers should be of Christian faith and have college degree or practical experience. MCC pays for preparation, travel,

and maintenance expenses during assignments, plus monthly allowances, full medical coverage, and assistance with educational loans. 96 domestic staff. ($25,000,000)

* *Mennonite Economic Development Associates, Inc.* (21 S. Twelfth St., Akron, PA 17501). An association of business and professional persons that works in self-help, economic-development projects with individuals and groups that have marketing, processing and manufacturing, or credit needs. Provides advisory services in financial and economic planning, business administration, and accounting. Works mainly in agriculture or small-business development. Also assists members in discerning biblical principles and their applications in the marketplace. Project sites in Bolivia, Paraguay, Uruguay, Colombia, Jamaica, Haiti, Dominican Republic, and Belize. Applicants, usually hired from within related Mennonite organizations, should have three years of experience in development work. Volunteers taken on short-term consulting basis as need arises. Six domestic staff, five overseas. ($775,000)

The Presiding Bishop's Fund for World Relief (The Episcopal Church Center, 815 Second Ave., New York, NY 10017). The official channel of the Episcopal Church's response to human need in the areas of relief, rehabilitation, refugee/migration, and development. The Fund supports the relief and development efforts of the World and National Council of Churches and of several other religious and private voluntary organizations. Programs in over 45 countries of Asia, Africa, Latin America, and the Middle East. ($4,890,000 in grants in 1983)

* *Salvation Army* (799 Bloomfield Ave., Verona, NJ 07044). A religious and charitable organization that provides financial and personnel assistance to projects in 83 countries, responding to local needs. Programs include community centers, disaster relief, medical services, education (primary, secondary, vocational, technical, and teacher training), feeding centers and food depots, day-care centers, agriculture projects, housing construction, nutrition programs, children's homes, and homes for the aged. While Salvation Army officers (clergy) are sent as administrators, nonofficers (usually Salvation Army members) may volunteer for minimum of one or two years. Must have educational background appropriate to position sought, as well as past occupational experience at home or abroad. Subsistence wage, transportation, room, board, and insurance provided. Overseas assignments are handled through the international headquarters in London. ($8,500,000 for programs in developing countries)

Summer Institute of Linguistics (19891 Beach Boulevard, Huntington Beach, CA 92647). Affiliated with Wycliffe Bible Translators (see p. 88).

Specializes in language research and applied linguistics among ethnic minority groups throughout the world. Works in alphabet formation, preparation of literacy materials, and translation of literature, including the Bible, into previously unwritten languages. Cooperates with local governments in bilingual education and literacy programs and in limited community-development activities in some areas. Interdenominational. Involved with more than 728 language groups from 46 countries. Citizens of all countries with a working knowledge of English are eligible. No age limitations. College or equivalent for linguistics. Appropriate training and/or experience for other specialists. Basic working knowledge of the Bible required. Three categories of service: guest helper (up to six months), short-term assistant (six months to two years), and career member (two to four years, required for linguistic assignments). Short-term assistants and career members attend orientation sessions before leaving. Career members also attend a field training course. Required to secure own financial backing to cover transportation, and no guaranteed salary or stipend provided. Active members: 4730 in various categories. ($41,500,000)

Unitarian Universalist Service Committee (78 Beacon St., Boston, MA 02108). Provides access to information and opportunities for community action to people working to build a society based on justice and freedom. Inspired by liberal, nonsectarian religious principles. Programs in areas such as public health, family planning, economic development, and women's rights are developed in partnership with local people within the context of their own cultures. Requirements for employment depend on position sought. Project sites in Senegal, Benin, India, St. Kitts, Jamaica, Haiti, and Central America. 30 domestic staff. ($2,000,000)

* *United Church Board for World Ministries* (475 Riverside Drive, New York, NY 10115). Divisions of World Missions and World Service of the United Church of Christ. In partnership with and under the direction of overseas partner churches and ecumenical ministries, UCBWM operates and supports programs in communications, community development, construction and housing, cooperatives and credit, education, enterprise development and management, food production and agriculture, material aid, medicine and public health, population and family services, and social welfare. Makes financial contributions to and maintains personnel in 25 developing countries around the world; makes financial and material contributions to an additional 41 countries. Uses both short- and long-term volunteers abroad. 55 domestic staff (including part-time interns), 252 overseas.

* *United Methodist Committee on Relief* (475 Riverside Drive, Rm. 1470, New York, NY 10115). Provides personnel and financial support to the

United Methodist Church and ecumenical agencies operating programs of relief, rehabilitation, land reclamation, child care, water resource management, afforestation, and development education. Supports resettlement projects, including programs of urban-to-rural transmigration. Six domestic staff executives. Sends more than 1000 short-termers for a maximum service period of three weeks. ($13,000,000)

* *World Concern* (Box 33000, Seattle, WA 98133). A Christian relief and development organization committed to: educating North America to the needs of the Third World; sending financial aid to existing Christian agencies working on development projects; and sending professional personnel to do relief and development work overseas. Applicants must have a personal relationship with Jesus Christ and must be willing to assist World Concern in the deputation process. Preferred skills vary with job descriptions. In general, accredited medical and veterinary doctors, dental administrators, and social workers are in greatest demand. Application process is lengthy, requiring seven references, psychological and medical examinations, and a personal interview. Accepts volunteers who are fully able to support themselves and who meet the same criteria of acceptance as salaried personnel. 52 domestic staff, 99 (including spouses) overseas in 67 countries. ($7,500,000)

* *World Relief* (P.O. Box WRC, Wheaton, IL 60189). World Relief is the relief, development, and refugee service arm of the National Association of Evangelicals. Carries out emergency relief efforts and long-term development projects in 24 nations. Also serves as an official resettlement agency for refugees entering the United States. It adheres to a statement of faith embraced by churches from the 75 denominations represented in the National Association of Evangelicals. A college degree is generally required for overseas placement, and fluency in a foreign language and/ or professional skills are often necessary. Between 40 and 50 volunteers are accepted each year for one- to two-year assignments. Usually a college degree and an evangelical orientation are the main requirements for volunteers. 34 domestic staff at headquarters, 111 staff assigned to refugee services, 72 staff overseas. ($15,000,000)

* *World Vision International* (919 W. Huntington Drive, Monrovia, CA 91016). Nondenominational Christian humanitarian agency that provides emergency relief in the event of human and natural disasters. Programs of development among rural poor in developing countries leading toward self-reliance. Areas of development include agriculture, health, nutrition, family planning, land regeneration, water systems, education, employment and income generation, and community development. Few interns. Staff persons on overseas assignment do administrative or advisory work. 1875 overseas staff in more than 70 countries. ($100,000,000)

General Humanitarian

CARE (660 First Ave., New York, NY 10016). Conducts programs in 37 countries in Asia, Africa, Latin America, and the Middle East. Major emphases: feeding programs (under Public Law 480) for school and preschool children; and self-help programs in which CARE, local communities, and host governments work together on housing, community development, school construction, roads, resource conservation, watersupply systems, mother-child nutrition systems, and training in primary health care. Active in immediate and long-range disaster relief. MEDICO, a service of CARE, trains local physicians, nurses, and other health-services personnel. CARE hires staff to monitor its programs, plus the professional and technical people required for specific projects. Publishes a pamphlet, "Career Information for International Personnel." More than 175 U.S. personnel overseas. ($242,359,000)

* *The Institute of Cultural Affairs* (4750 N. Sheridan Road, Chicago, IL 60640). A catalyst for grass-roots participation in improving the quality of life and for the self-development of local communities and organizations. ICA was originally a division of the Ecumenical Institute but was incorporated in 1973 as a separate entity. ICA trains people in leadership skills, helps create effective methods for self-development, and tries to demonstrate what people can accomplish. ICA believes that the local community is the origin of development, rather than the target. Having begun in Chicago, ICA now has 110 project sites in more than 40 countries. Its fulltime staff are members of "The Order: Ecumenical," which includes people from many different national and religious backgrounds who have volunteered to live a life of service based on their concern for creative renewal. ICA also provides opportunities for short-term volunteers, called "sojourners," to serve for periods of 3 to 12 months. "Sojourners" are responsible for their own travel and support expenses. 200 domestic staff, 450 overseas. ($4,000,000)

International Human Assistance Programs, Inc. (360 Park Ave. South, New York, NY 10010). Private development-aid agency helping impoverished people in developing countries raise their living standards with innovative self-help programs. Major projects designed as integrated ruraldevelopment activities focused on food production, health care, nutrition, family planning, environmental sanitation, vocational training, community-leadership training, and helping women and young people play more active roles in their village economies. Projects, planned and executed cooperatively with village people concerned, are designed to become self-supporting when IHAP phases out aid. Projects presently in the Philippines, Thailand, South Korea, Sri Lanka, the Maldives, the Solomon Islands, Cook Islands, Papua New Guinea, Vanuatu, Swaziland, Djibouti, and Equatorial Guinea. Looking for people with college degrees, certified professional skills, and at least three years overseas experience. 14 domestic staff, 18 overseas. ($4,000,000)

Overseas Education Fund (2101 L St. N.W., Suite 916, Washington, DC 20037). Assists indigenous organizations in Latin America, Asia, and Africa to develop and implement programs aimed at improving the social and economic life of the urban and rural poor. Projects focused on improving conditions of low-income women. Maintains a talent bank of resumés from which personnel are chosen as projects arise. Areas of interest include nonformal education and vocational-skills training, nutrition and health training, communications, organization development, management, adult-formation techniques, and income generation. Technical abilities, a second language, and overseas experience are preferred. Length and terms of projects vary. Currently active in Central America, Ecuador, Senegal, Nigeria, and Sri Lanka. 20 domestic staff, 15 overseas.

Oxfam America (115 Broadway, Boston, MA 02116). Funds local, grass-roots groups in poor countries in Asia, Africa, and Latin America. Oxfam is too well-known to omit from this list, but they offer virtually no opportunities for work abroad and already receive far too many applications. Oxfam also works to inform policymakers and the general public about the root causes of world hunger and poverty. Five domestic staff, two overseas. ($5,100,000)

Partnership for Productivity International (2001 S St. N.W., Suite 610, Washington, DC 20009). Offers assistance to people in a holistic, multi-disciplinary way, helping them to move toward self-reliance without losing their own culture and social structure. Key program elements include management training, credit, technical assistance, trade and investment development, and computer communications training. Works mainly in Africa (Burkina Faso, Botswana, Kenya, Liberia, Malawi, Togo) but also in the Caribbean Basin (Costa Rica, Haiti, Jamaica) and Asia. At least two years overseas development experience, working ability in the local professional language, and sensitivity to different cultures required of applicants. No volunteers overseas. 17 staff and several unpaid volunteers domestically, 140 staff overseas. ($4,500,000)

Serving Particular Regions

Accion International/AITEC (10-C Mount Auburn St., Cambridge, MA 02138). Dedicated to creating income and employment opportunities for the poor in Latin America, the Caribbean, and the United States through direct-assistance programs to rural and urban microenterprises. Includes a development education department, which investigates poverty and hunger problems in developing countries. Applicants must possess extensive overseas and technical experience and fluency in Spanish and/or Portuguese. No volunteers accepted for overseas placement. 10 domestic staff, 6 in Latin America and the Caribbean. ($1,000,000)

The Africa Fund (198 Broadway, New York, NY 10038). Provides humanitarian aid to African people struggling for independence and works toward increased American understanding of Africa issues. Provides relief to African refugees through shipments, grants, and emergency aid. Associated with American Committee on Africa. Project sites are in Angola, Zambia, Tanzania, and Algeria, where refugee facilities are located. Knowledge of southern Africa a bonus to potential employees. Nine domestic staff. ($300,000)

Africare (1601 Connecticut Ave. N.W., Washington, DC 20009). Works to improve the quality of life in rural Africa. Conducts self-help programs to cultivate the land's full potential, develop water resources, strengthen health care, and deliver emergency assistance to refugees. Applicants should have prior experience that suggests the ability to work in difficult cross-cultural situations. Most successful applicants possess an academic or technical degree in their career field. Africare maintains an extensive data bank on persons interested in development work and shares this information with other development agencies. No volunteers. 26 domestic staff; 30 U.S. personnel and more than 150 host-country nationals on 70 project sites throughout Africa. ($8,000,000)

American Near East Refugee Aid (1522 K St. N.W., Suite 202, Washington, DC 20005). Charitable development organization with activities in the West Bank, the Gaza Strip, Lebanon, and Jordan. Assists in economic and community development, health, and education. Bachelor's degree is the minimum requirement for employment; master's degree and overseas development experience are preferred. No volunteers accepted. Eight domestic staff, five in the Near East. ($1,500,000)

* *Foundation for the Peoples of the South Pacific* (158 W. 57th St., New York, NY 10019). Provides training and technical assistance for self-help community development groups and cooperatives. Also financial assistance for self-help projects, mainly for small-business development, fisheries, and agriculture. Active in Micronesia, Papua New Guinea, Fiji, Solomon Islands, Vanuatu, Kiribati, and other nations of the Pacific Basin. Applicants must have prior experience in overseas development. Advanced degree preferred but not required. Volunteers recruited on project-to-project basis. Seven domestic staff, nine overseas. ($1,000,000)

Near East Foundation (29 Broadway, Suite 1125, New York, NY 10006). Nonsectarian, nongovernmental organization assisting governments of developing nations in Asia and Africa in launching programs of rural improvement that later become the full responsibility of the host government. Provides experienced technicians for both operational and advisory positions. Current programs in 12 countries. These include agricultural schools, rural water development, agricultural research, irrigation, livestock and crop improvement, disease control, and conservation. Recruits experienced technicians in technical agriculture, agricultural education, extension, home economics, rural education, and environmental sanitation to serve for two-year periods. Five to seven years of professional experience, plus one or more degrees, generally required. Competitive salary provided, along with housing allowance, transportation, and travel. Currently 23 U.S. citizens serving abroad. ($900,000)

* *Pan American Development Foundation* (1889 F Street N.W., Washington, DC 20006). Encourages private-sector initiatives to respond to economic and social development needs of disadvantaged people throughout Latin America and Caribbean. Programs include: (a) work with local private-sector leaders to establish national development foundations, which provide business counseling and credit to microbusinessmen and women; (b) the provision of tools and machinery, medical equipment, and supplies to vocational schools and health-care institutions; and (c) the promotion of cash cropping of trees. Employment requirements depend on position sought. Volunteers used on specific projects according to project need and experience offered by volunteer. 25 domestic staff, 5 overseas.

Partners of the Americas (1424 K St. N.W., Washington, DC 20005). Links the citizens of 43 U.S. states together with those of 27 Latin American and Caribbean countries. The goal of these partnerships is to mobilize resources at the community level for technical and cultural projects that serve the goals of self-help and mutual benefit. Thousands of private citizens participate in partnership activities every year, conducting projects in agriculture, rehabilitation of the handicapped, sports, culture, community education, and health. The National Association of the Partners of the Americas functions as the advisory and administrative agency for all partnerships. Also provides grants for journalists to work abroad (p. 125).

Agriculture

Agricultural Development Council, Inc. (725 Park Ave., New York, NY 10021). Founded in 1953, aims to stimulate and support economic training and analysis related to human welfare in Asia. Programs centered around country-based Associates (mostly Ph.D's) who teach and direct research for Asian agricultural economists and rural social scientists. Focus on irrigation and water management, renewable resources, rural employment, and food policy. Programs in Bangladesh, China, India, Indonesia, Malaysia, Nepal, Pakistan, the Philippines, Sri Lanka, and Thailand. About 20 overseas.

* *Heifer Project International* (P.O. Box 808, 825 West Third St., Little Rock, AR 72203). Helps poor families around the world to produce more food and income from marginal resources by providing improved livestock and training. Cooperates with networks of churches, schools, self-help agricultural coops, and other voluntary agencies to provide for on-site supervision of projects (or works through local agencies in most countries). Minimum requirement is an agricultural background; development background preferred. Volunteers sent only for specific projects and usually for periods of one to three months. 62 domestic staff and 8 overseas. ($5,100,000)

* *International Institute of Rural Reconstruction* (1775 Broadway, New York, NY 10019). Objective is to generate and share knowledge and skills to enable poverty-stricken people in the Third World to build a better life for themselves. Originated from a grass-roots development movement 60 years ago. IIRR now carries out three interrelated activities from its base in the Philippines: field operational research, international training, and international extension. Foundation of work is an eight-village "social laboratory" in Cavite Province where people-oriented development programs are tested and refined. Cooperates with affiliated national movements in Colombia, Guatemala, Ghana, India, the Philippines, and Thailand. Minimum requirements for overseas employment are a Ph.D. in agronomy, public health, nonformal education or some other development-related field, and at least 10 years practical experience. Very limited openings for volunteers. 7 domestic staff, 121 overseas. ($1,900,000)

Technoserve (11 Belden Ave., Norwalk, CT 06850). A private, nonprofit organization providing training and technical assistance to community-based enterprises, projects, and related institutions committed to development. Primary emphasis is given to agriculture, including productivity, crop processing and marketing, along with savings and credit management.

Technoserve has 112 projects located in El Salvador, Peru, Panama, Costa Rica, Kenya, Ghana, Zaire, Uganda, Zimbabwe, and Rwanda. A degree in business administration and prior Third World working experience are the minimum requirements for employment. French, Spanish, or Swahili language and skills in management, finance, or accounting are preferred. 25 domestic staff, 93 overseas. ($3,400,000)

Children

Pearl S. Buck Foundation, Inc. (Green Hills Farm, Perkasie, PA 18944-0181). Nonsectarian charitable organization serving some 12,800 Amerasian children in various sponsorship, direct relief, outreach, and developmental programs. Amerasian advocate at home and abroad and actively involved in social-welfare remedial efforts. New outreach includes expanded adoption program and peripheral refugee support service. Developing-country programs in Korea, the Philippines, and Thailand. Program outreach to Vietnam and the Indochina region. 35 domestic staff, 146 overseas. ($3,014,000)

Save the Children Federation, Inc. (54 Wilton Road, Westport, CT 06880). Dedicated to improving the quality of life and defending the rights of children—particularly in underprivileged communities—without regard to race, religion, or place of origin. SCF believes children cannot be helped in isolation. Rather, their total environment must be enriched. Thus it works to unite the child, the family, and the community in development projects aimed at transforming need and dependence into plenty and self-reliance. Conducts child sponsorship programs and community development projects in areas such as housing, cooperatives and loans, education, agriculture, small industry development, nutrition, and health care. Emphasis is on community self-help through grass-roots organization as well as training and technical assistance. Programs in the United States and in 38 countries in Africa, Asia, Central America, Europe, and the Middle East. Minimum of two years prior overseas experience in community development required of applicants. No volunteers. 60 domestic staff, 63 overseas. ($40,000,000)

U.S. Committee for UNICEF (331 East 38th St., New York, NY 10016). UNICEF (p. 133) gets nearly a quarter of its funds from private contributions, and three-quarters of that through the U.S. Committee. UNICEF itself is part of the U.N. system, not a private agency, and the U.S. Committee has no staff overseas.

Christian Children's Fund, Inc. (Richmond, VA 23261). An international nonprofit and nonsectarian humanitarian organization founded in 1938 and dedicated to serving the needs of children worldwide through person-to-person assistance programs. Assistance is provided to children in family helper projects, children's homes, institutions for the blind or deaf, day nurseries, vocational training centers, and schools. CCF maintains programs in Argentina, Bolivia, Brazil, Colombia, Ecuador, Ethiopia, Gambia, Guatemala, Honduras, India, Indonesia, Kenya, Korea, Mexico, the Philippines, Thailand, Togo, Uganda, and Zambia. CCF employs nationals whenever possible because of language and cultural familiarity. CCF projects and offices overseas normally recruit personnel locally. No volunteers. ($47,400,000)

Christian Foundation for Children (13001 Wornall Road, Kansas City, MO 64145). Grass-roots movement dedicated to improving the condition of poor children around the world. Provides food, medical care, educational opportunities, and religious orientation to children with genuine need. Currently 11 staff in Chile, Colombia, Honduras, and Venezuela.

Foster Parents Plan International (P.O. Box 400, Warwick, RI 02886). Aims to help children, their families, and communities through social welfare, health, education, and community development programs. Self-help programs are designed to avoid long-term dependency by personal involvement between donor (the foster parent) and recipient (the foster child). Project sites in 22 countries in Asia, Latin America, and Africa. Only field directors and assistant directors are from the United States. Applicants must have fluency in a foreign language, five years experience in a Third World country and extensive administrative experience, including financial and personnel. No volunteers. 53 domestic staff; 3648 overseas, of which 65 from developed countries. ($38,238,000)

* *Holt International Children's Services* (P.O. Box 2880, Eugene, OR 97402). Nondenominational Christian agency that seeks to place homeless children and those children who are at risk of becoming separated from their biological parents with permanent families, usually through adoption. Offers counseling, family rehabilitation, temporary foster care, medical care, and adoption services. Has programs in six countries. Most positions require degree or background in social work and familiarity with Spanish or Asian languages. Few U.S. citizens used overseas, and volunteers accepted only under special conditions. 45 domestic staff, about 600 overseas. ($4,000,000)

Cooperatives

Agricultural Cooperative Development International (1012 Fourteenth St. N.W., Suite 600, Washington, DC 20005). An educational, consulting, and management-assistance organization created by the leading agricultural cooperative and farmer organizations of the United States. Its purpose is to respond to the needs of agricultural cooperatives and farm-credit systems and to support government agencies in developing countries with assistance in training, planning, operation, organization, and member involvement. Employment requirements include two or more years of experience in farm supply or marketing management, accounting and financial controls, combined with a degree in agricultural economics or a related field. Knowledge of a foreign language is desirable. Prior overseas work experience preferable. 23 domestic staff, 30 long-term advisors overseas. No volunteers. ($5,000,000)

Cooperative Housing Foundation (2501 M St. N.W., Suite 450, Washington, DC 20037). Works overseas at the invitation of local governments and cooperative organizations providing technical advice, training, and collaboration with local technicians in the development of self-help housing, cooperative housing, disaster-relief shelter, rural housing, and special programs for refugees. The main CHF concern is the social and human aspect of shelter programs, concentrating on establishing permanent community-based organizations that allow people to improve their homes and communities over a period of time. Overseas sites in more than 22 countries. No minimum requirements for employment, but advanced degrees and overseas experience are helpful. 22 domestic staff, 17 overseas. ($3,000,000)

Cooperative League of the U.S.A. (1828 L St. N.W., Suite 1100, Washington, DC 20036). The League is a national membership and trade association representing the United States' cooperative business community. Serves as a chamber of commerce for cooperative businesses, representing the unique and mutual needs of the various industries. Works to build, develop, and provide technical assistance in developing countries. Project sites in India, Indonesia, Gambia, Equatorial Guinea, Rwanda, Haiti, and Panama. Applicants preferably should have some cooperative or credit and accounting experience. 37 domestic staff, 13 overseas. ($4,100,000)

* *World Council of Credit Unions, Inc.* (P.O. Box 391, Madison, WI 53701). Apex organization of the organized credit-union movement. Promotes international credit-union development through service to regional credit-union associations and emerging credit-union organizations in 67 countries. Project sites in Cameroon, Malawi, Lesotho, Togo, Kenya, Barbados, and Sierra Leone. Purpose is to encourage self-help development through member-owned, member-controlled savings and credit cooperatives. Emphasis on development of self-sufficient credit-union institutions

and production-credit programs for small farmers. International staff and volunteers should have credit-union and cooperative experience, project-planning background, international work experience, and foreign-language capability. Project periods range from two to five years, short-term consultancies from two weeks to six months. Volunteers should also have good credit-cooperative experience and be currently involved or retired from working in the credit-union movement. Salary, benefits, and travel allowance commensurate with those of host organization. 25 domestic staff, 7 overseas.

Education

High/Scope Educational Research Foundation (600 North River St., Ypsilanti, MI 48197). Works with interested counterpart agencies in Latin America to design, implement, and evaluate educational components of early childhood projects. Provides consulting services, research assistance, information, and training programs for educators, ministers, and public service agencies. Also provides personnel for nutrition programs and other programs that serve young children and their parents. Project sites are in Bolivia, Ecuador, Mexico, Peru, St. Kitts-Nevis, and Venezuela. 80 U.S.-based staff involved in both domestic and overseas programs. ($600,000)

Laubach Literacy International (1320 Jamesville Ave., P.O. Box 131, Syracuse, NY 13210). Offers illiterate and newly literate adults instruction from trained tutors, primers, and follow-up materials, technical assistance in learning to plan and monitor their own programs, and financial assistance until programs become independent. Emphasis is on attitude change and the use of communications skills such as reading, writing, speaking, and listening. In the area of food production and agriculture, integrates literacy and agricultural development and tests new crops and improved seed. Assists citizens of Zimbabwe, Colombia, Mexico, Panama, and India. Two salaried domestic staff involved in overseas programs, 103 salaried and 60,000 volunteer host country personnel. ($259,000)

World Education Inc. (210 Lincoln St., Boston, MA 02111). Provides training and technical assistance in nonformal education to agencies in developing countries. Its goal is to strengthen local capacity to serve the needs to the very poorest sections of Third World countries. Applicants should possess an advanced degree in a field related to rural development or adult education, plus long-term experience working and living in a developing country. Relevant skills in training, materials development, program planning, and evaluation are also helpful. No volunteers. Eight domestic staff, 21 overseas at project sites in Thailand, Kenya, and Nepal. ($1,000,000)

Health

* *American Dentists for Foreign Service* (619 Church Ave., Brooklyn, NY 11218). Provides dental education and free equipment such as dental units, chairs, X-ray units, instruments, and supplies. Recipient country must pay for expenses and shipping. Places dentists, hygienists, assistants, and teachers, both graduate and undergraduate, for short-, intermediate-, and long-term service in about 35 countries. Volunteers must pay their own way. All activities oriented to foreign and domestic indigent people and to developing countries. More than 1700 complete dental operatories have been serviced and shipped overseas. Three domestic staff, three overseas. ($50,000)

* *Catholic Medical Mission Board, Inc.* (10 West 17th St., New York, NY 10011). A charitable organization in existence for over 52 years, engaged in the care of the sick, poor, and the shipment of cost-free medical supplies to overseas missions. A medical supply program sends medicines, instruments, and equipment to over 8000 Catholic hospitals and dispensaries in Africa, Asia, Latin America, and Oceania. CMMB's placement service recruits, screens, and introduces medical personnel to overseas Catholic medical mission institutions. Short- and long-term positions for persons skilled in the medical professions. Short-term commitments range from one to six months, with volunteers primarily relieving permanent staff during their leave periods. Volunteers receive a stipend for long-term service only. Two bimonthly publications, *Medical Mission News* and *Professional Placement Newsnotes*. 32 domestic staff, 52 domestic volunteers, and hundreds of volunteers placed overseas annually. Medicines and medical supplies valued at $9,700,000 were shipped to 54 countries in 1983.

Dental Health International (847 South Milledge Ave., Athens, GA 30605). Purpose is to establish dental care through clinics in developing countries' rural areas. Provides volunteer dentists and dental equipment. Volunteers must be accredited dental-school graduates in upper 50% of graduating class. Project sites in Cameroon, Lesotho, Rwanda, Thailand,

Nepal, El Salvador, and the Cook Islands. Two domestic staff. ($90,000 in dental equipment)

* *Direct Relief International* (P.O. Box 30820, Santa Barbara, CA 93130). Donates contributed pharmaceuticals, medical supplies, and new and used medical equipment to needy health facilities in medically less-developed areas of Latin America, South Asia, the Far East, and Africa. Also provides assistance to refugees and other victims of civil strife, famine, and other natural disasters. Through its Volunteer Services Program, DRI recruits medical, dental, and paramedical personnel for assignments at hospitals and clinics in these needy areas. Volunteers usually receive room and board but pay their own transportation. Long-term volunteers may receive a small stipend. DRI works directly with recipient health facilities or relief agencies, both U.S. and indigenous, and not through governments. 22 full-time and part-time domestic paid staff. Volunteer representatives stationed in about 25 countries. ($6,700,000)

* *Dooley Foundation/INTERMED-USA, Inc.* (420 Lexington Ave., Room 2428, New York, NY 10170). Formerly Thomas A. Dooley Foundation in San Francisco. Nonsectarian organization committed to assistance in health development in emerging nations through programs in immunization, health-manpower development, public health, education, nutrition, and family welfare. More recently, directing aid to primitive group survival through protection from Western diseases. Personnel must be fully accredited in health specialty, with a minimum of two years' practice in that specialty postaccrediting. Also has a three-month volunteer program in health development for airline employees. Five domestic staff and six overseas in three countries. ($1,000,000)

* *Esperanca, Inc.* (1911 West Earll Drive, Phoenix, AZ 85015). Inter-denominational agency organized for the purpose of promoting health of the human family and alleviating human suffering. Provides teaching, treatment, and consultative assistance in cooperation with other public and private entities. Sites in Brazil and Bolivia. For volunteer staff, coverage of expenses varies according to applicant's qualifications. Five domestic staff, four overseas. ($1,200,000)

Goodwill Industries International Department (9200 Wisconsin Ave., Bethesda, MD 20814). Provides technical assistance and training to local groups in developing countries engaged in vocational-skill training and employment of disabled persons. The international program relies on the support of individual and corporate contributors. Seven project sites (Panama, Peru, Honduras, Jamaica, Mauritania, Zimbabwe, and the Philippines) and 43 affiliate organizations in 30 countries. No volunteers accepted. Three full-time domestic staff. ($250,000 international budget)

Interchurch Medical Assistance, Inc. (P.O. Box 429, New Windsor, MD 21776). Serves primarily as a facility for the procurement and distribution of medical supplies for the overseas health care ministries of Protestant churches and relief organizations of the United States. Also responds to emergencies and disasters with medical and water-treatment supplies, food supplements, and other vital items and operates a nonprofit purchase service for medical missions. Five domestic staff. Shipped material aid valued at $4,728,000 in 1982.

* *International Eye Foundation* (7801 Norfolk Ave., Bethesda, MD 20814). Works to restore sight and prevent blindness worldwide through the training of local health personnel, through the use of ophthalmic-trained personnel, and by the utilization of volunteer doctors and nurses. Work involves surgical teaching and fellowship programs, shipment of eye tissue, organization of eye banks, and a paramedical-assistance training program in ophthalmology. Ten project sites in Latin America, Africa, and the Middle East. Graduate degree in ophthalmology or public health required. Also sends up to 10 volunteers per year to various locations, most of whom provide own travel and maintenance costs. 10 domestic staff, 15 overseas. ($4,000,000)

Helen Keller International (15 W. 16 St., New York, NY 10011). Works to prevent blindness and provide services for blind persons in developing countries. Accepts invitations from governments and private organizations to send consultants and experts to assess needs and to plan, carry out, and evaluate programs that can be ultimately self-sustainable. Trains teachers with objective of integrating blind children into regular school systems. In rural areas HKI-trained field workers teach blind adults to be self-sufficient and independent. Six project sites in Asia and the South Pacific, two in Africa, one in Latin America. Bachelor's degree and overseas experience required for employment. Public-health background or professional-level training for work with blind persons desired. No volunteers. 23 domestic staff, 9 overseas. ($2,494,000)

* *MAP International* (P.O. Box 50, Wheaton, IL 60189-0050). Interdenominational organization of evangelical tradition that works toward improved health care for people in developing countries. Provides donated medicines and supplies to treat disadvantaged people at mission hospitals,

emergency relief for disaster victims, and community-health assistance. Project sites in Ecuador and Kenya. Extends travel grants for fourth-year medical students to spend eight-week externships at mission hospitals in developing countries. Also sends volunteers. 70 domestic staff, 3 overseas. ($15,119,000)

The MEDEX Group (School of Medicine, University of Hawaii, 1833 Kalakaua Ave., Suite 700, Honolulu, HI 96815). Multidisciplinary team of specialists in primary health care. Designs and develops primary health care technology and assists Third World countries in its adaptation and use. The group has produced and published the MEDEX Primary Health Care Series. In general, background in primary health care (especially training or management) and a minimum of two years prior overseas work experience are required. Preference for candidates with advanced degrees. No volunteers. 19 domestic staff, 6 overseas in Liberia, Guyana, Lesotho. ($2,300,000)

* *Option* (3550 Afton Road, P.O. Box 85322, San Diego, CA 92138). A nonprofit referral and recruitment service. Helps direct health professionals into medically underserved areas of the world. Option offers assignments ranging from several weeks to several years. Short-term volunteers usually receive room and board and occasionally a salary. Programs offering long-term positions usually provide salaries, housing, and travel assistance. Specific opportunities are publicized in a bimonthly newsletter.

* *Orthopedics Overseas, Inc.* (c/o National Council for International Health, 2100 Pennsylvania Ave. N.W., Suite 740, Washington, DC 20037). Supports and promotes orthopedic and rehabilitation programs throughout the world, serving all races and religions on a nondiscriminatory basis. Provides voluntary assistance for the advancement of orthopedic education and care in developing countries. Has recently provided volunteer orthopedic surgeons to Ghana, Malawi, Indonesia, Dominican Republic, Honduras, Jamaica, and Peru. About 20 U.S. volunteers assigned on a short-term basis annually.

* *People to People Health Foundation, Inc. (Project HOPE)* (Personnel Department, Carter Hall, Millwood, VA 22646). Project HOPE is the principal activity of People to People Health Foundation, an independent organization that teaches medical science to medical, dental, nursing, and other health personnel in developing countries. Project sites include Belize, Guatemala, Honduras, St. Lucia, Antigua, Barbados, Jamaica, Grenada, Brazil, Colombia, Portugal, and Egypt. Requires a minimum of two years work experience after completion of certificate/license. Must have some

teaching experience and ability to learn host country's language. Cross-cultural experience preferred. Orientation at headquarters followed by a one- or two-year contract. Salary commensurate with degree and experience. Relocation allowance and full benefits included. Short-term assignments are not salaried. 100 staff at headquarters, 90 overseas. ($10,000,000)

Project Concern International (3550 Afton Road, P.O. Box 85323, San Diego, CA 92138). Independent health training and assistance organization. Founded in 1961 to develop physical well-being of people who lack basic elements of health, with self-sufficiency the ultimate goal. No church or government affiliation. Overseas employees include development specialists, administrators, and nurse trainers on 24-month renewable contracts. Salary, expenses, and benefits included. No volunteers other than in fund raising. ($2,891,000)

* *The Seva Foundation* (108 Spring Lake Drive, Chelsea, MI 48118). A nonprofit, international public health organization that focuses on programs in Nepal and India to prevent blindness and restore sight and on programs of relief to Guatemalan refugees. "Seva" is the Sanskrit word for "service"; the Seva Foundation seeks to reduce suffering through compassionate action. A few volunteer ophthalmologists are chosen for work in Nepal each year. Eight domestic staff, one overseas. ($500,000)

World Rehabilitation Fund (400 E. 34th St., New York, NY 10016). Trains technicians to make artificial limbs and braces, establishes workshops to provide these services, and trains physicians and health personnel in rehabilitation medicine, vocational evaluation, and placement training. Employment requires expertise in specific health-related fields. No volunteers.

Population

Association for Voluntary Sterilization (122 East 42nd St., 18th Floor, New York, NY 10168). AVS is both an international program (concerned with the design, development, and implementation of high-quality voluntary sterilization programs in developing countries) and a national program (concerned with government relations, public information, and increasing access to sterilization services in the United States). Active in 33 countries, AVS is devoted to insuring that sterilization is entirely voluntary, that people give truly informed consent, and that procedures are carried out safely and effectively. Its overseas programs are mainly funded by the U.S. Agency for International Development. Program positions require health professionals at the master's degree level or equivalent work experience, with areas of concentration in public health, public administration, or international affairs. 75 domestic staff, 42 at regional offices in South America/Caribbean, Asia, Africa, and the Middle East. ($10,000,000)

The Centre for Development of Population Activities (1717 Massachusetts Ave. N.W., Suite 202, Washington, DC 20036). A nonprofit organization that seeks to improve the management and supervisory skills of family planning, health, and development professionals from developing countries through specially designed training programs. For example, the Centre offers in-country "Women in Management" workshops to teach participants how to start programs that will reach villages and urban slums. It also offers training programs in the United States on management supervision and program evaluation for Third World family planning and health administrators. Short-term training sites and follow-up units located in Kenya, Mali, Togo, Indonesia, Peru, Bangladesh, Egypt, India, and Nepal. Personnel from 61 developing countries have attended workshops in the United States. 18 domestic staff. ($761,000)

Family Planning International Assistance (810 Seventh Ave., New York, NY 10019). The international affiliate of Planned Parenthood Federation of America (which is itself an affiliate of the International Planned Parenthood Federation). FPIA serves some 900,000 family planning clients in over 40 countries. It also provides contraceptives and medical supplies to governments. FPIA works in places where poverty, geography, culture, or politics make family planning programs especially difficult and helps to introduce family-planning information and services through a variety of non-governmental organizations. It is largely funded by the U.S. Agency for International Development. Planned Parenthood supports legalized abortions as a matter of policy, but FPIA does not finance abortion. ($20,000,000)

International Planned Parenthood Federation (18-20 Lower Regent St., London SW1Y 4PW, England). Founded 32 years ago in India. An international federation of 103 indigenous national family planning associations. IPPF serves some five million users of family planning services directly (at an average cost of roughly $2 per user per year) and another ten million indirectly. Over half its direct clients are in Latin America, concentrated in Brazil and Colombia. The national associations of IPPF advocate population policies and work for public understanding of family planning. IPPF receives almost all its funds from the development assistance programs of governments. IPPF does finance family planning programs that include abortion, which many Christians would consider ethically intolerable; support for abortion accounts for less than one percent of its budget. Most IPPF staff are nationals of the countries of their regions. Some staff with special expertise, in medicine for example, are recruited internationally. 40 staff in New York, 135 in London, 42 in developing countries. ($52,000,000)

Pathfinder Fund (1330 Boylston St., Chestnut, MA 02167). Encourages innovative approaches to foster family planning worldwide. Pathfinder usually makes relatively small grants for ''pathfinding'' activities that governments or other major institutions may be leery of trying but willing to replicate once tested. ($7,000,000)

The Population Council (One Dag Hammarskjold Plaza, New York, NY 10017). An international, nonprofit organization undertaking social science and biomedical research in demographic change and socioeconomic development, family planning, human reproduction, and contraceptive techniques. Produces publications for researchers, policymakers, and the concerned public, and supports advanced training for population specialists. Provides technical assistance to family planning and other population-related programs at local, national, and regional levels. The Council maintains area offices in Latin America and the Caribbean, West Asia and North Africa, and South and East Asia. The Council staff numbers approximately 200.

Other Specialized Areas of Action

* *American Institute for Free Labor Development* (1015 20th St. N.W., Washington, DC 20036). Assists labor movements in Latin America and the Caribbean through provision of basic leadership and technical seminars, regional and resident courses, and advanced-study courses in the United States. Social-aid programs include housing, community development, agricultural projects, and cooperative credit institutions. Offices or programs in all countries of the region except Cuba and Nicaragua. Only country program directors, recruited from the trade-union movement, are from the United States. Also employs as advisors bilingual people with expertise in cooperatives, agriculture, and dirt farming. Volunteers sent on rare occasions. 51 domestic staff, 19 overseas. ($10,000,000)

* *Fellowship of Reconciliation* (Box 271, Nyack, NY 10960). Interreligious, pacifist organization that works for peace education and nonviolent action against war and racism. Founded in 1914. Groups have been established in local communities and in 30 countries (with an international secretariat in Holland). Sells pacifist literature and supports projects for peace education and nonviolent social change in Africa, Asia, and Latin America. Applicants should be college-trained and have experience in peacemaking skills and projects. Some volunteers accepted. 28 domestic staff, 25 overseas. ($830,000)

* *Habitat for Humanity* (419 W. Church St., Americus, GA 31709). Helps poor persons improve their living conditions. Volunteers—most prominently, former president Jimmy Carter—help recipients build low-cost houses, which are then sold to the recipients on a nonprofit, no-interest basis. Works closely with local Christians. 155 staff. ($1,300,000)

Institute for International Development, Inc. (360 Maple Ave. West, Vienna, VA 22180). Helps families become self-sufficient by providing them with training and finance to start or expand their own small businesses and provide jobs for other needy families. Operates programs in Colombia, Costa Rica, Dominican Republic, Honduras, Indonesia, Kenya, Peru, and the Philippines. In the past five years, has helped establish more than 300 new businesses, resulting in new jobs that sustain some 4000 families. Raises funds mainly among U.S. Christians, and works with Christian congregations abroad to identify creditworthy entrepreneurs.

International Rescue Committee (386 Park Ave. S., New York, NY 10016). Nonsectarian agency that assists refugees from totalitarian countries and displaced victims of war. Services range from emergency relief to overseas resettlement for refugees from Europe, Asia, Africa, and Latin America. Activities include child care, medical and educational aid, job placement, self-help and training programs, family counseling, and assistance with asylum problems. Played a major role in Indochina-refugee resettlement in the United States. ($18,348,000)

Opportunities Industrialization Centers (240 West Tulpehocken St., Philadelphia, PA 19144). Operates a community-based, self-help skills training and community revitalization program that has been adapted to local communities in Ethiopia, Gambia, Ghana, Lesotho, Liberia, Nigeria, Sierra Leone, and Togo. Also developing programs in Zimbabwe, Cameroon, India, and Ivory Coast. Offers an innovative approach to vocational, technical, and agricultural skills training to help the disadvantaged become self-reliant and productively involved in the development of their countries. Applicants for staff positions must have a master's degree and French or

Spanish proficiency. Prefers applicants with work experience in Africa and technical or management skills. No volunteers. ($3,500,000)

Planning Assistance, Inc. (141 Fifth Ave., New York, NY 10010). Assists governmental and voluntary service-providing organizations to improve managerial performance, program performance, and their impact in improving the lives of the people they serve. More specifically, provides management assistance in food and nutrition, health, and rural development; also helps to develop the voluntary sector in targeted countries. Operates in Cameroon, Kenya, Lesotho, Mali, Senegal, Sierra Leone, Togo, Costa Rica, Guatemala, Haiti, Honduras, Jamaica, Bangladesh, India, and Sri Lanka. 14 domestic staff, 5 expatriate, and 5 host country employees. ($670,000)

Tolstoy Foundation, Inc. (250 West 57th St., Room 1101, New York, NY 10107). Assists victims of oppression by rehabilitation within the Free World. Facilitates immigration and resettlement to countries willing to offer asylum, integration, and assimilation in local communities without loss of distinctive values inherent in ethnic traditions. Cooperates with the U.S. Department of State, the U.N. High Commission for Refugees, the Intergovernmental Committee for Migration, and local agencies. Carries out programs in education, enterprise development and management, and social welfare (including legal counsel, operation of homes for aged refugees, and permanent care for the mentally disabled). Programs conducted in Argentina, Brazil, Chile, Paraguay, Uruguay, Venezuela, Greece, and Lebanon. 97 domestic, 94 salaried host-country staff. ($338,000)

* *VITA* (*Volunteers in Technical Assistance*) (1815 North Lynn St., Arlington, VA 22209). Gives appropriate technological information and assistance to individuals and institutions among low-income people in more than 100 developing countries. Services provided free of charge, mostly through mail, by worldwide corps of 4500 volunteer experts and a small central staff. VITA volunteers include scientists, engineers, sociologists, carpenters, agriculturalists, architects, information systems specialists, educators, electricians, and farmers. Most have language skills as well. Volunteers reply to requests for technical advice from people in developing countries, participating with them in the search for local solutions to local problems. Volunteers receive VITA newsletters, attend VITA seminars, and sometimes contribute to VITA publications. Names and backgrounds of volunteers are incorporated into a computerized skills roster at headquarters. Occasionally a volunteer may be asked to travel to a developing country for two to three weeks (all trip expenses reimbursed) to provide on-the-spot advice, sometimes free and sometimes as a paid consultant.

About 6 to 10 project sites at any one time. 35 domestic staff, 7 overseas. ($3,700,000)

YMCA International Division (101 North Wacker Drive, Chicago, IL 60606). YMCAs in the United States have helped to establish and strengthen YMCAs in Africa, Asia, and Latin America, until recently working mainly through this international office. But in 1981-82 the U.S. YMCAs decided that local YMCAs should manage some of their world-service funds themselves and become directly involved in international-awareness programs and in relationships with YMCAs in other countries. Your local YMCA may be moving along these lines. The central office of the YMCA is also still active in cooperation with YMCAs abroad, YMCA management training, programs related to the problems of refugees and urbanization, and development education. Programs involving U.S. personnel abroad include: Youth Exchanges, for youth and young adults in cooperation with the American Field Service; Young Professionals Abroad, for YMCA directors with two to five years' experience, to live and work abroad for two years; World Service Workers, for college graduates with YMCA experience; teachers of English as a second language, for recent college graduates to work for one or two years with the YMCA educational programs in Japan and Taiwan; and short-term specialists, sent in response to specific requests. Nine domestic staff work mainly with indigenous YMCA staff overseas. ($4,221,000)

There are a number of other sources of leads for positions with private development agencies. The best is the New Transcentury Foundation (1789 Columbia Road N.W., Washington, DC 20009). Transcentury is a development consulting group which (with partial funding from AID) has become an important clearinghouse for information about professional opportunities in private development agencies. Their bimonthly publication, *Job Opportunities Bulletin*, provides up-to-date, specific information on career opportunities in international development with private and voluntary organizations. Our most current figure for the price of an annual subscription is $15. The *Job Opportunities Bulletin* runs advertisements for agencies, and for $35 individuals can advertise their own availability.

In addition, several associations of private development agencies can furnish current sources of information about their member organizations. By far the largest is INTERACTION (200 Park Ave. South, New York, NY 10003), an association of over 100 private relief, refugee service, and development organizations. In 1984, the former American Council of Voluntary Agencies (ACVA) and the former Private Agencies in International Development merged to become InterACTION. One very useful source of information available from InterACTION is the report of their 1985 survey of U.S. private, voluntary agencies in Africa; it is called *Diversity in Development* ($12).

Until recently, ACVA maintained (with funding from AID) a Technical Assistance Information Clearing House (TAICH). This work has been discontinued because of a substantial cut in AID's contribution, but the TAICH directory, *U.S. Non-Profit Organizations in Development Assistance Abroad* (1983), remains the most complete catalog of private development programs available. It describes 535 U.S. agencies (including missionary agencies doing development work) and indicates which agencies are involved on a country-by-country basis. This directory costs $24.50. Other TAICH publications for sale include: directories on development assistance in East Africa (1984 edition, $14.50) and Central America and the Caribbean (1983 edition, $14.50); country-by-country reports of private agencies at work in nearly 70 countries; and annotated catalogs of agencies involved in both agricultural development and medical work. To order any of these publications, write: UNIPUB, P.O. Box 1222, Ann Arbor, MI 48106.

Another association of private development agencies is CODEL (Coordination in Development, 79 Madison Ave., New York, NY 10016), a consortium of 40 church-related (both Catholic and Protestant) organizations whose primary goal is to provide assistance to self-determined development projects in Third World areas. CODEL helps its member agencies with consultative services, network building, and assistance in pooling their resources. CODEL itself has no staff who are living abroad, but its regional representatives spend quite a bit of time traveling.

A third association of agencies is PACT (Private Agencies Collaborating Together, 777 U.N. Plaza, New York, NY 10017), an international consortium of some 22 private, technically oriented agencies working with people in developing countries who have limited access to resources. PACT provides funding to its member organizations for field-level development projects. During the 12 years of its existence, PACT has awarded over $15 million in grants.

Most of these projects are in Latin America. PACT also helps co-ordinate activities among its member agencies and sponsors activities that assist them in the areas of information exchange, personnel, financial management, and fund raising. Like CODEL, PACT has some staff who travel regularly to the developing countries, but none who live there.

Health professionals should acquaint themselves with The National Council for International Health (2100 Pennsylvania Ave. N.W., Suite 740, Washington, DC 20037), a nonprofit professional organization that works exclusively to strengthen participation in international health activities, especially in developing countries. NCIH includes more than 140 U.S. public and private organizational members and more than 2000 individual members from over 40 countries. It provides its members with services and technical assistance, including conferences and workshops, books and information, and job-placement services. NCIH publishes *U.S.-Based Agencies Involved in International Health Assistance* (1980 with a 1982 Addendum), which contains comprehensive and up-to-date information on more than 300 public and private U.S. agencies with health-related programs in developing countries.

The 156 private development agencies that have registered with AID are all described in a booklet titled *Voluntary Foreign Aid Programs*. Write: U.S. International Development Cooperation Agency, Agency for International Development, Washington, DC 20523.

Finally, there are two helpful publications that evaluate some of the best-known private development agencies. They both include agencies with programs abroad and agencies that try to influence public policy (as described in the section below). We especially recommend Louis L. Knowles' *A Guide to World Hunger Organizations*, a well-researched, reliable evaluation of about 20 agencies. It's currently available for $6 from Seeds/Alternatives, 222 East Lake Drive, Decatur, GA 30030. You might also get Mark Olson's *A Giver's Guide*, a magazine article reprint that evaluates the purposes, staff characteristics, financial practices, and administrative costs of 35 organizations. Request it from *The Other Side*, 300 West Apsley, Philadelphia, PA 19144.

Private groups focused on public policy

Most of this chapter is about private development agencies with operations in the Third World. But all the U.S.-based private development agencies together contribute about $1.3 billion to the developing countries. Their efforts, even taken together, are simply dwarfed by the need of the developing countries. By contrast, just one international agency, The World Bank, provided about $17 billion to the developing countries in its last fiscal year. Or, to take another example, developing-country exports to the industrial countries total $180 billion. Concerned people in the United States who really want to encourage economic and social progress in the developing countries need to influence these larger flows. That means getting informed—and then getting into politics.

So we are including this section on private organizations, many of them church-related, that help people in the United States understand Third World development issues and influence U.S. public policies that affect Third World development. These organizations seldom send staff abroad, which is generally our criterion for citing an organization in this book. But private organizations focused on public policy are just too important to Christian involvement in the Third World for us to omit them.

Private groups focused on public policy provide opportunities for service for many people who cannot, for some reason, actually go to developing countries. Staff are frequently people who have already had overseas experience, but there are also staff opportunities for people who haven't been abroad. These groups usually use lots of volunteers too, and placement is, of course, much easier than for an overseas program.

Here are some of the most prominent private organizations, most of them church-related, that work on public education and public policy issues in the United States:

American Friends Service Committee. See p. 35.

Amnesty International/USA (304 W. 58th St., New York, NY 10019). A worldwide movement, headquartered in London. Seeks the release of "prisoners of conscience" (people who are detained for their beliefs or ethnic background but have not used or advocated violence). Amnesty also works for fair and speedy trials of all political prisoners and opposes the death penalty and torture. It counts 325,000 members in 154 countries and territories. Amnesty's many local groups typically "adopt" specific prisoners in other countries on whose behalf they write letters and, in other ways, seek release from prison. 40 staff in the New York office. ($3,800,000)

Bread for the World (802 Rhode Island Ave. N.E., Washington, DC 20018). A Christian citizens' movement devoted to influencing U.S. government policy to speed the end of hunger. Bread for the World's 47,000 members are organized by congressional district. They are encouraged to study the causes and possible remedies for hunger, both domestic and international, and to lobby with their senators and representatives in favor of specific legislation of importance to hungry people. Some staff members study proposed federal legislation, others specialize in lobbying Congress, and a third group works with Bread's national network of members. Through its Educational Fund, Bread for the World also conducts an extensive education and publication program directed at church people and the general public. 52 full-time staff, 20 interns and short-term staff associates. ($2,500,000)

Center of Concern (3700 13th St. N.E., Washington, DC 20017). A Jesuit-related research and education center on justice and peace issues. Serves both policymakers and a network of 100 Justice and Peace Centers throughout the United States. One of the Center of Concern's four priorities is global rich/poor confrontation. Twelve full-time staff, three part-time research assistants/interns. ($350,000)

Interfaith Action for Economic Justice (110 Maryland Ave. N.E., Washington, DC 20002). Most of the large Protestant denominations, together with some Catholic and Jewish organizations, maintain this office to help them research and coordinate their efforts to affect public policy on behalf of poor people. Interfaith Action's primary means of mobilizing people in the religious community to support important legislation is the national alert system know as "IMPACT." The system provides subscribers with reports on the progress of legislation and special "action alerts" calling for letter writing, calls, and personal visits to congressional offices. Until 1983, Interfaith Action was known as the Inter-religious Task Force on U.S. Food Policy. Its present name reflects an expansion of purpose to include many public policy issues that have an impact on low-income people in the United States and throughout the world. Its work is focused in four areas of concern: agriculture, nutrition, development, and economics. Staff conducts research, writes reports and newsletters, and follows legislation in Congress and regulations in the Executive Branch. Interfaith Action also draws on staff working for its member organizations. Eight full-time staff. ($248,000)

The Hunger Project (2015 Steiner St., San Francisco, CA 94115). The Hunger Project works in North America and in 24 countries abroad to inform people about world hunger and encourage them to make a conscious commitment to end hunger. Much of the organization's activity is focused on getting more people to "enroll" in The Hunger Project; in practice, this means signing a card committing oneself to "making the end of hunger an idea whose time has come." So far, 4 million people have "enrolled." The Hunger Project also has an extensive educational program on ending hunger; it has provided four-hour briefings on ending hunger to over one-quarter of a million people in the last three years and publishes information about world hunger at various levels of sophistication. Werner Erhard, the founder of EST, also started The Hunger Project. The Hunger Project does not do relief or development work abroad; nor does it take positions on controversial political issues. Rather, it encourages people to commit themselves to ending hunger, helps them to become informed, and then urges them to decide for themselves how they can best contribute, as individuals and through other organizations, to actually ending hunger. 95 staff; 3000 active volunteers worldwide. ($5,500,000)

NETWORK (Merkle Building, 806 Rhode Island Ave. N.W., Washington, DC 20018). Lobbies in the U.S. Congress on justice and peace issues. Founded in 1971 by a group of Catholic sisters and informed by Catholic social teaching. Now includes men and women, lay and religious, throughout the country. NETWORK's prime Third World concerns are South Africa and Central America. Qualifications to work at NETWORK include a deep personal commitment to social justice and human rights and a feminist perspective which features participation, stewardship, mutuality, and integration as key values. Nine full-time staff, seven interns and volunteers. ($295,000)

Overseas Development Council (1717 Massachusetts Ave. N.W., Washington, DC 20036). An independent, nonprofit organization established in 1969 to increase American understanding of the economic and social problems confronting the developing countries and to promote awareness of the importance of these countries to the United States in an increasingly interdependent international system. In pursuit of these goals, ODC functions as a center for policy analysis, a forum for the exchange of ideas, and a resource for public education. Current projects fall within four broad areas of policy concern: trade and industrial policy, international financial issues, development strategies and development cooperation, and U.S. foreign policy toward the Third World. 27 permanent staff, plus four to seven volunteer interns each semester. ($1,200,000)

Oxfam America. See p. 43.

Many church bodies maintain programs to help their members understand Third World issues and bring Christian concern to bear on public policy. At the national level, some denominations maintain both an economic justice office, which usually devotes some of its attention to Third World issues, and another office focused entirely on world hunger. These national offices prepare church policy statements, organize conferences, work with church-related lobbies (such as Interfaith Action for Economic Justice or Bread for the World), and liaise with state and local networks of church members and officials concerned about Third World issues. The biggest Protestant hunger offices are:

Hunger Program
The American Lutheran Church
422 South Fifth St.
Minneapolis, MN 55415

Hunger Appeal
Lutheran Church in America
231 Madison Ave.
New York, NY 10016

Congregational Social
   Action Ministries
(Disciples of Christ)
P.O. Box 1986
Indianapolis, IN 46206

Staff Officer for Hunger
Episcopal Church
815 Second Ave.
New York, NY 10017

Presbyterian Hunger Program
Presbyterian Church in the U.S.A.
341 Ponce de Leon Ave. N.E.
Atlanta, GA 30365

Presbyterian Hunger Program
Presbyterian Church in the U.S.A.
475 Riverside Drive, 12th floor
New York, NY 10115

Hunger Office
American Baptist Churches
   in the U.S.A.
Valley Forge, PA 19482

Coordinator of Hunger Action
United Church Board for
   World Ministries
United Church of Christ
475 Riverside Drive, 16th floor
New York, NY 10115

United Methodist Committee on Relief
United Methodist Church
475 Riverside Drive, R 1374
New York, NY 10115

These offices offer few paid work opportunities, but they can certainly give you lots of ideas about how you can contribute as an unpaid volunteer, within the United States, to the cause of reducing world hunger.

The comparable office in the Roman Catholic Church is the Office of International Peace and Justice, U.S. Catholic Conference (1312 Massachusetts Ave. N.W., Washington, DC 20005). This office helps to draft pastoral letters on social issues for the bishops, lobbies in Congress, and works with an extensive network of concerned Catholics in the various dioceses and religious orders.

Robert McCan did a detailed evaluation of what the largest ecumenical Protestant denominations and the Roman Catholic Church are doing to shape public policy on international development issues in his *World Economy and World Hunger* (Frederick, Maryland: University Publications of America, 1982). McCan praised the quality of some of these efforts, but found them to be woefully understaffed, hesitant on controversial political issues, and often lacking in intellectual depth and creativity. His book is currently available for $5 from the Churches' Center for Theology and Public Policy, 4500 Massachusetts Ave. N.W., Washington, DC 20016.

This section has provided a very selective listing of U.S.-based groups working to shape public policy toward the developing countries. We haven't even listed all the explicitly church-related groups, let alone the host of purely political groups active in this area. For more extensive information, we refer you to the World Hunger Education Service (1317 G Street N.W., Washington, DC 20005). They publish *Who's Involved With Hunger: An Organization Guide for Education and Advocacy* by Patricia L. Kutzner and Nickola Lagoudakis (4th ed., 1985, $8). This fine reference includes a brief description of 400 organizations (U.N. agencies, U.S. federal agencies, religious organizations) which are sources of data, analysis, information, and educational materials on global or domestic hunger and related topics. Each entry gives address, telephone number, contact person, and major publications. The World Hunger Education Service also provides up-to-date information on hunger-related organizations in *Hunger Notes,* a journal on hunger education and advocacy (currently 10 issues per year for $15). Also see Thomas P. Fenton and Mary J. Heffron's *Third World Resource Directory* (Maryknoll, New York: Orbis, 1984). It describes key organizations (as well as printed and audiovisual resources) concerned with U.S. involvement in the Third World. Fenton and Heffron mainly feature organizations that favor radical change in the Third World. They have organized most of their information in separate sections for the various geographic regions of the Third World and also for certain issues: food, human rights, militarism, transnational corporations, and women.

Foundations

Charitable foundations are better funded and run more like business corporations than most private development agencies. Almost all of the major foundations direct a portion of their philanthropic giving to developing countries, and a number of smaller foundations specialize in Third World concerns. Foundations rarely place their own staff overseas and seldom have them travel abroad much. Several foundations specifically asked that we not mention them in this book because they are already deluged with job applications and offer very few opportunities for overseas travel.

The organizations that receive foundation grants, often university departments or private development agencies, offer more opportunities to live or travel abroad. Once you learn, for example, that the San Francisco Foundation funds a significant number of programs for Asian refugee assistance, you might check whether any of the groups they sponsor might need staff to implement programs in Thailand or the Philippines. A grant to a university for research abroad might be sufficient to provide for project support staff—a few "gophers" to accompany the Ph.D.'s. Write to the recipient organizations directly, not to the funding foundation, to inquire about possible employment.

Then, too, there is a slim possibility that with exhausting research and tenacity, you just might be successful in obtaining foundation funding for work that you yourself want to do. A grant seeker may need to write 200 letters to receive one affirmative reply, and you will probably need to be affiliated with some institution. Virtually all foundations make grants to institutions only, not directly to individuals.

The best source of information about foundations is the Foundation Center (Main Office, 79 Fifth Ave., New York, NY 10003; Washington Library, 1001 Connecticut Ave. N.W., Washington, DC 20036). Together with 150 cooperating libraries in all 50 states, the Foundation Center libraries provide free access to all of the materials necessary to identify funding recipients or develop a good proposal. Services that the Center makes available to grantseekers include reference librarians, weekly orientations, special orientations for groups or classes, and an Associates Program for those needing frequent and immediate access to foundation information.

The Foundation Center publishes a number of annually revised references. Among the most important are:

Foundation Directory. Describes over 4000 of the largest foundations.
Foundation Grants Index. A catalog of recent grant recipients.
Foundation Grants to Individuals. Describes programs of more than 900 foundations that make grants to individuals.
Grants for International and Foreign Programs. A catalog of recent grant recipients in the international field.
National Data Book. Brief descriptions of almost 22,000 foundations.

The Center also publishes a bimonthly volume of current information on grants and grantmakers.

Below are listed some of the foundations with the largest programs of funding related to developing countries, together with a few smaller foundations that specialize in fields related to developing countries. The figures in parentheses at the end of these listings indicate grant totals for a recent year.

The Asia Foundation (P.O. Box 3223, San Francisco, CA 94119). Works with organizations, institutions, and individuals in Asia and the Pacific dedicated to furthering social and economic progress. Conducts operations in 10 countries, providing financial support for education, law, public administration, business-management training, communications, and international studies. Since its founding in 1954, has awarded millions of dollars in small grants and has supplied more than 23 million books and journals through its Books for Asia Program. Requirements for staff: U.S.

citizenship, a master's degree in an appropriate subject, and previous experience living or working in Asia. Volunteers rarely used. 50 domestic staff, 20 U.S. citizens, and about 100 Asian nationals overseas. ($17,500,000)

Carnegie Corporation of New York (437 Madison Ave., New York, NY 10022). Devoted to advancement and diffusion of knowledge. One of its four broad goals is the strengthening of human resources in developing countries with initial foci on mothers' and children's health, nutrition, and basic education, especially for women and girls. Field efforts are concentrated in a few countries in the Caribbean and Africa for the present. About $500 million in assets. 40 domestic staff. ($20,000,000)

China Medical Board of New York, Inc. (622 Third Ave., New York, NY 10017). Supports programs of medical nursing and public-health education and research in East and Southeast Asia. Assets of $62 million. ($3,200,000)

Edna McConnell Clark Foundation (250 Park Ave., Rm. 900, New York, NY 10017). Funds research on one tropical disease, schistosomiasis. Assets of $275 million. Only two positions involved with international programs, both located in New York. ($15,000,000)

The William and Flora Hewlett Foundation (525 Middlefield Road, Menlo Park, CA 94025). Allocates substantial resources to activities in the population field, particularly those involving less-developed countries, where most of the unsustainable population growth occurs. Specific interests encompass the training of population experts, policy-related research on population issues, and support of family-planning services and other fertility-reducing programs.

W.K. Kellogg Foundation (400 North Ave., Battle Creek, MI 49016). Among the largest private philanthropic organizations in the United States. Established to "help people help themselves." Has distributed more than $700 million in support of programs in agriculture, education, and health. Areas of emphasis within those broad fields include adult continuing education; betterment of health; community-wide, cost-effective health services; nutritious-food provisions; and broadening leadership capacity of individuals. Supports projects in Latin America and the Caribbean as well as international fellowship programs in other countries. Assets over $1 billion. 23 professional staff and 41 support staff in the United States, 2 professional staff overseas.

The Rockefeller Foundation (1133 Avenue of the Americas, New York, NY 10036). Fourth largest U.S. foundation. Purpose is to provide for the well-being of people throughout the world. Carries out work in six fields: food and nutrition, population problems, health sciences, international relations, equal-opportunity promotion, and cultural development. Nairobi, Kenya, is the only project site in a developing country. Most professional staff have advanced degrees. No volunteers. Assets of more than $1 billion. 138 domestic staff, 11 overseas. ($63,871,000)

The fund-raising activities of pop musicians in response to the African famine have spawned several new foundations. An extraordinary gathering of British and Irish musicians made the record "Do They Know It's Christmas," and the revenues from it are being administered by *Band Aid Trust* (Band Aid Warehouse, Central London Garage, Burton St., London WC1, England). A group of U.S. artists made another record, "We Are the World," and set up *USA for Africa* (P.O. Box 67630, Los Angeles, CA 90067) to administer its revenues. In July 1985 more than one billion people in more than 100 countries watched the telecast of simultaneous "Live Aid" concerts in Philadelphia and London; the resulting contributions are being administered by the *Live Aid Foundation* (c/o Center for Immigration Policy and Refugee Assistance, P.O. Box 2298, Georgetown University, Washington, D.C. 20057). All these funds are to be channeled through existing development programs, mainly private agencies.

FOUR

Church Missions

Christians began going overseas to propagate their faith soon after the disciples first heard Jesus's injunction: "Go therefore and make disciples of all nations, baptizing them in the name of the Father and of the Son and of the Holy Spirit" (Matt. 28:19).

Today, there are an estimated 220,000 international Christian missionaries, of which 63,000 come from North America. At its best, missionary work offers exceptional opportunities for genuine intercultural dialog. Missionaries are normally the leaders among expatriates in learning non-Western languages, and they are often more sensitive to local culture and aspirations than are most other foreigners. Also, they interact with all types of people, including the humbler classes most foreigners know only as servants or employees.

Current trends and issues

The character of overseas mission has changed greatly since the Second World War. With the emergence of independent nations in much of the Third World, most churches already established in the developing countries accelerated their efforts to replace foreign with indigenous leaders. As the new nations made economic development their premier objective, Third World churches, too, assigned greater importance to economic improvement and social change. These trends have been pronounced within the Roman Catholic church and among ecumenical Protestant churches (those that belong to the

World Council of Churches). Conservative evangelical churches, on the other hand, have continued to increase their foreign missionary personnel in developing countries and to focus mainly on preaching and teaching.

The Roman Catholic church in the United States increased the number of its missionary personnel overseas, especially in Latin America, back in the 1960s. But the experience of North American missionaries in Latin America led to a deeper awareness of the importance of indigenous leadership and of the "liberation theology" that some Latin American Catholics were beginning to teach. The Roman Catholic church in the United States reduced the number of missionary personnel again, as a matter of deliberate policy. This fascinating story of how Roman Catholic mission thinking changed is best recounted in Gerald M. Costello's *Mission to Latin America* (Maryknoll, N.Y.: Orbis Books, 1979).

Ecumenical Protestant churches are also intent on avoiding any semblance of religious imperialism. They usually wait for invitations from their sister churches in developing countries before sending personnel abroad, and they have purposefully reduced the number of missionaries they send. They currently sponsor only about a fifth as many missionaries as they did 30 years ago, and they now account for only 6% of the total of Protestant missionaries.

The ecumenical Protestant churches are still contributing about a third of the national total of Protestant mission funds, but in response to Third World nationalism and the maturity of their sister churches in developing countries, they are supporting programs abroad without sending Americans to manage them. The ecumenical Protestant churches also provide major support for international and ecumenical organizations such as the World Council of Churches, the Baptist World Alliance, and the Lutheran World Federation.

Dr. William J. Danker, a distinguished professor of mission, says:

The mainline missionaries may be fewer in number, but they generally serve much larger and more autonomous national church bodies. One reason for their small numbers is that they have succeeded very well in reaching their objective of planting an indigenous church, which has less need of missionaries. The number of missionaries is not the bottom line. The number of Christians is much more significant.

By contrast, evangelical groups currently support three times as many missionaries as they did 30 years ago, and they are expanding their overseas staff by about 10% a year. Conservative evangelicals now account for 94% of U.S. Protestant missionaries abroad. Conservative evangelicals, too, espouse partnership with Third World churches, but the partnerships they fashion are typically with Third World churches of a similar outlook and conviction. U.S. evangelicals also concentrate much of their work in areas where national churches do not yet exist.

Most Third World churches (and the U.S. churches that cooperate with them) now supplement their ministry to souls with resourceful, small-scale efforts to meet a broad range of development needs— clinics and preventive health, schools and adult literacy work, community development, and advocacy for disadvantaged groups.

Among Roman Catholics, the Second Vatican Council and subsequent conferences of Latin American bishops—at Medellin, Colombia (1968), and Puebla, Mexico (1979)—affirmed the idea that religion should respond to the needs of the whole person, penetrating the social and economic realms as well as the spiritual. The struggle for social justice has assumed a more prominent place in Roman Catholic theology, and for many Catholic missionaries, identification with the cause of the poor means an overhaul of existing political and economic systems, perhaps even through revolutionary movements.

The leadership of many ecumenical Protestant churches has also taken outspokenly liberal positions on social issues, including issues of importance to developing countries, and U.S. Protestant funds support programs of economic development and social change throughout the Third World. Most controversially, the World Council of Churches has provided significant amounts of humanitarian assistance to liberation movements in southern Africa.

Among Roman Catholic and ecumenical Protestant mission agencies, there has been increasing emphasis on "reverse mission"— providing opportunities for Christians from the Third World to share both their faith and their perspective on social and political issues with North Americans.

Some evangelical Protestants, too, are attuned to the imperative of social change and advocate "holistic mission" (that is, mission to the whole person, in both material and spiritual ways). But the evangelical Protestant mission agencies—which provide the bulk of overseas opportunities for North Americans—still focus mainly on individual conversions in the developing countries.

The three main points of view on mission issues—Catholic, ecumenical Protestant, and evangelical Protestant—are represented in these three books:

Flanagan, Pedraig, ed. *A New Missionary Era*. Maryknoll, N.Y.: Orbis, 1982. An analysis of the changing face of missionary activities by leading Roman Catholic writers on the subject.

Hopkins, Paul A. *What Next in Mission?* Philadelphia: Westminister, 1977. An ecumenical Protestant perspective on directions for global mission.

Wagner, C. Peter. *On the Crest of the Wave: Becoming a World Christian*. Ventura, Calif.: Regal, 1983. An evangelical Protestant call to participate in the mission movement.

In addition, we recommend two periodicals:

Maryknoll Magazine (Maryknoll Fathers, Maryknoll, NY 10545). If you send as little as $1 to the Maryknoll Fathers, they will send you their colorful monthly magazine. It offers excellent, readable articles on mission issues generally, as well as accounts of Maryknoll activities.

International Bulletin of Missionary Research (Overseas Ministry Study Center, 6315 Ocean Ave., Ventor, NJ 08406). $14 per year. This more scholarly journal, published quarterly, includes articles and book reviews on Christian mission from Roman Catholic, ecumenical Protestant, and evangelical Protestant perspectives.

General information on work opportunities

Foreign missions are as diverse and decentralized as the rest of North American church life. By one count, there are 457 Protestant agencies and 300 Catholic agencies with overseas personnel. But among Protestants, 12 agencies account for 44% of overseas personnel; among Catholics, 10 agencies account for 43% of overseas personnel.

U.S. missionaries are concentrated in particular areas. A disproportionate number are in Latin America, for example. A quarter of all North American Protestant missionaries are in Brazil, the Philippines, Japan, Mexico, and India, and almost two-fifths of U.S. Catholic missionaries are in Brazil, the Philippines, Japan, Peru, Bolivia, and Puerto Rico.

Among both Protestants and Roman Catholics, about half of all missionaries are women.

Missionary agencies send both clergy and lay people abroad. Most agencies send some committed lay people abroad to preach and teach, and they also need administrators, accountants, and skilled trades people to support their evangelistic work. In addition, mission agencies and the churches they serve in developing countries need teachers for their schools, medical personnel for their clinics, and agriculturalists, microbusiness specialists, and community organizers for small development projects. Many church bodies and agencies maintain current lists of openings for professional and skilled people requested by sister churches abroad.

Mission personnel from North America are normally sent by their own church bodies. Christians with faith and skills to share might, however, contact a number of agencies in addition to those associated with their own church. A member of the American Lutheran Church, for instance, would surely want to find out what programs other Lutheran churches are sponsoring, and quite a few of the evangelical Protestant agencies are explicitly interdenominational.

Not too many years ago the term "missionary" denoted a lifetime commitment to service abroad. But most missionaries now serve for fixed terms, with the option to continue thereafter.

Both Protestant and Catholic mission agencies place many short-term workers abroad, including young and relatively inexperienced volunteers. About a third of the mission personnel overseas are serving terms of two years or less. Missions can sometimes use the talents of midcareer people who are willing to serve for low wages in a developing country but don't have any previous experience abroad. A number of programs allow North American youth to involve themselves briefly, in some cases for less than a month, in missionary work abroad.

Protestant agencies that regularly place short-term staff are marked with asterisks in the list on pp. 79-90. Catholic agencies that place lay people, normally on a short-term basis, are listed on pp. 92-95. Note that some Protestant programs for short-term workers are open to Catholics, and vice versa. Young people interested in short-term work with a mission agency might also check for further leads from youth groups or campus ministry offices.

Then, too, you may be able to use church contacts to arrange your own short-term program abroad or even to deepen what you learn during a tourist visit. Many pastors and lay people in the United States have direct relationships with church people abroad—with an American missionary, for example, or with a church official from another country who attended some international conference. Your priest or minister, or someone he or she knows, may be able to suggest a friendly contact for you in another country. Two examples:

• When David Beckmann traveled around the world after college, a friend of a friend, an executive of the American Bible Society, was kind enough to write colleagues in several countries; they, in turn, were kind enough to let him stay in their homes for a few days. They also helped him move quickly into local situations he could not have possibly found for himself.

• A young couple, teachers from Lincoln, Nebraska, made contact with a missionary in Kenya. They paid for their own tickets, but the missionary provided them a context for learning and helping (simple construction work on a new school building and a bit of teaching), plus room and board for the three weeks they stayed in Kenya.

You'll want to be careful about leaning on missionaries for hospitality, but some consider opening their doors to travelers as part of their ministry. Local church people are even better contacts because they are fully part of the local scene; on the basis of shared faith, they are often willing to go out of their way to welcome you into their lives.

Specifics for Protestants

The most comprehensive reference on Protestant mission agencies is the *Mission Handbook: North American Protestant Ministries Overseas*. It is the source of much information in this chapter. The 1980 edition provided summary data on 714 agencies, their activities, personnel, finances, and geographical coverage. Most seminary and religious libraries carry it, and it is also available from the publisher (Missions Advanced Research and Communications Center, 919 W. Huntington Drive, Monrovia, CA 91016).

Protestant clergy interested in working abroad might consider, in addition to missionary work, the possibility of serving a congregation of U.S. citizens and other expatriates in a developing country. There are hundreds of such churches in the Third World, and U.S. clergy can serve them effectively without first learning a foreign language or becoming thoroughly familiar with a foreign culture. Some of these churches recruit staff directly, some through denominational or interdenominational offices. The National Council of Churches of Christ maintains an information clearinghouse, but pastors normally apply through their own denominations.

There are four further sources of information that will be of particular interest to evangelical Protestants:

- *Intercristo* (P.O. Box 33487, Seattle, WA 98133) is a personnel information center listing about 20,000 openings among 400 mission agencies. For $35 individuals can register their intentions and qualifications using Intercristo's computerized Intermatch Personnel Profile system; they receive back a printout of appropriate job openings.

- *Global Opportunities* (1594 North Allen, No. 7, Pasadena, CA 91104). Assists mission-motivated Christians to find secular, salaried employment around the world. GO provides recruiting, job/mission counseling, computerized job referral, and cross-cultural orientation services as well as information on internship and study-abroad options. Through GO's computer job-matching service, applicants receive biweekly printouts of current openings, employment and mission counseling, cultural orientation materials, and liaison with Christians already working in the place of destination. The charge for six months of service is currently $36, or $48 if both spouses apply.

• Each year the Interdenominational Foreign Mission Association (P.O. Box 395, Wheaton, IL 60189-0395) publishes *Opportunities,* a pamphlet that lists hundreds of openings by type of position, mission society, and country. The Interdenominational Foreign Mission Association is a fellowship of 53 mission societies without denominational affiliation.

• The fourth reference of particular interest to evangelical Protestants is the *Student Mission Opportunities Guide,* an annual catalog of summer mission opportunities prepared by the Student Missionary Union (Biola University, 13800 Biola Ave., La Mirada, CA 90639). It lists hundreds of summer positions around the world among 50 mission agencies.

The following list of Protestant agencies includes agencies that send large numbers of personnel overseas and also agencies with large programs specifically for short-term personnel. It is drawn in part from the two latest editions of the *Mission Handbook* (p. 78) and from the Agency for International Development's *Voluntary Foreign Aid Programs* (p. 62). Annual income from a recent year, if available, is shown in parentheses at the end of each listing. Those mission agencies that use short-term staff are marked with asterisks:

* *Africa Evangelical Fellowship* (Box 1679, 733 Bloomfield Ave., Bloomfield, NJ 07003). Nondenominational sending agency in the evangelical tradition. Prime objectives are to preach the gospel and to establish and assist believers in a fellowship of local churches. Needs personnel skilled in aviation, literature, health care, education, secretarial services, and communications media. Missionaries must agree doctrinally and be sufficiently trained for their ministry, plus have a degree in Bible studies for Bible teaching. They are responsible for self-support through friends and churches. Commitments of two years or more. Summer student missionary opportunities also available. 12 domestic staff, 325 in Central and Southern Africa. ($1,800,000)

* *Africa Inland Mission* (P.O. Box 178, Pearl River, NY 10965). International, interdenominational, evangelical organization dedicated to the work of evangelism and church planting by means of education, medicine, literature, mass media, agriculture, and personal witness. Also sends volunteers to East and Central Africa for a 10- to 12-week period during the summer or from two to six months at any time throughout the year. Volunteers should be at least 19 years old and have some specific skill to offer the local church. Approximate cost $2400. About 35 domestic staff, 700 overseas. ($5,000,000)

* *Agape Movement* (Arrowhead Springs, San Bernardino, CA 92414). Interdenominational sending agency of evangelical tradition, training and equipping vocationally qualified lay persons for spiritual impact through aggressive evangelism. Engaged in agricultural development, community-health education, medical and engineering assistance. Thorough application process involving extensive biblical training and orientation to the organization. Original commitment two to three years; average stay about eight years. Volunteers must raise funds for all program costs. 130 staff overseas in 24 countries. ($1,200,000)

American Bible Society (1865 Broadway, New York, NY 10023). Assists churches and Christian missions in developing countries in education and evangelism through scripture reading materials. Has helped to translate scripture into over 500 languages by training local people in linguistic and communications theory. Also provides materials for the translation and production of scripture literacy texts for use in church and government programs. Conducts worldwide program through the auspices of the United Bible Societies; the American Bible Society contributes about 50% of the budget of the United Bible Societies. Six domestic staff. ($7,410,000)

* *American Lutheran Church* (Division for World Missions and Inter-Church Cooperation, 422 S. Fifth St., Minneapolis, MN 55415). A denominational sending agency of Lutheran tradition providing personnel and funds for support and nurture of national churches. Engaged in community development, theological education, and medical work. Also sponsors four to five short-term volunteers annually through its Young Adults in Overseas Ministries for two- to three-year terms of service. 305 staff in 19 countries.

* *Assemblies of God* (Division of Foreign Missions, 1445 Boonville Ave., Springfield, MO 65802). Provides general missionary ministry and more specialized, technical skills to 115 countries. Projects include schools, orphanages, medical clinics, and disaster-relief programs. Vocational opportunities include both general ministries (evangelism, church planting,

child sponsorship and feeding programs, disaster relief, Sunday school, lay training, children and youth, women's groups, Bible school teaching and administration, literature publishing and distribution, bookstore ministries, writing, translating, radio and television) and specialized ministries (nursing, secular school teaching, printing, resident counseling for missionary children, business management, secretarial and office work). Must be member in good standing of the General Council of the Assemblies of God, between ages 23 and 35, and, if married, have no more than three children. Men must be married; some single women accepted. Bible school or college training highly recommended. 72 domestic staff, 1,261 overseas. Also sponsors volunteer program. Volunteers are self-supporting. Strict requirements for eligibility. Waiting list of applicants; when accepted, they are given a one-week orientation and work under the direct supervision of career missionaries. From three-week to two-year commitment. 1,148 volunteers in 115 countries. ($56,800,000)

Baptist Bible Fellowship International (P.O. Box 191, Springfield, MO 65801). Sending agency of independent fundamental Baptist character active in evangelism, church planting, church construction, and ministry to military personnel. Training in Bible college and at least one year of pastoral experience required of applicants. 26 domestic staff, 715 overseas in 67 countries. ($14,900,000)

Baptist International Missions, Inc. (P.O. Box 9215, Chattanooga, TN 37412). Nondenominational sending agency of fundamentalist and Baptist traditions engaged in evangelism, church planting, education, broadcasting, aviation, and ministry to people in military service. Testimony of faith in Christ required. Th.B. or its equivalent in Bible or Christian education helpful. 35 domestic staff and 1,100 overseas in 60 countries. ($10,200,000)

* *Baptist Mid Missions* (4205 Chester Ave., Cleveland, OH 44103). Denominational sending agency of Independent Baptist and fundamentalist traditions active in evangelism, church planting, Bible translation, aviation, and medicine. Applicants should be Bible college graduates, members of an orthodox Baptist church, and have professional certification in a specialized field. Project sites in 42 countries. Also sends some 60 volunteers each year. Volunteers need church endorsement and self-support. About 800 staff overseas. ($15,000,000)

* *Bethany Fellowship Missions* (6810 Auto Club Road, Minneapolis, MN 55438). Interdenominational sending agency of evangelical tradition establishing churches, Bible schools, and seminaries. Engaged in literature

production and distribution and in missionary and theological education. Operates in 28 centers in Brazil, Dominican Republic, Indonesia, Mexico, the Philippines, Puerto Rico, and U.S. Virgin Islands. Must be a graduate of Bethany Missionary Training Center. Occasionally sends volunteers on short-term assignments. Four domestic staff, 176 overseas. ($1,035,000)

* *Campus Crusade for Christ International* (Clay Gender, Dept. 30-40, San Bernardino, CA 92414). Interdenominational sending agency of evangelical tradition engaged in evangelism and serving national churches. Each summer 700-800 students recruited for short-term projects in 15-20 countries on every continent. Service opportunities of up to one year in 151 countries. Three months of cross-cultural training for overseas assignments. All staff and short-termers must develop own financial support. Costs range from $1500 to $4000. ($50,000,000)

* *Child Evangelism Fellowship* (P.O. Box 348, Warrenton, MO 63383). International organization composed of born-again believers whose purpose is to evangelize children and to disciple them in the local church. Enlists nationals in each country to carry out the program through a teacher training network. A Bible-school diploma or college degree plus a year of Bible school required. Also must attend CEF Leadership Training Institute, plus a minimum of one year domestic internship with CEF. Accepts volunteers having experience with CEF suited to ministry. 85 domestic staff, 181 expatriate missionaries in 91 countries. ($2,300,000 for overseas ministries)

Christian and Missionary Alliance Overseas Ministries (P.O. Box C, Nyack, NY 10960). Denominational sending agency of evangelical tradition conducting evangelism and serving national churches. Active in literature, linguistics, translation, theological education, and medicine. In addition to career missionaries, also needs missionary associates (office workers, teachers, skilled technicians). 1000 overseas staff in over 35 countries. ($18,000,000)

* *Christian Church (Disciples of Christ)* (Department of Interpretation and Personnel, Division of Overseas Ministries, Box 1986, Indianapolis, IN 46206). Involved in ecumenical movements around the world. Seeks to participate in the world mission of the church in service, witness, and support for justice. Employment opportunities contingent upon invitation by overseas body for the kind of skills proposed; active and articulate Christian faith; preparation in foreign languages; and professional training in a field such as development, education, or theology. Through the National Council of Churches, volunteers are sent to serve in church-related

schools in Thailand as English teachers. Also opportunities for work camp and other volunteer service. Open to all denominations, although most persons sent are Protestant. Three- to four-year term for regular overseas staff. Short-term overseas staff work from a few weeks to three years. 16 domestic staff, 100 overseas. ($3,000,000)

* *Christian Service Corps* (P.O. Box 56518, Washington, DC 20011). Interdenominational sending agency involved in evangelism, medicine, agriculture, communications, construction, social services, and education. Seven weeks intensive spiritual and cross-cultural training prior to 15-, 30-, or 42-month terms of service with missions and Christian institutions abroad. Accepts volunteers age 18 to 70, married or single, with a basic skill or profession, plus a Christian commitment. Volunteers must raise own financial support. 25-30 new volunteers sent annually. Most staff are former CSC volunteers. 15 paid domestic staff, 40 overseas volunteers. ($511,000)

* *Christians in Action, Inc.* (350 E. Market St., Long Beach, CA 90805). Cross-cultural missionary society specializing in personal evangelism and indigenous church planting. Founded in 1957, Christians in Action allows all who meet their entrance requirements to take part in decisions on policy and leadership. Requirements include two years as member of Christian church, completion of in-house training program, and willingness to function as team member. Some college or Bible school preferred. Business skills are a plus. Applicant must raise own support funds. Also 15 volunteer positions for six- to eight-week summer mission program. 30 domestic staff, 130 overseas in 25 countries. ($980,000)

* *Church of God World Missions Department* (P.O. Box 2430, Cleveland, TN 37311). Operates churches, mission stations, day-care centers, food-distribution centers, evangelism centers, nursing schools, medical clinics, and communication centers in 107 countries. College degree or its equivalent, with additional training in specialized area, required of all applicants. Volunteer program recruits for three-week to four-year terms of service. 50 domestic staff, 385 overseas. ($10,000,000)

Church of the Nazarene (Division of World Mission, 6401 The Paseo, Kansas City, MO 64131). Denominational sending agency of Wesleyan tradition engaged in evangelism, church planting, and support of national churches. Also involved in relief, Bible translation and distribution, education, literature, and medicine. 580 staff in 75 countries.

* *Conservative Baptist Foreign Mission Society* (P.O. Box 5, Wheaton, IL 60189). Denominational sending agency of Baptist tradition doing evangelism, establishing churches, and serving national churches. Involved in

education, literature, linguistics, medicine, radio, and support of nationals. At least a two-year seminary degree needed for career service. Short-term service requires at least one year out of high school. 55 domestic staff; 700 overseas in 23 countries, of which some 100 are short-termers. ($13,000,000)

* *Eastern Mennonite Board of Missions* (Oak Lane and Brandt Boulevard, Salunga, PA 17538). Mennonite organization involved in developing, supporting, and directing mission, relief, and development efforts of the church. Candidates should be Mennonite or willing to cooperate with and support the Mennonite tenets of faith, with particular reference to nonviolence and peace. Normally, candidates have a minimum of a bachelor's degree, having majored in a relevant field of study. Three years' overseas experience normally required for long-term employment. Short-term volunteers should have cross-cultural experience and be committed to Christian faith and doctrine. Six full-time domestic staff, 145 adults in 20 countries on all five continents. ($4,000,000)

* *Evangelical Covenant Church* (5101 N. Francisco Ave., Chicago, IL 60625). Carries on missionary work in Colombia, Ecuador, Mexico, Thailand, and Zaire. Emphasis on evangelism and planting of churches as well as on educational and medical ministries. Must be a member of an Evangelical Covenant local church, a U.S. or Canadian citizen, and in good health. Master of Divinity required for evangelism and church planting; appropriate technical degrees for medical and educational work plus one year at ECC's theological seminary. Approximately 40 volunteers age 20 to 70 sent on short-term mission program. Short-term missionaries serve one to two years and must raise their own support. Six domestic staff, about 95 overseas. ($1,800,000)

Lutheran Church in America (Division for World Mission and Ecumenism, 231 Madison Ave., New York, NY 10016). Denominational mission agency. Active in 32 countries. Recruits mainly from Lutheran Church in America membership. Looks for firm Christian commitment, flexibility, and sensitivity. Requires a bachelor's degree; prefers a master's or doctor's degree. 14 domestic staff, 260 overseas. ($8,400,000)

* *Messengers of Christ Lutheran Bible Translators, Inc.* (1114 N. Batavia St., P.O. Box 92667, Orange, CA 92267). Independent Christian mission organization operating within the Lutheran confessional position. Primary purpose is to help bring people to faith in Jesus Christ through Bible translation and literacy work. Also does linguistic research in support of translation and preparation of literary materials. Missionaries must be in

good standing in a Lutheran congregation and agree to the organization's doctrinal position; have a B.A. degree or its equivalent, plus additional training in theology, linguistics, and language acquisition; pass religious, medical, and psychological tests. Volunteers considered, provided they have a needed skill and can provide for themselves financially. Project sites under direct supervision in Liberia, Sierra Leone, Cameroon, and Ecuador. Sites in 10 other countries in conjunction with Wycliffe Bible Translators. 28 domestic staff, 145 overseas. ($2,800,000)

* *Mission Aviation Fellowship* (Box 202, Redlands, CA 92373). Nonprofit, interdenominational service agency providing flight and radio service to missionaries and the national population in remote areas of the Third World. Candidates should be at least 21 years old, preferably Bible institute or college graduates. In addition, technical qualifications required for pilots, mechanics, avionics specialists, and business-related professionals. Very limited number of short-term volunteers recruited; they are generally highly qualified for a specific technical need related to flying, mechanical repair, or radio work/avionics. 100 domestic staff, 200 families stationed at flight bases throughout 25 countries of Asia, Africa, and Latin America. ($14,000,000)

Mission Service Association (Box 2427, Knoxville, TN 37901). A fellowship of autonomous congregations supporting more than 200 foreign missions. Considers the congregation as the sending agency for missionaries and, with that end, provides reference and publicity resources for the American missionary overseas but does not directly sponsor volunteers. Represents Christian missionaries in 60 countries.

* *Mission to the World* (4151 Memorial Drive, Suite 209C, Decatur, GA 30032). The foreign sending-agency for the Presbyterian Church in America. Project sites include India, Kenya, Mexico, and Ecuador. Presently studying plans for a volunteer program. 25 domestic staff, 411 overseas ($9,087,000)

North Africa Mission (239 Fairfield Ave., Upper Darby, PA 19082). Committed to planting churches with national elders among the Arabic-speaking Muslims of North Africa and the Middle East. An interdenominational mission whose major ministries are low-key evangelism and discipleship. A college degree is required and graduate training in teaching or a professional field preferred. No volunteers. Project sites in Tunisia, Morocco, Algeria, Mauritania, and Egypt. 16 domestic staff, 200 overseas. ($2,000,000)

* *North American Baptist General Missionary Society, Inc.* (1 S. 210 Summit Ave., Oakbrook Terrace, IL 60181). Conservative and evangelical organization that draws its constituency predominantly from the North American Baptist Conference. Establishes and nurtures national churches. Also engaged in church construction, fund raising, evangelism, and relief. Undergraduate degree a minimum. Volunteers accepted for a two-year appointment. Generally from 12 to 15 volunteers in the field. Ten domestic staff, 90 overseas in Cameroon, Japan, Nigeria, and Brazil. ($1,800,000)

* *OMS International, Inc.* (P.O. Box A, Greenwood, IN 46142). A nondenominational faith mission that concentrates on evangelism, church planting, and training of national church leaders. Works in Brazil, Colombia, Ecuador, Haiti, India, Indonesia, Korea, and the Philippines. Applicants should have had a conversion experience and be motivated to propagate the gospel. Also sends summer volunteers. 150 domestic staff, 287 overseas. ($10,000,000)

* *Operation Mobilization* (P.O. Box 148, Midland Park, NJ 07432). International, interdenominational fellowship of young adults learning about and serving Christ on the "frontiers of world evangelization." Specializes in international training teams for worship, Christian discipleship, and cross-cultural evangelism in the Muslim world, the Indian subcontinent, Mexico, and from aboard two ships. Must be 17 or older and be recommended by local church or assembly before initiating application procedure. Provides travel to field and $300 per month in support. 1700 volunteers in 30 countries for one- or two-year programs, 1900 volunteers in 10 countries for two-month summer terms. ($2,000,000)

Overseas Crusades (OC Ministries, Inc.) (25 Corning Ave., Milpitas, CA 95035). Interdenominational mission that is interchurch in ministry and international in vision. "Discipling Nations by Equipping Nationals" is its slogan. Applicants must evidence a personal conversion experience, conviction, and a thorough knowledge and appreciation of the teachings of the Word of God. They must also have experience in Christian service and a college education plus seminary or Bible school. Must raise own support funds. Activities in Taiwan, the Philippines, Indonesia, India, Kenya, Colombia, Brazil, Mexico, and Guatemala. No volunteers. 40 domestic staff, 170 overseas.

* *Overseas Mission Fellowship* (404 South Church St., Robesonia, PA 19551). Interdenominational organization whose objective is the evangelization of East Asia through Christian teaching, church planting, and facilitating the growth and witness of already established churches. Two

years' theological study, two years' Christian work, and/or two years' secular employment required. Foreign language aptitude desired. Training includes three weeks in the United States and 10 weeks in Singapore. Travel to overseas mission, housing, local travel, and personal allowance provided. Minimum age 22. Short-term missionary opportunities through student program. 120 overseas staff, 840 missionaries in all countries of East Asia. ($8,000,000)

* Presbyterian Church in the U.S.A. (475 Riverside Drive, Room 1126, New York, NY 10115). Denominational agency of Presbyterian tradition. Interdependently relates to overseas national churches through the exchange of personnel. Also engaged in education, health concerns, community development, and evangelism. Wide variety of service possibilities. Working relationships in more than 50 countries. Volunteers in Mission program provides information on full-time voluntary service needs that are defined by requesting churches, institutions, and agencies. Volunteer teachers working in Thailand and Egypt; medical volunteers in India, Egypt, Thailand, Kenya, and Pakistan. Overseas volunteers must be church members, but not necessarily of the Presbyterian Church. Most are college graduates or medical professionals. Must have no dependents. Length of commitment varies, but teaching positions are normally two years and medical positions short-term. Room, board, and some stipend paid to teachers; medical personnel provide for own expenses. 212 staff in the United States, 494 staff and 116 volunteers overseas. ($15,239,000)

* Reformed Church in America (General Program Council, 475 Riverside Drive, New York, NY 10115). Supports missionary personnel in several countries. Minimum requirements for employment include membership in the Reformed Church in America, technical qualifications appropriate to position, and a strong Christian commitment. Specific skills depend on position sought. Uses volunteers.

* SEND International (Box 513, Farmington, MI 48024). A nondenominational sending agency of evangelical and Baptist tradition establishing churches and engaged in education and evangelism. Project sites in the Far East. Applicants should have at least one year of Bible school plus ministry experience. Also sends short-term volunteers to work in specialized areas such as construction, guest-house hosting, and medicine. 39 domestic staff, 270 overseas. ($5,200,000)

* Seventh Day Adventist Church (6840 Eastern Ave. N.W., Washington, DC 20012). Responsible for promoting missions and recruiting, training,

and sending church workers to all parts of the world for medical, educational, publishing, and evangelistic activities. Assists in rehabilitation for needy through self-help projects. Also operates and provides equipment and material aid for programs in education, agriculture, public health, and social welfare. Criteria for employment: SDA church membership; successful experience; suitable recommendations; bachelor's degree (although master's or doctor's degree often required); plus medical, educational, and administrative skills most in demand. Also sends volunteers for periods between three months and two years. Living expenses provided for volunteers. 996 U.S. staff and 100 volunteers in 60 developing countries. ($60,000,000 for work in developing countries).

* *South America Mission* (P.O. Box 6560, Lake Worth, FL 33466). Interdenominational mission society seeking to "preach the gospel to every creature," using mass media to expand its ministries. Involved in literature distribution, radio broadcasting, films, and Bible courses. Programs in Bolivia, Brazil, Colombia, and Peru. Applicants should be born-again Christians, normally 21 to 30 years old, and high-school graduates with one year of Bible training. Each candidate is required to raise his or her own support. Also runs an eight-week volunteer program in teams of up to 30 members. 33 domestic staff, 127 overseas. ($1,800,000)

* *Southern Baptist Convention* (Foreign Mission Board, Box 6767, Richmond, VA 23230). Denominational sending agency of Baptist tradition that establishes churches, supports national churches, and engages in evangelism, education, literature, medical ministries, broadcasting, aid, and relief. All programs undertaken in cooperation with local Baptist organizations in each area. Bachelor's degree plus appropriate seminary and professional training in a specific field required for career and associate missionaries. For other categories of personnel, requirements vary with assignment. Age requirements: 24-45 for career missionaries, 35-60 for associates, 26 and under for journeymen. Volunteers sent in response to requests received from Baptist organizations abroad. 415 domestic staff, 3,342 overseas in 103 countries. ($111,956,000)

T.E.A.M. (P.O. Box 969, Wheaton, IL 60189). Interdenominational missionary agency of evangelical tradition committed primarily to church planting. Involved in literature, linguistics, and education. Applicants should have a minimum of 30 semester hours in Bible study and theology at the college level. 86 domestic staff, 990 overseas in 27 countries. ($16,000,000)

* *Teen Missions International, Inc.* (P.O. Box 1056, Merritt Island, FL 32952). Interdenominational sending agency of evangelical tradition with

emphasis on summer work projects and evangelistic teams. Trains youth 13 years and older to assist existing missions with building projects, youth outreaches, and evangelism. Project duration, eight to nine weeks. Cost ranges from $1200 to $2700. Also seeks team leaders, age 22 and up. About 1200 team members and 250 team leaders volunteer each summer for work in over 38 countries. ($3,000,000)

* *United Methodist Church, General Board of Global Ministries* (475 Riverside Drive, New York, NY 10115). Coordinates relationships and administers personnel and programs of the United Methodist Church as it relates to areas outside the United States. Engages mutually in mission with related churches and ecumenical agencies in 77 countries of Africa, Pacific Asia, Latin America, and the Caribbean. Bachelor's degree required; master's degree plus specialized training and experience as called for by technical assignments an asset. Volunteers sent in short-term work teams when requested by local hospitals, churches, or agencies. 33 executive staff, 39 domestic support staff, 630 U.S. missionary personnel overseas. ($23,463,000)

* *Worldteam* (P.O. Box 143038, Coral Gables, FL 33114 or Box 333, Brantford, ON, Canada N3T 5N3). Interdenominational faith mission involved in church planting, church nurture, and ministries of mercy. Church-planting ministries done by teams of missionaries who cooperate together in starting several churches in one metropolitan area at a given time. Testimony of faith in Jesus Christ and participation in a church team required of candidates. Volunteers are used in building projects throughout the Caribbean. Also places medical volunteers. Summer ministries available. 55 domestic staff, 230 overseas in 14 countries of the Caribbean, Latin America, and Europe. ($3,600,000)

* *Wycliffe Bible Translators, Inc.* (Huntington Beach, CA 92648). International, interdenominational agency of evangelical tradition doing linguistic analysis and Bible translation. About 800 language programs in over 40 countries. Applicants normally have college degree or Bible school training. Total overseas staff of around 2700, including both career members and short-term assistants. About 200 short-termers accepted each year, typically for one-year assignments. Short-termers are expected to obtain their own financial support. ($35,000,000)

* *Youth with a Mission* (P.O. Box 296, Sunland, CA 91040-0296). Movement of Christians from more than 100 nations and many denominations working in a spectrum of evangelistic activities. Ministries include agricultural training, nutrition services, construction, medical services, vocational rehabilitation, relocation assistance for refugees, and food and

clothing distribution. No salaries, volunteers responsible for self-support. Close to 1000 staff working in permanent ministries in over 40 countries. Short-term projects pioneer where permanent ministries have not yet been established.

The Church of Jesus Christ of Latter-Day Saints (47 East South Temple, Salt Lake City, UT 84150) is worthy of special note. The Mormons, as they are popularly known, are not included among Protestant churches in the *Mission Handbook* because their teachings are markedly different from those of other churches. But they are an intensely missionary church, with approximately 27,000 of their members currently serving as volunteer missionaries, 17,000 of them outside the United States (compared to 63,000 missionaries from all Protestant and Roman Catholic sending agencies in North America combined). The Church of Jesus Christ of Latter-Day Saints includes congregations in 90 nations, and missionary work is carried on in 179 missions, including 115 outside the United States.

Missionaries must be members of The Church of Jesus Christ of Latter-day Saints in good standing and in good health. Single men age 19 and above, single women age 21 and above, and mature couples whose families have already been raised are eligible for missionary service. The church reviews candidates through personal interviews and decides where to send them partly on the basis of a language-aptitude test. Missionaries normally serve 18 months. Most expenses are paid by the missionaries themselves, their families, or other members; the church pays only for transportation to and from the area of mission. A president is appointed for each mission; these presidents normally serve for three years and are provided a budget for food, housing, office, and transportation. The church also employs some of its members, preferably local members, to oversee the construction and maintenance of buildings, for translation and printing, to administer finances, and to operate schools, institutes of religious education, and seminaries.

Specifics for Roman Catholics

There are 6,128 full-time U.S. Roman Catholic foreign missionaries overseas, in the following categories:

Religious priests	2,603
Religious sisters	2,492
Religious brothers	549
Lay men	87
Lay women	170
Diocesan priests	187
Seminarians	40

The largest of the Catholic missionary orders is Maryknoll (537 fathers and brothers, 369 sisters, and 87 lay missionaries abroad). Maryknoll sometimes welcomes priests and sisters outside their own order to join them in their overseas work. Maryknoll's lay mission program is described on p. 94. We recommend *Maryknoll Magazine* (p. 75).

Some of the U.S. offices of international congregations also send personnel to developing countries. The predominant ones are the Jesuits (552 priests abroad), Franciscan Friars (201), Capuchin Franciscans (135), Marianists (122), Benedictines (87), and School Sisters of Notre Dame (104). The Jesuits, for example, have nine geographical "provinces" in the United States. Each province has its own missionary concerns and thus must be contacted directly. The Jesuit International Volunteer Corps was started in 1984 in response to the great number of inquiries from lay people interested in overseas service (p. 93).

In addition, some U.S. religious orders are active in overseas mission. The Divine Word Missionaries (153 abroad), Medical Mission Sisters (59), and Franciscan Missionaries of Mary (37) are among the largest. Smaller religious congregations may also sponsor a few missionaries; a large proportion of the sisters serving abroad come from relatively small congregations. Individual dioceses, parishes, and schools sometimes also sponsor priests, sisters, brothers, and lay people for work abroad.

If you want to know more about Roman Catholic mission agencies, you can review the mission section of *The Official Catholic Directory* (published annually by P. J. Kennedy and Sons in New York and available from most libraries). It lists (with addresses) the major foreign missions of the U.S. provinces of all the major international orders, all religious orders in the United States that engage in missionary work, and all U.S. missionary societies, mission boards, and their diocesan branches. You could also write the United States Catholic Mission Association (1233 Lawrence St. N.E., Washington, DC 20017). It is the coordinating agency for Catholic missions and publishes an annual handbook ($1.50) with current statistics on Catholic missionaries by sending agency and by country served.

Nearly all orders send only their own members abroad, and recruitment into an order often depends on personal contact with some priest, brother, or sister, perhaps through school or college. However, Catholics considering a missionary vocation would be wise to learn about orders with which they have not had personal contact. Most orders publish newsletters about their traditions, devotions, emphases, and mission programs to inform supporters and potential candidates.

Lay Catholics interested in exploring volunteer service should contact International Liaison, an affiliate of the U.S. Catholic Conference. Their main office is in Washington (1234 Massachusetts Ave. N.W., Washington, DC 20005), and they also maintain two regional information centers:

> International Liaison Midwest
> 225 South Euclid St.
> St. Louis, MO 63110

> International Liaison West
> 2451 Ridge Road
> Berkeley, CA 94709

International Liaison is an information clearinghouse and referral agency for many missions and ministries in both the United States and developing countries. It is interdenominational in intention but works mainly with Catholic agencies and volunteers. International Liaison publishes *Response,* an excellent annual directory of lay volunteer opportunities. *Response* is available by mail from any of the International Liaison offices.

Roman Catholic programs for lay missioners in developing countries are listed below:

Associates of the Sisters of the Holy Cross Volunteer Program (Bertrand Hall, Saint Mary's College, Notre Dame, IN 46556). Placement opportunities include teaching, nursing, pastoral ministry (youth work, catechetics, adult education), community outreach, and social work. Placement based on individual talents and education. Longer terms of service require a college degree or its equivalent. Completion of a degree not required for summer programs. Two-year commitment for overseas service. Room and board, health insurance, a small stipend, and travel expenses are provided. Presently five volunteers in Peru, Ghana, and Uganda.

Davenport Diocesan Volunteer Program (2706 Gaines St., Davenport, IA 52804). Sends volunteers to Latin America, the Caribbean, Central America, Africa, and India. Current project sites in Peru, Ecuador, the West Indies, Zambia, Cambodian refugee camps, and Mexico. Volunteers must be at least 21 years of age and possess a needed skill such as nursing, farming, or teaching. Long- or short-term volunteers accepted. Stipend given depends on host country. 18 volunteers overseas. ($32,000)

Erie Diocesan Mission Office (246 W. Tenth St., Erie, PA 16501). Sends volunteers to Yucatan, Mexico, and Arusha, Tanzania. Active in agriculture, health, community organizations, pastoral ministry, and education. In particular solicits qualified nurses, aids, medical technologists, and teachers. Must be 21 or older, may be single or married without dependents. Spanish proficiency necessary for Yucatan volunteers. Minimum commitment of one year for Mexico or two years for Tanzania. Volunteers receive room and board, stipend, insurance, travel expenses, and (for terms of commitment longer than three years) also language training. Six volunteers in Yucatan, three in Tanzania.

Jesuit International Volunteer Corps (P.O. Box 24578, Washington, DC 20007). International branch of the Jesuit Volunteer Corps. A Christian service organization that offers men and women an opportunity to work at subsistence level wages in developing countries. Its first year of operation was 1984-85. Involved in teaching, pastoral work, and social service projects with refugees, youth groups, and others. Jesuit volunteers are challenged to integrate Christian faith in service among the poor and marginalized while living simply in communities with other volunteers. Work began at inaugural project site, Belize, in 1984. Future project sites include Jamaica, Micronesia, the Turks and Caicos Islands, and others. One- or two-year term of service in collaboration with members of the Jesuit religious order. Summer programs may be started in 1985 or 1986. Must be 20 or older and Christian to participate in one- or two-year programs; no requirements for summer programs. Stipend of $50 per month plus room, board, and health insurance. Assists in fund raising for airfare. Three staff and 10 volunteers in pilot group. In future 10-15 volunteers per country. ($50,000)

Lay Mission-Helpers Association (1531 West Ninth St., Los Angeles, CA 90015). Activities include catechetics, teaching, paramedical and nursing fields, medical and hospital projects, construction of buildings, mechanical tasks, accountancy, and secretarial work. Must be Catholic, 21 or older. May be single or married, with or without dependents. Volunteers provided with room and board, travel to and from country site, small stipend, and medical insurance. Minimum three-year term includes a nine-month training course in Los Angeles.

Maryknoll Lay Missioners (Maryknoll, NY 10545). Lay men and women are placed in response to specific requests from Maryknoll mission areas (13 countries in Latin America, Africa, and Asia) for missioners with skills in pastoral, medical, educational, agricultural, or other community-development fields. Acceptance limited by these specific requests. Must be between 23 and 40, married or single, have college degrees and work experience, or work experience following technical education. Minimum commitment is three years, beginning with four months of training at Maryknoll, New York, in theology, area/regional studies, communication, intercultural communications, ministry, missiology, and health/first aid. Volunteers receive monthly stipend, travel expenses, insurance, and room and board. U.S. Catholics only. 87 serving abroad.

Mission Corps International (7685 Quartz St., Golden, CO 80403). Seeks volunteers with medical, educational, engineering, and mechanical skills. High-school diploma required for some sites; college degree preferred. Six-month to one-year commitment with a spiritual, cultural, and professional preparation period in Colorado. Volunteers receive room, board, and medical insurance and are assisted in raising their transportation costs to and from project sites. About 15 volunteers currently overseas in Sudan, Kenya, and Tanzania. Has plans for programs in South America and Haiti. Open to non-Catholics. ($24,000)

Missionaries of Africa (2020 W. Morse Ave., Chicago, IL 60645). Roman Catholic mission society specializing in the African apostolate. Seeks Catholic men, 23 to 40 years old and single, with strong religious commitment and a professional skill. Stresses the international character of the society (15 nationalities represented), adaptation to local cultures in Africa, and team ministry. Volunteers receive room and board, health and accident coverage, plus $150 monthly allowance. All volunteers are integrated into international communities in Africa and are posted with at least two other individuals for community and professional support. Six-month training program in the United States, then two-and-a-half years of overseas service. Almost 2000 missionaries currently serving in 25 African countries.

Society of African Missions (337 Common St., Dedham, MA 02026). Sends and receives volunteers motivated by a Christian missionary commitment. Work ranges from teaching high school to building maintenance and construction, from catechetical work to assisting local farmers in improving crop yields. Must be 22 to 45, single and without dependents, and possess a skill or talent that can be used in service to African peoples. No language requirement, but degree required for teaching. Three-month in-service training program in Liberia, followed by three-year minimum commitment. No non-Catholics.

Volunteer Missionary Movement (7320 Route 71, Yorkville, IL 60560). Recruits, prepares, and sends lay missionaries to work in Papua New Guinea, India, Brazil, and 12 countries in Africa. Involved in rural health centers, high schools, trade and technical schools, and rural community-development projects. Ecumenical Christian movement working out of Catholic tradition. Professional qualifications required of volunteers, including one-year work experience. Must be 21 or older, without dependents of school age. Minimum commitment of two years. One-week introductory course in Yorkville, plus five-week preparation course in London Colney, England. Volunteers receive living allowance and board, but are requested to pay airfare to England and contribute toward cost of courses. 15 permanent staff in England, 120 volunteers overseas.

Study and Tourism

Exposure to another country and culture is almost always a powerful educational experience, and many programs have been established to encourage students and scholars at all levels to include a period abroad in their studies.

There are a number of good general references on international education; they are described in the next few paragraphs. Subsequent sections describe:

- programs for high-school students;

- programs for university study from the undergraduate to the postdoctoral level;

- fellowships for study in developing countries;

- nonformal educational programs, including tourism.

The best general source of information on study-abroad opportunities of all kinds is the commercially run Council on International Educational Exchange. CIEE's main office is at 205 E. 42nd St., New York, NY 10017, but international programs offices on more than 500 U.S. campuses and in Europe and Asia are affiliated with the organization. CIEE issues the International Student Identity

Card, which entitles students to discounts in many countries. They also publish several excellent general references:

Basic Facts on Foreign Study. 50 cents. Outlines formal study and teaching opportunities from the high school to graduate and professional levels. Also discusses financial information, scholarships and internships, and guidelines for selecting programs.

CIEE Student Travel Catalog. Free. Catalog of CIEE's discount travel, study, and work abroad offerings. Especially strong on basic travel details. Also advertises programs offered by other commercial travel groups. Published annually.

Work, Study, Travel Abroad: The Whole World Handbook 1984-1985. $6.95. A cornucopia of details and tips—extensive and frank. Includes information by geographical regions on inexpensive travel: charters and special fares, lodging, work camps, study programs, and jobs. More than 800 summer, semester, and year-long study-abroad programs sponsored by U.S. schools are listed. This is the best all-around guide to study and student travel abroad.

The Division of International Education, U.S. Department of Education (400 Maryland Ave. S.W., Washington, DC 20202) provides:

American Students and Teachers Abroad. $1. Brief, up-to-date information guide.

Study and Teaching Opportunities Abroad: Sources of Information about Overseas Study, Teaching, Work and Travel. $4.50. Clues on where to find overseas employment. Also lists services of organizations and agencies concerned with international travel, study, and employment. Includes highlighted section of answers to questions most frequently asked by prospective travelers.

In addition, the following books provide general information on study abroad, including information relevant to more than one section of this chapter:

Cohen, Gail A., ed. *The Learning Traveler.* Two volumes. Institute of International Education (809 United Nations Plaza, New York, NY 10017), annual. The first volume, *Vacation Study Abroad* ($8), describes more than

900 spring, summer, and fall study-abroad programs offered by U.S. and foreign institutions and private groups. Programs designed for secondary school and college students, teachers, professionals, and retirees. Includes information on many and unusual fields of study, admissions, credit, costs, and housing. The second volume, *U.S. College-Sponsored Programs Abroad: Academic Year* (also $8), describes more than 800 semester and academic-year foreign-study programs in countries all over the world. Each entry includes fields of study, eligibility requirements, credits, teaching methods, costs, housing, and scholarships or work-study opportunities.

Garraty, John A., Lily Von Klemperer, and Cyril S. Taylor. *The New Guide to Study Abroad, 1981-1982 Edition.* New York: Harper and Row, 1981. $7.95. Helpful sections on planning for study abroad; academic-year and summer programs for college and graduate students; the secondary school student abroad; the teacher abroad; and foreign experience outside the classroom (mainly summer work and travel). Comprehensive, but does not treat developing countries at length.

One Friendship at a Time: Your Guide to International Youth Exchange. International Youth Exchange Institute (Pueblo, CO 81009). Gives some general advice and then lists specific exchange programs. The programs noted in *One Friendship at a Time* that send students to developing countries are also listed in this chapter. President Reagan created the International Youth Exchange Institute, a joint venture between the government and the private sector, to encourage citizens to take part in international educational and cultural exchange programs.

Students Abroad: A Guide for Selecting a Foreign Education. National Association for Foreign Student Affairs (1860 19th St. N.W., Washington, DC 20009). Free. Provides basic information about choosing academic programs, work, travel, and voluntary service opportunities.

For discussion of the problems and advantages of study abroad you might refer to:

Learning Across Cultures. National Association for Foreign Student Affairs (1860 19th St. N.W., Washington, DC 20009), 1981. Intended for people who work with students or scholars involved in international educational exchange. Discusses various issues in intercultural communication, including problems of cross-cultural adjustment, English-language training from an intercultural viewpoint, and communication and problem solving across cultures.

Mathies, Lorraine and William G. Thomas. *Overseas Opportunities for American Educators and Students, Perspectives and Possibilities.* New York: MacMillan Information, 1973. An on-target collection of essays on overseas educational programs and service.

Trans Cultural Study Guide. Volunteers in Asia (Box 4543, Stanford, CA 94305). $4. Also available from Council Travel Offices of the Council on International Exchange (205 East 42nd St., New York, NY 10017).

The Experiment in International Living (Brattleboro, VT 05301; Western Regional Office, Suite 442, San Francisco, CA 94108) is the oldest educational-exchange institution in the United States. EIL maintains national offices in 60 countries and an exceptionally broad range of programs. EIL offers summer-abroad programs in 31 countries for high school and college students (ages 14-21). EIL also offers semester and school-year abroad programs for high school students (minimum age 16), recent high school graduates, and college students. Applicants should have a good academic record, including one to three years' of language experience for Spanish- and French-speaking countries. Programs cost $2,090-$3,790, varying with destination. Positions as leaders of high school or college groups and as semester academic directors are filled from among applicants who meet the following qualifications: a minimum age of 21; fluency in French, Spanish, or German; experience in cross-cultural living; and demonstrated skills in group leadership. Finally, EIL's School of International Training also offers an undergraduate degree in international studies and two graduate programs (in intercultural management and the teaching of languages).

High school programs

The pamphlet *Secondary School Study Abroad: Fact Sheet on Program Selection* (Council on International Educational Exchange, 205 E. 42nd St., New York, NY 10017) helps high school students, together with their parents and teachers, select the program that is best for them. It gives further details on the following and some smaller programs:

AFS International/Intercultural Programs (313 E. 43rd St., New York, NY 10017). Summer or year homestay and study opportunities for high-school students to and from more than 60 countries. Language study options, college credit, college scholarships for AFS alumni, teacher and professional exchange, hosting program. Apply through a local AFS chapter or contact the AFS Program Information Office. In 1983-84 program 3060 American students living in 53 countries.

Children's International Summer Villages, Inc. (206 North Main St., Box YX, Casstown, OH 45312). Conducts multinational summer camps for preadolescents emphasizing international friendship, cross-cultural communication and cooperative living. CISV has chapters in 14 U.S. cities and 54 countries with nearly 38,000 alumni. CISV offers a Village Program (a four-week international summer camp for boys and girls age 11 and junior counselors ages 16-17), an Interchange Program (a bilateral family-centered two-summer exchange for youth ages 12-16), and a Seminar Camp (a three-week summer camp for youth ages 17-18 that features seminars on cross-cultural communication). Program costs include fees of approximately $200 plus travel. Living expenses are covered by hosting families or local chapters. Limited travel grants are available. Developing-country program sites in Jamaica, Kenya, Jordan, Lebanon, Tanzania, Pakistan, Thailand, Tunisia, Zambia, Guatemala, India, Liberia, Nigeria, Senegal, Sierra Leone, Sudan, Venezuela, Argentina, and Colombia. Sponsors approximately 500 U.S. youth abroad in a given year.

Future Farmers of America (P.O. Box 15160, Alexandria, VA 22309). Offers international exchange opportunities for agricultural students in more than 25 countries. These allow for a practical working experience with a host family. Participants select a desired country, length of stay, and programs in production agriculture, ornamental horticulture, or agribusiness. College credit can sometimes be arranged. Basic program fees range from $1500 for a three-month program to $5000 for a twelve-month around-the-world program. Some financial assistance is available.

National 4-H Council (International Relations, 7100 Connecticut Ave., Chevy Chase, MD 20815). Supports the 4-H program of the Cooperative Extension Service in a variety of educational programs, including international exchange and training programs with more than 40 countries around the world. The International 4-H Youth Exchange program, begun in 1948, pioneered the 4-H international experience of living and working with families in another land and provides a six-week summer experience for 15- 19-year-olds in 17 countries. Programs emphasize cross-cultural understanding plus some focus on a specific 4-H project study area (such as animal science, clothing, dairy, or foods-nutrition). Costs range from $700 to $2300 (depending on the country) and include orientation, international travel, insurance, and other services.

Open Door Student Exchange (124 East Merrick Road, P.O. Box 1150, Valley Stream, NY 11582). Offers high-school students in grades 10-12 with a good academic record international-exchange opportunities. Founded in 1963, it has active programs in 27 countries in Latin America, Europe, and the Middle East. Three-month summer programs range in cost from $950 to $1900, while five-month semester and fall programs are $1200 to $1900 (according to destination). Fees cover orientation, insurance, international transportation, and administrative costs. April 30 application deadline.

People to People International (2420 Pershing Road, Suite 300, Kansas City, MO 64108). Promotes international understanding through direct contact among people of all countries. Among People to People International's various programs is the High School Student Ambassador Program. It offers a 42-day summer program of economic, political, and cultural overviews in East Asia through field visits to factories and offices and through guided programs at historical sites and museums. Approximately 1000 Young Ambassadors per year, ages 15-19, live with families for five-day periods in three separate countries. People to People also offers an agricultural exchange program for young farmers. Current fees are approximately $3600 and usually cover all costs.

School Exchange Service (National Association of Secondary School Principals, 1904 Association Drive, Reston, VA 20091). Jointly sponsored by the NASSP and the Council on International Educational Exchange. Links U.S. secondary schools to partner schools in nine countries to permit a regular international exchange of students, teachers, and administrators. Each participating school is both a hosting and sending school. Venezuela is the only developing country involved. Open to secondary-school students, teachers, and administrators with two years of French or Spanish. Academic credit can be earned according to individual school policy. Program costs, $320 to $1,425, cover airfare and homestay with local families; there is no enrollment fee or tuition. Three- to four-week summer programs.

Sister Cities International (1625 Eye St. N.W., Washington, DC 20006 or 527 Ashberry, El Cerrito, CA 94530 or your city hall). A national association linking 712 U.S. cities with 995 foreign cities in 79 countries in a long-term, two-way relationship. Fosters international communication and exchanges of persons, things, and ideas through cultural, educational, technical, professional, municipal, youth/student, and sports activities. Programs are planned at the local community level by Sister Cities committees of city officials and citizen volunteers. Academic short-term and nonacademic arrangements. Age requirement varies, but applicants are generally in high school. Good academic standing and some language ability desired. Generally a participant furnishes airfare and personal spending money.

Youth for Understanding International Student Exchange (885 San Antonio Road, Suite C, Los Altos, CA 94022). An exchange organization for high schools, with 14 U.S. regional and 24 overseas offices. Programs in developing countries all located in Central and South America. Students live with host families and attend school (year student only); also attend language orientations in most countries. Year, summer, semester, and summer sports exchange programs. Open to students ages 14-18. Two years of language training required for French- and Spanish-speaking countries. Minimum academic average 3.0 for year programs, 2.0 for summer. Costs $4100 for the year, $2150 for summer sessions, including tranportation. April 15 application deadline.

Note that several of the volunteer-sending programs listed on pp. 28-31 include high school students.

University study

University—the roots of the word mean "the world of human experience." So why not include some time abroad in your university studies? This section surveys the major programs and sources of information regarding study in developing countries from the undergraduate to the postdoctoral level.

University study-abroad opportunities in developing countries abound, but you will have to search them out with a keener eye than required for the prosaic junior year in France. For reasons of practicality, most undergraduate students abroad rely on study programs organized and accredited by U.S. colleges and educational organizations. Such programs are tailored to the needs of U.S. students, providing training and housing arrangements as required.

Linda Powers spent one of her college years studying in Mexico City through such a U.S.-sponsored program. She was initially disappointed, because instead of the "cultural integration" promised her, the program kept her together with a large group of U.S. students, segregated from the rest of the university. She found that admission requirements and prerequisites excluded her from virtually all university-level courses for Mexicans in the area, but was finally able to enroll in an economics course—which met at 7:00 a.m. and at some distance from her residence. Powers found that the experience of being the sole *gringa* (with little background in Spanish and none in economics) among 54 Mexicans more than compensated for the predawn wake-up calls. The act of consciously stepping out of one's prescribed group invited friendships that extended beyond the university campus, as people reached out to her as an individual, whereas they found a large group of foreign students unapproachable. Mastering Spanish, learning about Mexican culture, and acquiring new and lasting friendships made this period of study abroad among the most enriching times of her life.

Relatively few U.S. students simply enroll at universities in the Third World. Language is barrier enough for many students, and, in addition, admission requirements may be markedly different than at a U.S. university. Most Third World universities are modeled after universities in Britain, France, and Spain, and students in the European system specialize earlier than U.S. students do. Local requirements (Spanish literature in Latin America, African history at African institutions) or national examinations (for which local students prepare throughout secondary school) may also make it difficult for U.S. students to get started in a Third World university. Then, too, universities in developing countries often suffer from relatively large classes and, in some countries, from a long history of extremist politics and repeated political disruptions. Finally, some special arrangement is usually necessary to transfer credit for study at a foreign university back to a U.S. degree program. If a student could overcome such obstacles and enroll independently at a foreign university, he would spend less than is charged for the study-abroad programs organized by U.S. institutions. But what these programs charge generally reflects the real costs of facilitating international study.

Those adventurous souls who do enroll at Third World universities have usually already graduated from U.S. universities, and they normally opt for programs of independent study. Some are specialists in area studies—deepening their knowledge of African art at the University of Ghana, for example, or of Latin American literature in Lima, Peru. There are a scattering of U.S.-style universities in

Asia, the Middle East, and Latin America, and U.S. students tend to gravitate toward these because of their known reputation at home. If you are ready to look for specific study-abroad programs at the university level, we suggest:

Handbook on International Study for U.S. Nationals. New York: Institute of International Education, 1973. No longer in print, but still quite useful and available from many libraries. Lists study programs sponsored by U.S. colleges and universities as well as awards for study and research in institutions abroad. Also describes higher-education systems of 120 countries and territories, including all university-level institutions.

Resource Book for International Education, U.S. Jesuit Colleges and Universities (Association of Jesuit Colleges and Universities, 1717 Massachusetts Ave. N.W., Suite 402, Washington, DC 20036). Lists, by country and by college, opportunities for study abroad with a profile on international students.

Study and Research Opportunities in the Middle East and North Africa. AMIDEAST (1717 Massachusetts Ave. N.W., Suite 100, Washington, DC 20036), forthcoming. Includes U.S. institutions that offer study-abroad and study-tour programs in the Middle East and North Africa, Middle Eastern institutions that admit U.S. students, and organizations that offer financial assistance for study or research in the region. Other sources of information and tips on preparation for study abroad also included.

Study in American Republics Area. Institute of International Education (809 United Nations Plaza, New York, NY 10017), 1976. Comprehensive guide to university-level study in South America, Mexico, Central America, and the Caribbean. Distinguished by a field-of-study guide that lists 196 major fields and the institutions that offer them. Also details scholarships, volunteer, trainee, and work opportunities, government regulations, agencies providing services, and sources for additional information.

UNESCO. *Study Abroad.* Switzerland. Presses Centrales de Lausanne, annual. Lists 2600 international study programs in all academic and professional fields, plus financial-aid possibilities, in more than 115 countries.

The International Student Exchange Program (Georgetown University, 1236 36th St. N.W., Washington, DC 20547) provides an administrative and financial structure to facilitate the regular exchange of university-level students on a one-to-one basis between participating institutions in the United States and institutions around the world. More than 120 institutions in 20 countries are currently members of ISEP. Exchanges can occur at any academic level and in any discipline and can range in length from one semester to two years. To be eligible to participate in an ISEP exchange, a student must be attending an ISEP member institution. He or she must also have a good academic record and the necessary language skills. Applicants apply to, and are selected by, their home institution. There is currently a $100 fee for ISEP exchanges.

The Committee on Scholarly Communication, together with the People's Republic of China and the National Association for Foreign Student Affairs, publishes three useful guides for students interested in China.

Finger, Thomas. *Higher Education and Research in the PRC: Institutional Profiles.* 1981. Provides profiles on 701 four-year universities in the People's Republic of China.

Finger, Thomas and Linda A. Reed. *An Introduction to Education in the PRC and U.S. China Educational Exchanges.* 1982. Outlines China's educational system (structure, evolution, university system) and lists institutions of higher education.

Gottschang, Karen Turner. *China Bound: A Handbook for American Students, Researchers, and Teachers.* 1981. Preparatory guide describing study and research facilities, banking facilities, professional relationships, and other aspects of educational exchange with China.

These are available from the Committee on Scholarly Communication with the People's Republic of China, National Academy of Sciences (2101 Constitution Ave. N.W., Washington, DC 20418) or from the National Association for Foreign Student Affairs (1860 19th St. N.W., Washington, DC 20009).

Students interested in China might also contact the American Institute for Foreign Study Scholarship (100 Greenwich Ave., Greenwich, CT 06830), which sponsors academic year and summer programs in Beijing. Information on Taiwan is available both in Gail Cohen's book (pp. 97-98) and from the Coordination Council for North American Affairs (5161 River Road, Bethesda, MD 20816).

For information on study, employment, and volunteer opportunities in Africa, you might get the African-American Institute's free brochure, *Opportunities in Africa* (833 United Nations Plaza, New York, NY 10017).

Advanced scholars, as well as students who hope to enroll independently in a foreign university, might also refer to library references that catalog educational institutions around the world, such as:

Commonwealth Universities Yearbook 1984. London: Association of Commonwealth Universities. Comprehensive guide to 356 universities within the British Commonwealth. Includes information on courses, organization, staff, admission requirements, and degrees.

Keys, H. M. R. and D. J. Aitkens, International Association of Universities. *The World List of Universities.* New York: De Gruyter Publishers, 1978.

International Association of Universities. *International Handbook of Universities,* 8th ed. New York: De Gruyter Publishers, 1981.

Research Strengths of Universities in Developing Countries of the Commonwealth. Association of Commonwealth Universities, 1978. Notes areas of research strength in more than 90 universities in 18 Commonwealth countries.

World Directory of Social Science Institutions, 3rd. ed. UNESCO, 1982. Lists address, staff coverage, activities, finances, and publications.

World Guide to Higher Education, 2nd ed. New York: Bowker Publishing Co., Epping, and Unipub, 1982.

The World of Learning, 1983-1984. London, Europa Publications, Ltd. A comprehensive directory for the advanced scholar. Lists academies, learned societies, research institutes, libraries, cultural institutions, and universities by country. Also includes a section on the activities of international organizations in the humanities, technical, and professional fields.

The Foundation Center Libraries (p. 69) have an impressive collection of catalogs and bulletins from educational institutions around the world; these libraries are in New York and Washington but are linked together with cooperating libraries across the country. If you can get to New York or Washington, you could also do your own research about universities and study programs abroad at the resource centers of the Academy of Educational Development (680 Fifth Ave., New York, NY 10020, and Suite 400, 1255 23rd St. N.W., Washington, DC 20037).

Fellowships

Fellowships for international study are highly competitive and nearly all limited to graduate students and mature scholars. The following are the biggest international fellowship programs:

The *G.I. Bill* allows veterans, in-service students, and eligible dependents to receive educational benefits from the Veterans Administration for study at any approved institution of higher learning in countries with which the United States has diplomatic relations. For details and a list of already approved institutions, write to your regional VA office or to: Veterans Administration, Department of Veterans Benefits, 941 N. Capitol St. N.E., Washington, DC 20421.

The *Higher Education Act Title VI* provides funds (not including travel expenses) for foreign-language study abroad in very specific situations. To qualify for these Foreign Language Area Studies Fellowships candidates must have completed all course work requirements for the doctorate and need access to materials not available in the United States in order to complete their dissertations, or plan to use their awards in one of the participating U.S. university-sponsored foreign-language or area-study programs abroad. No awards are made for the study of English or related area studies. Specific information is available from the appropriate financial aid officer at the student's own university.

The *Institute of International Education* administers international fellow-ships in all fields of study at the graduate level, including U.S. government grants under the Fulbright-Hays Act and fellowships and travel grants offered by foreign governments, universities, and private donors. Currently enrolled university students should contact their campus Fulbright Program Advisers. Prospective applicants not currently matriculated at a U.S. uni-versity should write to Study Abroad Programs, Institute of International Education, 809 U.N. Plaza, New York, NY 10017.

The *Rotary Foundation* offers fellowships to highly qualified undergrad-uates and graduate students for study abroad. Timothy Mitchell spent the year after his college graduation studying Spanish and foreign affairs at the University of Salamanca, Spain, on a Rotary Fellowship. From that base, he also traveled widely in Europe, North Africa, and the Middle East as a Rotarian "ambassador of good will." Rotary fellowships cover all the costs of study abroad (airfare; tuition, fees, books and educational supplies; room, board, and incidental living expenses). They also pay for limited educational travel during the study year and, if necessary, for intensive language training. An award may be used for almost any field of study. Applicants for graduate fellowships must have earned the bachelor's degree or its equivalent and be 20 to 28 years of age. Applicants for undergraduate scholarships must have completed two years of university work, be currently enrolled, and be 18 to 24 years of age. The selection process for Rotary fellowships is lengthy, so it is best to apply at least a year before you would like to begin your study abroad (for example, a college student should meet the spring deadline of his or her junior year for a fellowship that would commence in the fall after graduation). Further information is available from local Rotary clubs or from the Rotary Foundation, 1600 Ridge Ave., Evanston, IL 60201.

The *U.S. Department of Education* administers Fulbright study grants for senior scholars and for advanced research in most academic fields, particularly in modern foreign languages and area studies. Information is available from foreign-studies advisers at most universities or from: International Studies Branch, Division of International Education, Department of Education, 400 Maryland Ave. S.W., Washington, DC 20202.

Most universities have a campus office for international studies. Your university's graduate student office and foreign-language departments are also likely to be good sources of current information. You might also review these books on international fellowships:

CISP International Studies Funding Book. Council for Intercultural Studies and Programs (60 E. 42nd St., New York, NY 10017). Information on funding for international/intercultural education. Contains profiles of sponsoring institutions. Updated periodically in the Council's monthly bulletin.

The Directory of Financial Aids for International Activities. International Programs, University of Minnesota (Minneapolis, MN 55455), 1981. Information on 453 award opportunities available to academic staff, graduate and undergraduate students, advanced scholars, and young professionals for study, research, travel, and teaching abroad. Also includes a section on awards for study in degree programs at international schools, centers, and universities in foreign countries.

Grants and Fellowships in International Studies. International Studies Association, Department of Government and International Studies, University of South Carolina (Columbia, SC 29208), 1977. A brief but thorough listing of grants and fellowships available on both the predoctoral and postdoctoral levels.

A Selected List of Fellowship Opportunities and Aids to Advanced Education. Fellowship Office, Commission on Human Resources, National Research Council (2101 Constitution Ave. N.W., Washington, DC 20418). The most exhaustive guide to grants for advanced study.

Note that a few of the references on pp. 96-99 and 104-5 also include fellowship information.

The following agencies provide fellowships for advanced scholars in their respective areas and also information on other sources of financial assistance:

National Endowment for the Arts
1100 Pennsylvania Ave. N.W.
Washington, DC 20506

National Endowment for the Humanities
1100 Pennsylvania Ave. N.W.
Washington, DC 20506

Social Science Research Council
    Fellowships and Grants
605 Third Ave.
New York, NY 10016

Information on grants is also available from:

American Council of Learned Societies
800 Third Ave.
New York, NY 10022

Check, too, whether your state's arts and humanities agencies offer fellowships or information on fellowships.

The Agency for International Development (pp. 151-52) contracts with U.S. universities to provide technical assistance to institutions in developing countries and to conduct research on development problems. The total value of obligations for the contracts and grants made in AID's fiscal year 1983 was over $53 million, with 117 universities involved. This program has made it possible for many faculty members to work in developing countries, either on brief visits or longer periods of residence. Check whether your university has a contract with AID or, for further information, write: Bureau for Science and Technology/Research and University Relations, Agency for International Development, Washington, DC 20523.

Nonformal education and tourism

You can design your own study-abroad program, finance part of it yourself, and perhaps get help by applying specially to your university, your church, or some agency that might be interested in your findings. We recommend serious consideration of this strategy, especially for bright, self-motivated people. You might, for example, do an on-site evaluation of a foreign-aided project. You would need to be familiar with other literature on the subject of aid effectiveness, and you would need to find out (maybe from the aid agency) about a particular foreign-aided project for which an on-site evaluation might be useful. Another quite specific idea: a church group in Africa might welcome you to study some aspect of religious or cultural life, again assuming that you have done your homework, have a fairly clear idea of what you want to study, and that your visit would represent little or no cost to your African hosts.

If you take this do-it-yourself approach, and if you can't cover the costs with a postgraduate research fellowship, you will probably need some money of your own to invest. You will also need a solid project proposal—an imaginative idea with appeal to potential funding sources—and enough details about your arrangements so that the proposal seems likely to work. With such a proposal in hand, you might be able to get someone at your college, your congregation, or a local foundation to contribute part of the cost. You might also plan to work as well as study in the Third World situation, thus giving your hosts more reason to cooperate with you and also perhaps earning board and room.

Some of the references listed on pp. 96-99 and 104-5 include sections on study-abroad programs, often of short duration, that are outside the normal progression of accredited academic study; see especially CIEE's *Work, Study, and Travel Abroad: The Whole World Handbook.* Also refer back to the section in our Chapter 1 directed to people who are going abroad for the first time (pp. 10-14); nearly all these opportunities include a substantial educational component. The volunteer-sending programs sponsored by private development agencies (pp. 28-32) are particularly worthy of note in this regard.

You could also check the *Directory of Overseas Summer Jobs,* an annual guide devoted entirely to workcamps, tourism jobs, and other summer employment. It is published in England, but distributed here ($7.95) by Writer's Digest Books (9933 Alliance Road, Cincinnati, OH 45242). Most listings are for summer jobs in Europe, but there are about 20 listings from 10 developing countries.

For information on internship programs for undergraduates or recent graduates, see the *Overseas Development Network Opportunities Catalog.* It is written by students for students and describes over 50 meaningful internships, employment, or research opportunities with development agencies in the United States and abroad. The *Catalog* currently costs $10 (or $8 for students), plus $2.50 for postage and handling. It's available from Overseas Development Network (Harvard University, P.O. Box 1430, Cambridge, MA 02238).

Some specific programs of nonformal education are listed below:

AIESEC-United States, Inc. (14 W. 23rd St., New York, NY 10010). Acronym for the International Association of Students in Economics and Commerce. Offers a reciprocal job internship program for students in the fields of economics and business. Criterion for eligibility is membership in any of AIESEC's more than 60 member colleges and universities in the United States. Academic credit for participation must be arranged by the student. Program costs $70 to $110 in fees and dues, plus transportation and insurance. Employers provide a stipend that covers room, board, and other living expenses. More than four-fifths of applicants are matched to jobs; of those, two-thirds realize their traineeships. Length of stay varies from 6 weeks to 18 months. Language proficiency required in French, Spanish, and German-speaking countries.

AMIDEAST (America-Mideast Educational and Training Service, Inc.) (1717 Massachusetts Ave. N.W., Suite 100, Washington, DC 20036). Established in 1951, seeks to further human resource development in the

Middle East/North Africa and to promote mutual respect and understanding between peoples of the Arab world and the United States. Has programs of education, training, research, and information, focusing on appropriate U.S. training for Middle East development. Administers short-term educational programs for individuals or groups visiting the Middle East/North Africa. Also offers publications, including *Study and Research Opportunities in the Middle East and North Africa* (p. 104). AMIDEAST's program for teachers is described on pp. 116-17.

Archaeological Institute of America (P.O. Box 1901, Kenmore Station, Boston, MA 02215). Each February the AIA publishes the *Fieldwork Opportunities Bulletin*, which includes a listing of excavations seeking volunteers and staff, study tours, and special programs with an archaeological focus. The price of the 1984 edition is $6. AIA will also send a free brochure titled *Archaeology as a Career*.

Archaeology Abroad (31-34 Gordon Square, London, England WCIH OPY). Issues an annual bulletin and two news sheets (available by subscription) which list overseas excavations requiring volunteers, usually for two to twelve weeks. Does not organize courses or offer academic credit. Seeks applicants with some excavation or academic training in archaeology. Working knowledge of country's language useful. No fees required of applicant other than airfare and sometimes contributions toward food costs. Students usually accommodated on a campsite with their own equipment or in a hotel. Digs located in the Near East, East, southern Africa, and other regions.

Council of International Programs (1001 Huron Road, Suite 209, Cleveland, OH 44115). Sponsors young people in the human service professions (including teachers and counselors for teenage youth) to work abroad. Applicants should have practical experience in their fields. The person going abroad pays for air travel and insurance, but expenses in the host country are assumed by the cooperating program. Nearly all placements are in Europe, but CIP is beginning a pilot project in India.

Earthwatch Research Corps (International Exchange, 10 Juniper Road, Box 127-Z, Belmont, MA 02178). Recruits interested amateurs, age 16 and up, to help prominent researchers on their field expeditions worldwide. Since 1971, more than 6000 people have funded and joined over 450 projects in 55 countries. Earthwatch projects include expeditions, environmental impact studies, and art history, architecture, or dance. Volunteers do not need to have special skills to participate. Costs currently range from $500 to $2000 for two- to three-week expeditions. Contributions are tax deductible and cover meals, lodging, equipment, and field transportation. Airfare is not included. Developing-country sites in Zimbabwe, Central America, and Southeast Asia.

IAESTE Trainee Program, Association for International Practical Training (American City Bldg., Suite 217, Columbia, MD 21044). Reciprocal exchange program offered by the International Association for the Exchange of Students for Technical Experience. Provides on-the-job training for students in engineering, architecture, agriculture, mathematics, and the natural and physical sciences in 46 countries. Some 5500-6000 openings worldwide. Applicants must be in good standing at accredited four-year college or university and have completed sophomore year. Graduate students also eligible. Trainee is paid maintenance allowance adequate to cover living costs while in training. Students pay $50 application fee, travel expenses, and fees for passport and visa. About $700-900 in expenses typically incurred during 8-12 week summer assignment. Fluency in the language required for some countries and useful for all others. Deadline for summer placements is December 15; for long-term placements (three to twelve months) and for placements outside of summer months, a four- to six-months' processing time is minimum. Students who secure places in the United States for foreign trainees are given first consideration for jobs abroad.

International Camp Counselor Program/Abroad (YMCA of Greater New York, 422 Ninth Ave., New York, NY 10001). Camp counseling positions are available for four to eight weeks in a number of YMCA and other camps in 10 countries, including Colombia and Ghana. Fluency in Spanish required in Colombia. Open to men and women, 18 to 25 years of age, who have completed at least one year of college, as well as camp counseling, teaching, or similar experience working with groups. Participants pay a $100 application fee, which includes insurance coverage, placement services, and flight information. Counselors receive room and board and, occasionally, pocket money. They are responsible for all international transportation costs. Applications due January 1 (late applications may be accepted until March 1 if there are vacancies). For more information send a stamped, self-addressed envelope.

People to People International (South 110 Ferrall St. TAF-39-C, Spokane, WA 99202). Sponsors a Citizen Ambassador Program for adults similar to the High School Student Ambassador Program (p. 101). Programs are of two- to three-week duration, and about two-thirds of all programs include visits to developing countries.

Finally, don't forget the possibilities of tourism. You need not wait for a job opportunity, fellowship, or carefully planned program to take you to the Third World. You may learn as much by spontaneous exposure to the people, culture, and everyday life of a foreign country. See pp. 204-5 for ideas about discount travel.

If you have already had quite a bit of travel experience, you could inquire with a commercial travel agency about leading a tour group. Normally a tour group leader's own expenses are paid, but he or she has to recruit the tour participants. A pastor who is a seasoned traveler, for example, might be able to attract a sufficiently large group to comprise a tour.

All places look alike from the inside of your hotel room, and many tourists so surround themselves with other Americans and the conveniences of home that they miss much of the excitement of unknown environments. So be adventurous and accept a few discomforts as you travel, if that's what it takes to win new friends and have genuinely new experiences.

SIX

Teaching and Journalism

The information gap between the developing and developed countries is just as wide as the gap between income levels. There are obvious needs for people to teach (as well as learn) in the Third World and to report the news back home.

This chapter includes the following sections:

- books and programs relevant to teaching abroad at all levels;

- teaching abroad at the elementary and secondary levels, including special education;

- teaching English as a foreign language;

- teaching at the university level.

The chapter closes with a section on jobs in journalism related to the developing countries.

Teaching abroad

Of all the professions, teachers probably have the broadest range of placement opportunities in the developing world. Education is a precious commodity in any area of the world, but education's fundamental role in economic development, coupled with a burgeoning population of young people, makes teachers especially in demand in the developing countries.

Some of the references cited at the beginning of the last chapter (pp. 97-99) discuss opportunities for teaching as well as learning abroad. Also note that teachers are needed by some of the private development agencies described in Chapter 3 (see especially the sections on "Children" and "Education," pp. 47-48 and p. 50). Teachers are also recruited by some of the mission agencies described in Chapter 4 (see "Education" in the Index to Activities for specific references) as well as by the Peace Corps (p. 152-53). UNESCO sends educational experts to provide high-level technical assistance in the educational field to developing countries (p. 135).

For background reading on education in the developing countries, refer to *Overseas Opportunities for American Educators and Students* (p. 99). Some of UNESCO's publications will also be of interest; you can get their catalog from: Unipub, P.O. Box 1222, Ann Arbor, MI 48106.

There are many general references for people interested in teaching abroad, among them:

Brett, Richard J. *World Study and Travel for Teachers*. American Federation of Teachers (11 Dupont Circle N.W., Washington, DC 20036), revised annually. Currently $4. Information about 300 study and travel programs for teachers sponsored by U.S. colleges and universities in 119 countries.

Fine, Janet. *Teaching*. Chicago: VGM Career Horizons, 1984. Detailed information of teaching as a career, including international opportunities.

Teaching Abroad. Institute of International Education (809 U.N. Plaza, New York, NY 10017), 1984. $11.95 (including first-class postage and handling). Describes opportunities in 100 countries, with information from the U.S. government, foreign governments, and U.S. and international schools abroad. Each entry includes information on faculty positions and needs, requirements, duration, salary and benefits, and contracts.

Teaching Opportunities in Latin America for U.S. Citizens. Department of Educational Affairs, Organization of American States (17th and Constitution Ave. N.W., Washington, DC 20006), annual. Free.

Teaching Opportunities in the Middle East and North Africa. American Friends of the Middle East (1717 Massachusetts Ave. N.W., Suite 100,

Washington, DC 20036), forthcoming. Lists organizations, companies, and government agencies that recruit teachers, as well as schools and universities in the region that hire English-speaking teachers on a regular basis. AMIDEAST maintains a computerized resource bank to locate professionally qualified personnel for short- and long-term assignments in the region. General information on traveling in the Middle East also included.

The U.S. government operates two programs that take teachers (at the elementary, secondary, and college levels) to developing countries:

The *Teacher Exchange Program* of the Department of Education is open to U.S. citizens currently employed as teachers who have a B.A. degree, at least three years' teaching experience, and often facility in the language of the host country. The program includes teaching assignments for elementary, secondary, and university-level teachers, as well as short-term seminars abroad for teachers. An annually published booklet, *Opportunities Abroad for Educators,* describes the program in detail. Write: Teacher Exchange Section, Division of International Education, U.S. Department of Education, Washington, DC 20202.

Overseas Dependent Schools of the Department of Defense, with 36,000 students and 11,000 employees, comprise the United States' largest school system. It recruits U.S. teachers for positions in 270 elementary, junior and senior high schools, and community colleges to instruct dependents of Department of Defense personnel stationed in some 20 countries overseas. These are generally one- to two-year assignments. Many are in the Caribbean area (notably Panama and Bermuda) or the Pacific region. Candidates should have at least one year of successful full-time employment as teacher, counselor, librarian, vocational-education instructor, or administrator in an educational institution during the five-year period before application. The descriptive booklet about the program, *Overseas Employment Opportunities for Educators,* is free, and includes an application form. Write: U.S. Department of Defense, Office of Overseas Dependents Schools, Teacher Recruitment Section, 2461 Eisenhower Ave., Alexandria, VA 22331.

Elementary and secondary teachers

In addition to those noted above, major avenues of placement for elementary and secondary teachers are:

Educational Career Services (Placement and Career Planning Center, Educational Career Services, UCLA, Los Angeles, CA 90024). Provides educators in all disciplines and at all levels with the opportunity to meet and interview with school administrators from around the world for potential overseas placement. Hosts the International Schools Recruitment Conference every year in February for headmasters of American schools overseas. B.A. and credentials are minimum requirements for employment; candidates need not in all cases be certified to teach English as a foreign language. Registration fee is currently $20 for single applicants, $30 for couples. More than 250 applicants registered in 1984. One- to two-year assignments.

Fulbright-Hays Program. Places elementary and secondary schoolteachers abroad, but currently no programs in developing countries. For brochure, *Opportunities Abroad for Educators,* write: Teacher Exchange Section, U.S. Information Agency, E/ASX, 301 4th St. S.W., Washington, DC 20547.

International Schools Service (P.O. Box 5910, Princeton, NJ 08540). Services all aspects of overseas education, including educational staffing, school management, curricular materials and supplies, personnel services, residential student placement, consultation, and publications. Maintains a bank of approximately 1200 candidates, both teachers (kindergarten through 12th grade) and administrators. Bachelor's degree and two years of current experience usually required. Candidate need not be certified to teach English as a foreign language. Domestic recruitment center in New York City. One- or two-year renewable contracts made directly with schools. Registration fee of $50; placement fee of $600 (which may be absorbed by school). Salaries contracted with individual schools. A typical overseas school salary will not support more than two dependents. A brochure, *Teaching and Administrative Opportunities Abroad,* describes ISS programs, services, and registration procedure.

The Register for International Service in Education (RISE) (809 United Nations Plaza, New York, NY 10017). An information service of the Institute of International Education. Matches individuals with schools, universities, research centers, and development projects. Maintains an updated computer listing of more than 500 individuals and more than 1000 assignments. Educational background of applicants generally includes an advanced degree and/or certification in field of expertise. Positions for teachers of English as a foreign language generally require a higher degree, certification, and previous experience in the field. Ability to speak a foreign language and prior overseas experience are useful assets. $45 fee for a one-year listing with RISE; employers are also charged for listing assignments. Stipend usually includes international transportation, support for family members, insurance and housing assistance in addition to salary. Assignments available worldwide, with the majority in Asia, Africa, Latin America, and Oceania.

School Exchange Service. See p. 101.

School Exchange Service. See p. 101.

Lists of schools likely to hire U.S. citizens might be helpful, especially for teachers who know they are going to a particular country, to accompany a spouse for example. The two most widely cited lists of this kind are Anne Maher's *Schools Abroad of Interest to Americans* (1983), available from Porter Sargent (11 Beacon St., Boston, MA 02108), and the *1984-1985 ISS Directory of Overseas Schools,* available from International Schools Service (13 Roselle Road, P.O. Box 5910, Princeton, NJ 08540).

Special-education teachers will be interested in the Partners Appropriate Technology for the Handicapped (PATH). This program matches U.S. states with Latin American and Caribbean countries and areas to exchange personnel, financial aid, and information about special education and rehabilitation. PATH designs projects, funds specialists in rehabilitation or special education to work overseas, and also uses volunteers to implement its projects. Foreign language skills are not required. PATH pays for international transportation and $100 of expenses. Write: Partners of the Americas, 1424 K St. N.W., Suite 700, Washington, DC 20005.

Teachers who have taught physically, mentally, or educationally handicapped students for at least two years may also apply for Rotary International grants for an academic year of study in a foreign country. Write: Rotary International, 1600 Ridge Ave., Evanston, IL 60201.

English as a foreign language

Teaching English to people whose native language is not English has, since the Second World War, grown to become a profession unto itself. The world has become more interdependent, economically, politically, and culturally, and English is the most important international language. Some of the Americans teaching English abroad have a master's degree in ESL (English as a Second Language), plus knowledge of the host country's language. But some upper-level college students with virtually no teaching experience and no previous exposure to the local language are also teaching English abroad. Salaries, conditions for employment, and channels for job finding also vary widely.

The major national organization of ESL teachers, TESOL (Teachers of English to Speakers of Other Languages), has 10,000 members and training centers around the country. TESOL's members are working in 106 countries. TESOL publishes a monthly newsletter detailing job opportunities abroad and also sponsors an annual conference of employers and prospective employees. Write: Teachers of English to Speakers of Other Languages, 481 Intercultural Center, Georgetown University, Washington, DC 20057.

In many developing countries, privately organized binational centers teach English, offer library services, and present social and cultural events. The U.S. Information Agency provides binational centers in Latin America about 15 ESL teachers a year. Its English Teaching Fellow Program is open to any U.S. citizen who has or is working toward a degree in linguistics with emphasis on teaching English as a foreign language. An ETFP Fellow signs a contract with a binational center for one year, and contracts are sometimes renewed. The United States and the host-country government each contribute half of the salary and expenses of the Fellow, who is provided a subsistence level stipend, shared housing accommodations, round-trip travel expenses, and health insurance. Details and applications are available from: English Teaching Fellow Program, U.S. Information Agency, 301 Fourth St. S.W., Room 310, Washington, DC 20547. Applicant profiles are also given to TESOL, which acts as a job bank for ESL teaching positions at U.S. cultural centers in Africa and Southeast Asia.

The Center for Applied Linguistics (3520 Prospect St. N.W., Washington, DC 20007) also provides services and acts as an information clearinghouse for people interested in teaching English overseas. Their Education Resource Information Center will send you lists of schools and binational centers that are looking for English teachers.

Some people find their own teaching positions abroad. Many schools in developing countries, although not part of any formal program, would be glad to have a U.S. liberal-arts graduate on their staff. They won't be willing to pay for your plane ticket, and they will probably pay you the same wage they pay local teachers. But, on the other hand, they might not insist on any credential other than a B.A. or B.S. degree.

The trick is to make contact with a school abroad that might hire you. You should ask people who have lived in the Third World if they know of particular schools you might write. When David Beckmann was in college, he learned of specific opportunities to teach English in Nepal and Thailand—one by writing a U.S. citizen living in Nepal, the other by talking to another college student who had just returned from a year in Thailand. Some years later, when Beckmann and a friend were traveling through the Caribbean, they were both offered jobs teaching English at a Catholic school in the Dominican Republic. If you go abroad as a tourist, you should not count on such luck, but you could at least check for similar opportunities. Keep an eye out for English-language "conversation schools," usually privately run centers for adults and professionals interested in improving their conversation ability.

Teachers of higher education

University-level educators often find teaching positions abroad through personal contacts, or sometimes through professional societies or by writing directly to a university department abroad. The best published information on currently available positions are the advertisements in *The Times Higher Education Supplement* and *The Times Literary Supplement*. Both are published weekly and available from Times Newspapers of Great Britain (Subscriptions, 210 South St., New York, NY 10002). Overseas positions for educators are also advertised in various education periodicals, including *The Chronicle of Higher Education,* Canada's *University Affairs,* UNESCO's *International Social Science Journal,* and journals of regional studies (such as the African Studies Association's *ASA News*).

The Modern Language Association of America maintains an information service that publicizes openings in English and foreign-language departments at institutions of higher education. The service helps candidates for faculty positions learn about opportunities and also seeks to keep the profession as a whole informed about current hiring trends. The *MLA Job Information List* focuses primarily on domestic teaching positions but is likely to include at least a few openings in developing countries. Subscription rates for U.S. and Canadian addresses are $25 for a full year (four issues) or $13 for a half year (two issues). Inquiries should be addressed to Subscription Office, MLA Job Information Service, 62 Fifth Ave., New York, NY 10011.

In addition, university educators might investigate the Fulbright Scholar Program, which offers both travel-only grants and full fellowships for lecturing and research positions abroad. Information on the Fulbright Scholar Program is available on campuses or from the Council for International Exchange of Scholars (11 Dupont Circle N.W., Suite 300, Washington, DC 20036).

See also the Register for International Service in Education (pp. 118-119).

Journalism

Aspiring foreign correspondents have often thrown themselves into foreign lands to escape the humdrum, familiar life in which they were raised. Yet most have also continued to feel the force of the American landscape on them, long after leaving, and like foreign correspondent Eric Sevareid found themselves asking, "Why have I not returned [home] for so many years?" If anything, life in foreign places has sharpened their sense of being American. Serving as the eyes and ears of Americans has been a high calling as well as a personal adventure.

Of course, much has changed in the nearly 50 years since Sevareid left his North Dakota home for Europe. In his youth the world was, especially for Americans, a simpler place. The United States had not yet taken a commanding role in world affairs, had not made the mistakes and enemies that great powers traditionally do. Decades of colonization by the European powers had served to open borders. More than one American youngster eager to reach the Far East simply stowed away on a ship heading his way. With a readership that was curious about the rest of the world, U.S. editors paid fat fees for free-lance stories and set up bureaus abroad. A casual visit to the Paris office of a U.S. newspaper could turn into a job—and a career.

Today, in contrast, Cold War tensions and the emergence of scores of new nations in Africa and Asia have made vast regions of the world less accessible, more dangerous. The U.S. government's need to lay out clear, sharp policies abroad have made American reporters appear less neutral. Indeed, many of the new nations have expressly sought to keep out foreign reporters. They argue that such interlopers misrepresent their countries, concentrating on coups and earthquakes.

Meanwhile, the economics of journalism have helped confound foreign news coverage. It costs *The Washington Post* about one-third of a million dollars a year to keep each of its two foreign correspondents in Africa. Many of the papers that once had large corps of foreign correspondents abroad—like *The Chicago Daily News* or the *New York Herald-Tribune*—have gone out of business, the victims of a trend toward one-newspaper towns. Not surprisingly, the number of reporters working abroad has also declined during the past several years.

Yet if the world is not as simple as it once was, the mission of the foreign correspondent is more important than ever. Increasingly complex international problems demand that Americans have access to more reliable, sophisticated information. Economic prosperity at home depends more and more on trade with other countries. The United States can no longer be just curious about the rest of the world.

As a practical matter, most of today's foreign correspondents have worked their way up through the ranks of a newspaper, wire service, or network. They started at the bottom, covering fires and writing obituaries. Only when they prove themselves, a process that can take several years, do reporters get the chance at an overseas assignment. And then the first posting is often to a country where living conditions are more difficult. Few foreign correspondents have their first posting in Rome or Rio.

An aspiring foreign correspondent can also strike out on his own as a free-lance writer. While that will get a person overseas more quickly, it has several major liabilities. One is that free-lance journalists often find it difficult to get their stories into print. Anyone taking this more adventurous course should try to persuade one or two American editors to hire him on as a stringer—that is, to allow him to represent the newspaper or radio overseas. Stringers are paid by the story; some receive a modest retainer. Such an approach gives a free-lance journalist formal backing—and hence better credibility with officials in the country he is covering—and some assurance of income. A free-lancer must still sell articles to other publications, of course, and therefore must be sensitive to media markets. He must find angles that will sell to special interest publications. Very few free-lance journalists make good incomes. On the other hand, they have more freedom than many reporters who work full-time for a media outfit.

A third way of breaking in as a foreign correspondent is to seek employment with English-language publications in foreign cities where there are large numbers of expatriates. Pay is usually low, but the experience can be wide, including editing as well as reporting. Often such jobs are combined with stringer assignments with media back in the United States.

In any of these approaches, one fact stands out. Foreign correspondents need more specialized knowledge to meet today's complex problems. In recognition of this, news organizations increasingly prefer to send abroad reporters who know the language and customs of the country they will work in. Such an attitude may ultimately help allay concerns in developing countries about the quality of U.S. reporting overseas. Advanced academic training or prior experience in the country, perhaps with the Peace Corps, is a big plus.

The following programs prepare journalists specifically for work in developing countries. Some of these programs themselves involve travel to developing countries:

East Asia Journalism Program, funded by the U.S.-Japan Friendship Commission, aids students who wish to specialize in Japan or China. Two years of study. Contact: Graduate School of Journalism, Columbia University, New York, NY 10027.

Fulbright Grants are made for journalism and communications specialists with U.S. citizenship for travel abroad. Apply to Council for International Exchange of Scholars, Suite 300, 11 Dupont Circle N.W., Washington, DC 20036.

Gannett Fellowships in Asian Studies provide tuition and fees, transportation expenses, and a $15,250 stipend for midcareer journalists and recent graduates of journalism school who are U.S. citizens and meet standards at the University of Hawaii. Apply before March 1 to: Asian Studies Program, Moore Hall 315, 1890 East-West Road, Honolulu, HI 96822.

IAPA Scholarship Fund provides up to $5000 for U.S. and Canadian journalists or journalism school graduates between the ages of 21 and 35 for six to nine months of study and work in Latin America. Applicants must be fluent in Spanish or Portuguese. Apply before September 1 to: Inter-American Press Association, 2911 N.W. 39th St., Miami, FL 33142.

National Press Foundation gives tuition and stipends for journalists for study and research in the Spanish language at a school in Mexico. Contact: Don Larrabee, Suite 261, National Press Building, Washington, DC 20045.

Partners of the Americas Program, with grants from the Tinker Foundation, Time Inc., and Gannett Company, allows U.S. journalists to work for one month in Latin America or the Caribbean. Contact: Hunter Farrell, 2001 S St. N.W., Washington, DC 20009.

Rotary Foundation Educational Program is open to journalists between 21 and 28 years of age for study abroad. Apply to: Rotary International Foundation, 1600 Ridge Ave., Evanston, IL, 60201, or contact local Rotary Club.

SEVEN

International Organizations

Official international organizations—the United Nations, its specialized agencies, regional development banks, and other associations of nations—have more than 60,000 permanent employees and many more fixed-term personnel. These organizations deal with a broad range of issues, but much of their work is focused on Third World issues and involves dealing with Third World governments. In addition, there are a host of private international organizations and associations, many of which also include Third World members.

International interdependence makes international organizations essential. The International Monetary Fund, for example, plays a necessary (albeit sometimes controversial) role in assisting nations with balance-of-payments problems and in maintaining global systems of money and trade. The World Bank and the regional development banks intermediate between the international capital markets and developing countries whose ability to attract capital directly from commercial sources is limited. Together with other multilateral and bilateral agencies, the multilateral development banks also provide technical assistance and some concessional finance to developing countries. Finally, the United Nations provides vital forums for the discussion of controversial international issues, especially issues of importance to developing countries, as well as mechanisms for international cooperation on more routine matters such as international air travel and copyright law.

There has been growing impatience with some U.N. agencies in some quarters, however, especially in the United States. The U.S. government has more than once withdrawn, at least temporarily, from a U.N. agency. A major complaint is that U.N. forums have become unduly politicized, with the developing-country majority often adopting resolutions that the United States opposes. Critics are also concerned, as are supporters of the United Nations, about inefficiencies in the system—overlap and duplication among agencies, lax administration in some agencies, the adverse effects of political considerations in hiring, and the allegation that salaries in some international agencies are too high.

Supporters of the international agencies are concerned that the U.S. government has become increasingly reticent to contribute to cooperative efforts with the other nations of the world. The developing countries have called for sweeping reforms of the global economic order to make it more supportive of Third World development; they envision a larger role for international agencies, and representatives of the developing countries have expressed bitter disappointment at what seems to them U.S. recalcitrance in U.N. forums.

For further discussion of the virtues and problems of international organizations, and of the United States' role as a member nation, you may want to read:

The Brandt Commission. *Common Crisis: North-South Cooperation for World Recovery.* London and Sydney: Pan Books, 1984. Argues that global economic reform, including an expanded role for international institutions, is urgently needed by the developing countries and is also in the self-interest of the developed countries.

Chen, Samuel Shih-Tsai. *The Theory and Practice of International Organizations.* Dubuque, Iowa: Kendall/Hunt Publishing Co., 1979. Good history and description of international organizations.

Committee on Government Operations, U.S. Congress, Senate, 95th Congress, lst Session. *U.S. Participation in International Organizations.* Washington: U.S. Government, 1977. Updated in 1982 by U.S. General Accounting Office. Assesses international organizations from a U.S. government perspective. Generally critical.

Finger, Seymour Maxwell and Joseph R. Herber, eds. *U.S. Policy in International Institutions: Defining Reasonable Options in an Unreason-*

able World. Boulder, Colorado: Westview Press, 1982. A collection of essays about changes in international relations, effects on international institutions, and the impact on U.S. interests.

It is quite difficult to get a position in one of the international organizations, for several reasons. First, international organizations aim to recruit a broadly international staff. They are especially eager to hire people from underrepresented countries, and that often puts U.S. citizens at a disadvantage. Many of the U.N. agencies use a quota system to assure that their staff is representative of all their member nations.

Second, the international agencies aim to recruit highly qualified personnel. The Food and Agriculture Organization, for instance, requires five to seven years experience of its applicants. In a recent year, according to U.N. figures, only 4% of the professional staff of its combined agencies were under 30 years old, and only 14% were younger than 35. The international agencies usually have somewhat higher salary scales than member governments, a practice that has sometimes been criticized but allows international agencies to attract genuinely expert people.

Finally, member nations, notably the United States, have curbed their financial contributions to many international organizations. The organizations have therefore been forced to limit new hiring and, in some cases, to cut back on their personnel.

Categories of employees

In general, international organizations recruit for the following four categories:

Permanent professional staff: Professional staff nearly all have advanced degrees, successful work experience, and facility in at least one major language other than English. For employment with the United Nations, fluency in at least two of their three working languages (English, French, Spanish) is required. Economists are employed in great numbers. There are also relatively frequent openings for professionals in public administration, agriculture, education, statistics, demography, finance, engineering, health services, computers, public information, social services, and transportation. Occasionally there are openings for translators, interpreters, editors, and media technicians. Very few openings exist for political scientists, specialists in international affairs, lawyers, general administrators, or individuals with military experience.

Secretarial and support staff: The intergovernmental agencies try to get a broad international mix among secretarial and support staff, too, but people are generally recruited locally for these positions. A secretary wanting to work at the United Nations in New York, for example, would have to pay her own transportation expenses for the interview and to begin the job. Particularly in demand are qualified bilingual secretaries, high-speed conference typists, computer programmers, librarians, and telecommunications specialists.

Most of the international agencies also have research assistants, many of them people with master's degrees, a second language, and perhaps some facility with computers. In addition to the formal channels described below, someone who wants a research assistantship should knock on the doors of people who might use research assistants and try to nurture personal contacts.

Short-term consultants: Most international agencies recruit highly qualified professionals to advise and assist agency staff. The World Bank, for example, might need a planner to join a staff mission in the evaluation of an urban-poverty project, or the United Nations might have a consultant spend several months in Tunisia studying rural development needs in order to suggest a possible project. (Consulting is discussed on pp. 190-94.) The international agencies often recruit as permanent staff people whose work they have first learned to respect under consulting arrangements. In fact, this may be the most likely way to a permanent professional appointment in one of the international organizations: first work for them on consulting assignments. If you prove yourself effective as part of the team, you may be hired again and again, finally for a permanent position.

Technical-assistance experts: The United Nations and its specialized agencies provide technical assistance for development by hiring experts and loaning them to Third World governments. These experts usually serve as advisors and planners rather than as administrators of projects in execution. Assignments vary from several weeks to a year or more. Experts normally have an advanced degree and have attained a recognized standing in their profession, several years of relevant experience (preferably some of it in developing countries), and any necessary language facility. On occasion, retirees in good health are selected. Since the selection process may involve more than one agency and the host government, several months may elapse between application and appointment. Although the official literature doesn't say so, these positions can also be a stepping-stone to consulting for the funding agency itself and, eventually, to a permanent position with the agency.

Opportunities for young people to intern in the U.N. agencies are few. We note those of any size in our descriptions of the agencies (on pp. 132-38), but you might find some further useful leads in the *International Directory for Youth Internships With the United Nations, Its Specialized Agencies, and Nongovernmental Organizations* ($6.75 from Learning Resources in International Studies, Suite 9A, 777 United Nations Plaza, New York, NY 10017). The most promising section would be their chapter on nongovernmental organizations; although few of the nongovernmental organizations they list send people to developing countries, some of them work closely with U.N. agencies.

The United Nations family of agencies

The purposes of the United Nations, as defined in its charter, are to maintain international peace and security through the peaceful settlement of disputes, to develop friendly relations among nations based on respect for the equal rights and self-determination of peoples, to achieve cooperation in dealing with matters of concern to humanity, and to be a center for harmonizing the actions of nations in attaining these ends. The charter was signed by 51 nations in 1945, and 106 more nations have joined the United Nations since then.

Almost all the intergovernmental organizations with nearly worldwide membership are, in one way or another, linked into the United Nations system (see diagram on p. 131). In general, the specialized agencies (ILO, FAO, and the others listed on the bottom right of the diagram) are autonomous, while the other U.N. bodies (UNRWA, UNCTAD, and the others listed on the bottom left) are responsible to the Economic and Social Council and the U.N. General Assembly.

THE UNITED NATIONS SYSTEM

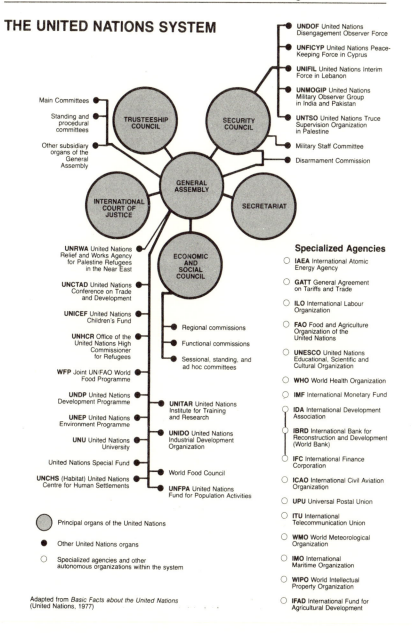

- **UNDOF** United Nations Disengagement Observer Force
- **UNFICYP** United Nations Peace-Keeping Force in Cyprus
- **UNIFIL** United Nations Interim Force in Lebanon
- **UNMOGIP** United Nations Military Observer Group in India and Pakistan
- **UNTSO** United Nations Truce Supervision Organization in Palestine
- Military Staff Committee
- Disarmament Commission

Main Committees

Standing and procedural committees

Other subsidiary organs of the General Assembly

TRUSTEESHIP COUNCIL

SECURITY COUNCIL

GENERAL ASSEMBLY

INTERNATIONAL COURT OF JUSTICE

SECRETARIAT

ECONOMIC AND SOCIAL COUNCIL

- **UNRWA** United Nations Relief and Works Agency for Palestine Refugees in the Near East
- **UNCTAD** United Nations Conference on Trade and Development
- **UNICEF** United Nations Children's Fund
- **UNHCR** Office of the United Nations High Commissioner for Refugees
- **WFP** Joint UN/FAO World Food Programme
- **UNDP** United Nations Development Programme
- **UNEP** United Nations Environment Programme
- **UNU** United Nations University
- United Nations Special Fund
- **UNCHS** (Habitat) United Nations Centre for Human Settlements

- Regional commissions
- Functional commissions
- Sessional, standing, and ad hoc committees

- **UNITAR** United Nations Institute for Training and Research
- **UNIDO** United Nations Industrial Development Organization
- World Food Council
- **UNFPA** United Nations Fund for Population Activities

Specialized Agencies

- ○ **IAEA** International Atomic Energy Agency
- ○ **GATT** General Agreement on Tariffs and Trade
- ○ **ILO** International Labour Organization
- ○ **FAO** Food and Agriculture Organization of the United Nations
- ○ **UNESCO** United Nations Educational, Scientific and Cultural Organization
- ○ **WHO** World Health Organization
- ○ **IMF** International Monetary Fund
- ○ **IDA** International Development Association
- ○ **IBRD** International Bank for Reconstruction and Development (World Bank)
- ○ **IFC** International Finance Corporation
- ○ **ICAO** International Civil Aviation Organization
- ○ **UPU** Universal Postal Union
- ○ **ITU** International Telecommunication Union
- ○ **WMO** World Meteorological Organization
- ○ **IMO** International Maritime Organization
- ○ **WIPO** World Intellectual Property Organization
- ○ **IFAD** International Fund for Agricultural Development

● Principal organs of the United Nations

● Other United Nations organs

○ Specialized agencies and other autonomous organizations within the system

Adapted from *Basic Facts about the United Nations* (United Nations, 1977)

All the specialized agencies and some of the other U.N. bodies recruit staff separately from the United Nations itself. A number of agencies are involved in selecting experts for recommendation to Third World governments (as discussed on pp. 129-30); the United Nations itself for the fields of economic development, welfare, and public administration; UNCTAD for trade and development; UNIDO for industrial development; UNEP for environment; and 10 of the specialized agencies in their own areas of concern.

Below are listed the ten largest employers in the U.N. system. They all deal primarily with developing countries.

Agency	*Employees*
United Nations Secretariat	16,019
Food and Agriculture Organization	6,884
World Bank	6,117
United Nations Development Program	5,931
World Health Organization	4,403
UNESCO	3,512
UNICEF	2,796
International Labor Office	2,752
International Monetary Fund	1,743
International Atomic Energy Agency	1,526

These ten agencies and their personnel requirements are described, in alphabetical order, below:

Food and Agriculture Organization (Via della Terme di Caracalla, 00100 Rome, Italy. For U.S. applicants: FAO Liaison Office for North America, 1001 22nd St. N.W., Washington, DC 20437). The FAO was established to fight malnutrition and hunger and to serve as a coordinating agency for development programs in all areas of food and agriculture, including rural development, nutrition, forestry, and fisheries. It assists developing countries with the promotion of educational and training facilities and institution building. It also finances special relief operations, quick and flexible projects in response to urgent needs, and studies to prepare the way for larger investments. FAO regional offices are located in Ghana, Ethiopia, Thailand, Chile, and Egypt. FAO's staff includes 129 U.S. citizens.

International Atomic Energy Agency (Vienna International Center, Wagramerstrasse 5, 1220 Vienna, Austria). The IAEA is an autonomous intergovernmental agency, founded in 1957, with responsibility for international activities concerned with the peaceful uses of atomic energy. It seeks to develop the use of atomic energy, ensuring that it is not used for military purposes. As of 1983, IAEA employed 555 professional staff and 971 general-service staff. Each year the IAEA renders assistance to more than 75 developing countries, including the services of over 600 experts, fellowships for individual study, and equipment and supplies valued at around $11 million.

International Labor Office (Personnel Department, 4 route des Morillons, 1211 Geneva 22, Switzerland, or ILO Office, 1750 New York Ave. N.W., Suite 330, Washington, DC 20007). The ILO is the senior specialized agency of the U.N. system responsible for international labor and social affairs. It is unique in the system in having a tripartite (government/employer/worker) composition. The ILO's main fields of technical action include employment and development, vocational and management development, conditions of work, labor law and administration, industrial relations, social security, and sectoral activities dealing with major branches of industry and occupations. Its means of action are setting international labor standards in the form of conventions and recommendations; technical cooperation, chiefly in developing countries; technical meetings; and research and publishing. Staff employed at Geneva headquarters and 40 field offices with 110 nationalities represented, including 54 U.S. citizens.

International Monetary Fund (700 19th St. N.W., Washington, DC 20431). Established in 1946, the principal objective of the Fund is to promote international monetary cooperation and a freer system of world trade and payments as means of helping its member countries achieve economic growth, high levels of employment, and improved standards of living. It maintains close contact with members on their economic situations and has set up facilities for making available technical and financial assistance, especially with regard to foreign exchange and balance of payments difficulties. The Fund's staff is drawn from over 100 countries. About half are in the professional categories, and two-thirds of these are economic staff. Relatively few staff are stationed outside the United States, but there is opportunity for frequent travel abroad. The Fund recruits about 50 economists per year, about half of whom enter through its Economist Program, open to candidates below age 33. Most applicants have Ph.D.'s in economics, finance, or statistics. Some M.A.'s are accepted if they have exceptional practical experience in economic or finance areas. There is also a Summer Intern Program for those who have completed at least one year of graduate work in macroeconomics.

United Nations Children's Fund (866 U.N. Plaza, New York, NY 10017). UNICEF, established in 1946, aims to improve the situation of children everywhere, especially those in developing countries who are in the greatest need. Its programs include mother-and-child care, nutrition, inoculation campaigns, schools and education, and emergency relief. UNICEF is financed separately from the regular U.N. budget, through voluntary contributions from governments supplemented by private and individual contributions (see U.S. Committee for UNICEF, p. 47). UNICEF hires mostly generalist administrators who have experience in developing countries and a graduate degree in economics, social development, or related fields. Three-quarters of UNICEF's staff are located in its 87 field offices. As of 1983, professional staff totaled 735, and general services staff totaled 2061.

United Nations Development Program (One United Nations Plaza, New York, NY 10017). The UNDP was founded in 1965 to assist developing countries increase the wealth-producing capabilities of their natural and human resources. As the world's largest agency for coordinating technical assistance, UNDP focuses its project work in five main areas: activating latent natural resources and other development assets, stimulating capital investment, supporting professional and vocational training, expanding scientific research and applied technology, and strengthening national and regional development planning. Much UNDP assistance is channeled into preinvestment studies, leading toward large-scale development projects. UNDP maintains resident offices in nearly all developing countries. In 1981 UNDP supported 5074 projects at a cost of $732 million.

UNDP directs a Junior Professional Officer Program (JPOP) that trains young professionals sponsored by their governments. The JPOP is one or two years in duration, after which the young officers are expected to return to their own countries. At any given time, there are more than 100 JPOs on active assignment. While some JPOs go on to become permanent UNDP employees, the program is not considered a backdoor entry to a career with UNDP. Applicants should have a background in economic development and economics.

UNDP also has a summer internship program that lasts from eight to ten weeks. Providing on-the-job training for participants, the internships are filled by graduate students specializing in development areas.

The United Nations Volunteers (UNV), a UNDP affiliate, serves as an important source of midlevel skills for the U.N. development system. In 1981 more than 1000 volunteers, including agronomists, architects, health workers, teachers, and engineers, were working in 92 developing countries. Volunteers receive a small stipend and transportation expenses. UNV does not recruit volunteers directly; U.S. citizens apply to UNV through the U.S. ACTION/Peace Corps. Additional information can be obtained by writing the Peace Corps (pp. 152-53) or: U.N. Volunteers, Palais des Nations, 1211 Geneva 10, Switzerland.

United Nations Educational, Scientific, and Cultural Organization (7 place de Fontenay, 75700 Paris, France. For U.S. applicants to UNESCO Secretariat: Office of International Organizations Recruitment, Department of State, Washington, DC 20520. For U.S. applicants for UNESCO technical assistance: International Organizations Recruitment, Division of International Education, Department of Education, 400 Massachusetts Ave. S.W., Washington, DC 20202). UNESCO was established to advance, through the educational, scientific, and cultural relations of the peoples of the world, the objectives of international peace and the common welfare. UNESCO's activities can be grouped in three main areas: international intellectual cooperation, operational assistance, and promotion of peace. Its activities include helping with literacy campaigns, providing refugee schools, sponsoring training programs to strengthen the scientific capacity of Third World nations, leading rescue operations for ancient monuments that may be endangered, financing the study of literature and art around the world, and assisting in efforts to strengthen the news media of developing countries. Job applicants are expected to have at least three to five years professional experience in educational, scientific, or cultural work. Regional offices are located throughout the Third World. About two-thirds of UNESCO's professional staff are posted outside headquarters on technical assistance missions to member countries. In 1984 the U.S. government withdrew from UNESCO after a dispute over its policies and programs. Thus, the chances of UNESCO employment are very limited for U.S. citizens.

United Nations Secretariat (Recruitment Programmes Section, Division of Recruitment, Office of Personnel Services, New York, NY 10017). The United Nations Secretariat (U.N.) is the largest employer of international civil servants. If interested in working for the U.N., you should apply through the Recruitment Programmes Section, but also contact particular offices where you would like to work. Most permanent U.N. staff live in New York. Others are based in Geneva, Rome, Paris, Vienna, Nairobi, and at U.N. regional economic commission offices in Santiago, Baghdad, Addis Ababa, and Bangkok. In addition, there are some 50 information centers around the world and offices of UNDP resident representatives in most developing countries. As of 1983 the U.N. Secretariat employed 6,198 professional staff (564 U.S. citizens) and 9,821 in general services (1,166 U.S. citizens).

Most administrative and professional vacancies overseas are filled by transferring staff already working at headquarters, but some specialized staff (including economists, sociologists, industrial experts, and statisticians) may be recruited directly for overseas positions. Would-be government advisors for technical assistance positions in the fields for which the U.N. is responsible (see p. 132) should apply to: Technical Assistance Recruitment Service, Department of Technical Cooperation, United Nations, New York, NY 10017.

The United Nations is looking for good support personnel, especially high-speed conference typists, stenographers and secretaries, accounting and statistical clerks. The only vacancies in the secretarial categories, however, are at junior levels (ages 18 to 35), since senior levels are filled by promotion. Clerical and secretarial staff are normally recruited locally, from among residents of the area in which the office is located. A staff member with a permanent appointment (normally granted after two years of service) who has reached the age of 24 may, however, apply for a mission assignment abroad.

Some support staff for peace-keeping missions abroad is supplied through the United Nations Field Service, a corps of security officers, vehicle mechanics, radio technicians and officers, and experienced secretaries who are rotated from mission to mission. Qualifications: 23 to 40 years of age, high-school graduation or equivalent, second language desirable, top-notch health, personal suitability, and relevant experience (military or police experience for security officers; five years of experience and certified competence in repair and maintenance for vehicle mechanics; radio training and experience for radio technicians and operators; five years of secretarial training and/or experience and tested typing and stenographic speeds for secretaries).

There are annual summer internship programs for selected college and graduate students in the fields of economics, law, international relations, sociology, communications, and other related areas. About 50 candidates are chosen for the New York program and 80 for a similar program in Geneva. Write: UNDPI, U.N. Secretariat, United Nations, New York, NY 10017; or United Nations Office at Geneva, Information Service, Palais des Nations, CH-1211, Geneva 10, Switzerland.

In addition, ad hoc internships in U.N. offices can occasionally be arranged for graduate students specializing in fields related to U.N. work. As in the summer program, participants do not receive a stipend, and internships in developing countries are rare. Address inquiries to: Recruitment Programmes Section, Division of Recruitment, Office of Personnel Services, United Nations, New York, NY 10017.

U.N. guides are recruited on a local basis, normally once a year, and begin their training in March. Candidates should be 20 to 30 years old, with a college education or equivalent. They must be fluent in English and another official U.N. language, with a good speaking voice. A personal interview at U.N. Headquarters is required, usually in the fall, and candidates must pay their own travel expenses to the interview. If interested, write: U.N. Central Employment Service, United Nations, New York, NY 10017. The Non-Governmental Liaison Service (Room DC2-1103, United Nations, New York, NY 10017) offers six-month to one-year internships for students who have completed their undergraduate education. Both voluntary and paid positions are available, with stipends of up to $500 a month. The Non-Governmental Liaison Service is a link between governmental organizations and the U.N. system. It focuses on public education regarding economic and social issues.

The World Bank (Staffing Division, 1818 H St. N.W., Washington, DC 20433). The World Bank's objectives are economic growth and the reduction of poverty in the developing countries. The World Bank comprises three legally separate institutions—IBRD (International Bank for Reconstruction and Development), IFC (International Finance Corporation), and IDA (International Development Association)—each of which provides a different mechanism for channeling finance to the developing countries. The three sister institutions of The World Bank invested a total of $15.3 billion in the developing countries in the Bank's 1985 fiscal year. In addition, the Bank helps developing countries with policy advice and assistance in the preparation and supervision of investment projects.

The World Bank is involved in nearly every aspect of Third World development, but about half the Bank's lending supports projects in energy and in agriculture and rural development. The Bank has recently placed increased emphasis on support for broad policy reforms to revive rapid growth in the developing countries and on its programs of cofinancing with commercial banks and other investors. After a period of very rapid growth in the 1970s, the Bank's staff has grown only 15% over the last five years. Recruitment by The World Bank, always very competitive, has become even more so.

The Bank hires highly qualified, experienced professionals: economists, financial analysts, M.B.A.'s, engineers, lawyers, and specialists in diverse sectors (such as energy, agriculture, population, industry, education, water supply, power, and transportation). The Bank also needs computer programmers, accountants, translators, and personnel specialists. The Bank recruits professional staff internationally, and most of them come to the Bank after years of successful professional experience; many have already demonstrated their effectiveness as consultants to the Bank. A small group of people under the age of 30 come into the Bank through its Young Professionals Program; they each begin with two six-month assignments in two different aspects of the Bank's work.

About half the jobs in The World Bank are support-level: research and administrative assistants, secretaries, and operation and maintenance personnel. Competition is also keen for support-level positions. Nearly all support staff are recruited from the Washington, D.C. area.

Over 90% of the Bank's staff is headquartered in Washington. The rest are posted to the Bank's offices around the world. Travel opportunities are very limited for support staff, but most higher-level staff travel in developing countries one to three months per year.

World Health Organization (Avenue Appia, 1211 Geneva 27, Switzerland, or Pan American Sanitary Bureau, 525 23rd St. N.W., Washington, DC 20037). WHO is the main agency directing international health work. WHO assists member governments in fighting disease and providing health care, finances relevant health research, and leads worldwide efforts to control communicable diseases. Its most impressive accomplishment to date has been leadership of the international effort that wiped out smallpox globally. WHO's most important activities involve technical cooperation with national health administrations, particularly in developing countries. The staff consists mainly of physicians, medical scientists, nurses, and health administrators, as well as specialists in planning and management techniques. They work at headquarters in Geneva, at six regional offices around the world, and in most member countries. WHO's staff includes 179 U.S. citizens.

The following list includes smaller agencies within the U.N. family that also employ some staff in work related to developing countries:

General Agreement on Tariffs and Trade
Centre William Rappard
154 rue de Lausanne
1211 Geneva 21, Switzerland

International Civil Aviation Organization
P.O. Box 400
1000 Sherbrooke St. W.
Montreal H3A 2R2, Canada

International Fund for Agricultural Development
Via del Serafico 107
00142 Rome, Italy

International Maritime Organization
4 Albert Embankment
London SE1 7SR, England

International Telecommunication Union
Palais des Nations
1211 Geneva 20, Switzerland

U.N. Conference on Trade and Development
Palais des Nations
1211 Geneva 20, Switzerland

U.N. Environment Program
P.O. Box 30552
Nairobi, Kenya

U.N. High Commissioner for Refugees
Palais des Nations
1211 Geneva 20, Switzerland

U.N. Industrial Development Organization
P.O. Box 300
1400 Vienna, Austria

Universal Postal Union
Weltpost Strasse
3000 Berne, Switzerland

World Intellectual Property Organization
32, Chemin des Colombettes
1211 Geneva 20, Switzerland

World Meteorological Organization
Case Postale No. 5
1211 Geneva 20, Switzerland

The U.S. government publicizes positions and helps recruit candidates for many of the intergovernmental organizations. While it does not maintain a public mailing list for the vacancy announcements from these organizations, the U.S. government does keep a computerized roster of qualified professional candidates whose background can be checked against the qualifications sought for referral as vacancies arise. The main office for this purpose is:

Office of U.N. System Recruitment
Bureau of International Organization Affairs
Department of State
Washington, DC 20520

U.S. citizens are also eligible to apply directly to the organization in which they are interested. In the end, each organization makes its own final selection, so you should contact each directly and not depend entirely on U.S. government channels.

Intergovernmental work outside the U.N. system

The major intergovernmental agencies outside the U.N. system are the regional banks (principally the Inter-American Development Bank, African Development Bank, and Asian Development Bank) and regional or other associations of nations (such as the Organization of American States [OAS] and the Organization for Economic Cooperation and Development [OECD]). This section also includes information about the Consultative Group on International Agricultural Research and about opportunities to work directly for a developing-country government.

The regional development banks were established on The World Bank model. Their activities are similar to those of The World Bank, but they are smaller and regional in scope. They were founded in the late 1950s and 1960s in attempts to raise more capital and, to some extent, also to create banks in which the Third World members would have more power than they did in The World Bank. Each regional bank recruits heavily from the region it serves, but there are employment opportunities for U.S. citizens too. Of the three main regional banks, the African Development Bank hires the fewest U.S. citizens.

The regional banks look for people with the same qualifications as does The World Bank, but with emphasis on experience in the region and knowledge of regional languages. The Inter-American Development Bank has a Junior Professional Program and summer programs for graduate students and administrative support staff. The headquarters of the regional banks are:

African Development Bank
BP 1387
Abidjan 01, Ivory Coast

Asian Development Bank
2330 Roxas Boulevard
Metro Manila, Philippines

Inter-American Development Bank
808 17th St. N.W.
Washington, DC 20577

There is also the Caribbean Development Bank (P.O. Box 408 Wildey, St. Michael, Barbados), but it is quite small and offers few employment opportunities. The oil-rich Arab states have established over half a dozen official development banks. They employ U.S. citizens as consultants from time to time, but offer U.S. citizens virtually no opportunities for permanent employment.

The Organization of American States (OAS) is one of the oldest international organizations. It fosters peace, security, mutual understanding, and cooperation among the nations of the Western Hemisphere. While in recent years the OAS has been charged with being weak and ineffectual, it is still influential in mediating disputes, providing technical assistance, and encouraging economic, social, and cultural development in the Americas. OAS is headquartered in Washington, D.C., with offices in each active member state. It has more than 1100 employees. The OAS is involved in a wide variety of fields (finance and trade; human rights; public administration and planning; science, music, arts and letters; education), so staff are recruited from diverse backgrounds. Write:

Office of Personnel
Organization of American States
17th St. and Constitution Ave. N.W.
Washington, DC 20006.

The Organization for Economic Cooperation and Development (OECD) includes most of the nations of Europe and North America as well as Japan, Australia, and New Zealand. It was founded to assist member governments in formulating policies to promote economic and social welfare and to stimulate and harmonize members' assistance to developing countries. The bulk of its work is carried out in specialized committees and working parties, which number more than 200. The OECD is sometimes called "the club of rich countries," but its staff does a good deal of research on Third World development and Third World relations with the industrial countries. Travel is limited to ad hoc missions by experts and consultants. Applicants should have graduate degrees and experience; competition is keen. Inquiries can be addressed to either of two offices:

OECD
2 rue Andre-Pascal
75775 Paris Cedex 16
France

Office of OECD Affairs (EUR/RPE)
Rm. 6517
U.S. Department of State
Washington, DC 20520

The Consultative Group on International Agricultural Research (CGIAR) is a network of 13 agricultural-research centers throughout the developing regions of the world. They include the institutes in Mexico and the Philippines that pioneered the high-yielding varieties of wheat and rice which led to the "Green Revolution." These high-yielding varieties are now grown on over a third of the wheat and rice lands of the developing world, and the resulting increase in production is enough to meet the needs of over 300 million people. At the present time, the CGIAR institutes are giving priority to high-yield crop varieties that require a minimum of purchased inputs (such as chemical fertilizer) and that can withstand drought, disease, and pests. This line of research is important for poor farmers and for water-scarce environments (including much of Africa).

The CGIAR institutes together employ more than 7000 people. These include some 750 senior scientists (about a fourth of them U.S. citizens), and there are also opportunities for postdoctoral fellows and graduate students in the relevant sciences. Each center recruits separately, but the CGIAR Secretariat (at The World Bank) will send you more information on CGIAR and a directory of the centers and their addresses. Write:

> Consultative Group on International
>   Agricultural Research Secretariat
> 1818 H Street N.W.
> Washington, DC 20433.

Finally, some U.S. citizens work directly for Third World governments, mainly in Africa and a few of the least developed Asian countries. Typically, foreigners are first sent by their own government or an international organization, but prove their worth and make personal contacts that lead to an extension of their tour within the host government's own bureaucracy. One young man from the United States, for example, went to Botswana as a Peace Corps volunteer. He worked three years in a rapidly growing town, first as an assistant, then as the town's housing officer. About that time the government of Botswana began preparing a large low-income housing project for World Bank financing, and they contracted with this man to help in their planning efforts.

Very few U.S. citizens make long-term careers serving in the governments of developing countries, not only because of the governments' reluctance to rely too heavily on foreigners, but because of the wide divergence between U.S. and Third World salary scales. A U.S. architect with several years of experience in Zambia took a contract with the government of Sierra Leone, on a Sierra Leone salary, because she wanted to join her husband there. But they left when his contract finished, mostly because her salary was much lower than what she could earn at home.

Before taking a position in a foreign government, be sure to check with the U.S. embassy or the State Department. In some cases, working for a foreign government can be cause for revoking a person's U.S. citizenship.

Nongovernmental international organizations

There are thousands of nongovernmental international organizations. Some are well-known, such as the World Council of Churches, International Red Cross, or Lions International. Some represent particular points of view, such as the World Assembly for Moral Rearmament or the European Socialist Movement. Others are very specialized—the International Committee on Alcohol, Drugs and Traffic Safety, for example, or the International Association of Professional Congress Organizers. All such organizations require staff such as technical specialists, writers, and administrators. Most of them have their headquarters in international cities such as Geneva, Brussels, or Washington, but many of them also send staff to or hold conferences in the Third World.

We have made extensive use of the *Europa Yearbook* (London: Europa Publications Limited, annual) for parts of this chapter, and it is a good reference for information on nongovernmental as well as official international organizations. *The Yearbook of International Organizations,* edited by the Union of International Associations (Munich: K.G. Saur, annual), lists almost 20,000 international bodies, most of them nongovernmental.

Contrary to popular opinion, the Red Cross does not offer substantial employment opportunities in international relief work. The American National Red Cross provides services to U.S. military personnel abroad (pp. 172-73), but only rarely loans its staff members to the international League of Red Cross Societies for relief work.

More generally, jobs in the international associations are difficult to get, especially for outsiders. International organizations can usually get top-notch people who have long been active within their own ranks. The way into this type of work is normally via successful participation in international organizations at the local level and the gradual cultivation of international contacts.

EIGHT

The U.S. Government

The U.S. government employs about 55,000 civilians abroad, including 40,000 in the Third World. The government also has more than 500,000 military personnel stationed overseas, a third of them in Asia, Africa, and Latin America. In addition, thousands of federal employees live in Washington but do work related to the Third World, some of them traveling there from time to time.

The U.S. government represents the interests of the United States worldwide. It wields its power and influence in the name of global peace and security. It works with other governments on international problems, encourages U.S. business and global commerce, and provides both economic and security assistance to developing countries.

Some critics stress the inefficiencies of the federal government, implying that many government employees do not really earn their salaries. Partly because of such sentiments, the number of federal employees has been held virtually constant since the beginning of the Carter Administration, and civil service salaries have not kept pace with inflation.

Other critics argue that U.S. policy is often opposed to the interests of developing countries (frustrating needed change in Central America, for example), so that U.S. government personnel who relate to developing countries do more harm than good. L.S. Stavrianos has chronicled, at depressing length (and in a one-sided way), the long history of violence and exploitation, official as well as commercial, against Third World countries in *The Global Rift: The Third World*

Comes of Age. (New York: William Morrow and Company, Inc., 1981). A less radical, but even more disturbing chronicle is Stanley Karnow's *Vietnam: A History* (New York: Penguin Books, 1984). Karnow details how U.S. officialdom, all too understandably, took the wrong course and persisted in it. The Vietnam War was one situation—but there have been many others—in which some civil servants eventually became so opposed to the government's policy that they felt compelled to resign.

Despite frequent criticism of the U.S. government—from all sides—few would dispute the need for highly motivated, competent people in government. The U.S. government is a frequent target of criticism precisely because it is so powerful, and people of conscience in public service can make a big difference in how that power is used in developing countries.

The section below offers general information on federal jobs overseas and on the U.S. Office of Personnel Management (created in 1979 out of the former Civil Service Commission). In the five sections following, different types of federal jobs involving residence or travel in developing countries are discussed. There are jobs with:

- economic-assistance agencies that deal mainly with developing countries,

- diplomatic agencies,

- other federal agencies with staff stationed in the Third World,

- agencies with Third World responsibilities that have Washington-based staff who sometimes travel to the Third World,

- military and military-related agencies.

Getting a federal job overseas

Recruitment for most federal civilian jobs overseas falls under the competitive service administered by the U.S. Office of Personnel Management. Some of the government agencies that provide employment opportunities abroad are excepted from the competitive service, and even the agencies within the normal competitive service often have distinctive personnel practices. The hiring idiosyncrasies of particular agencies are noted in the following descriptions. But first—some general comments about federal jobs abroad and the U.S. civil service.

U.S. government employees abroad are found in almost every occupational field. The government hires construction workers, doctors, nurses, teachers, technical experts, mining engineers, meteorologists, clerks, stenographers, computer technicians, typists, geologists, skilled trades workers, social workers, agricultural marketing specialists, and economists for work overseas. Most in demand are highly qualified and hard-to-find professional personnel, skilled technicians, and, in some cases, stenographers, clerical personnel, teachers, librarians, and medical staff.

Qualifications for federal jobs abroad are normally the same as for like positions in the United States. In some cases, applicants are required to meet additional or higher standards, and knowledge of a foreign language is often a valuable qualification. Salaries are normally the same as for federal employment domestically, plus hardship or cost-of-living allowances for certain posts. In addition to the normal benefits of federal employment, U.S. employees abroad may receive free housing, travel to the post, transportation and storage for household goods, additional paid vacations with free travel home between tours of duty, and the benefit of government-operated schools for their children.

Most of the people employed by the U.S. government in developing countries are citizens of the host country. Drivers, clerks, secretaries, and even some expert staff are recruited locally. That's less expensive than resettling staff from the United States, and host governments prefer that U.S. installations generate as much local employment as possible. U.S. staff are brought in for most of the senior positions and other positions that cannot be filled locally, but in filling these openings strong preference is given to career government employees.

Candidates for overseas employment with the U.S. government are recruited through the standard application procedure that applies also to domestic civil servants. Applicants for entry-level, nontechnical, professional and administrative positions must be college graduates or have three years' qualifying experience or an equivalent combination of education and experience. They should register their candidacy through Professional and Administrative Careers (PAC), which replaced the PACE examination system in 1982. Applicants for mid-level positions (GS-9 to GS-12) should normally have either a master's degree or two to three years' work experience beyond college graduation. Candidates for both entry- and mid-level positions must submit a Standard Form 171 and another form on which applicants indicate their particular areas of professional interest. Candidates must also submit either a college transcript or a special form listing their college courses. Agencies directly hire candidates who have received a PAC rating based on such factors as class standing, grades, and previous work experience. There are few GS-14 and GS-15 level jobs. Preference is given to military veterans in the competition for all federal jobs.

There are Federal Job Information Centers in many cities across the country; check under U.S. Government Office of Personnel Management in the white pages of your local telephone book. Two basic pamphlets, *Working for the U.S.A.* (BRE-37) and *Federal Jobs Overseas* (BRE-18), are available at Job Information Centers or from the Superintendent of Documents, Government Printing Office, Washington, DC 20402. For specific information on possible openings overseas, write:

For Pacific area:
San Francisco Area Office
U.S. Office of Personnel Management
525 Market St.
San Francisco, CA 94105

For Atlantic area:
Washington Area Office
U.S. Office of Personnel Management
1900 East St. N.W.
Washington, DC 20415

But anyone who hopes to find a position in government must be aggressive, especially during the present period of no growth in government employment. Simply qualifying through the Office of Personnel Management will not get you a job. OPM sends the names of rated applicants to agencies with vacancies, but an agency usually has several eligible candidates from whom to choose. The serious job seeker should contact potential employers in government directly, preferably in person.

You should allow months to get your examination results, find a job, and have all the necessary papers processed. For some jobs it may be helpful to move to Washington for part of that time. You'll need to do some research. Many job openings are listed in the weekly newspaper, the *Federal Times*. You should also ferret out offices doing work that would be interesting to you and sell yourself to potential employers before vacancies occur. Information about what particular offices do and who is in charge can be obtained from:

The Federal Executive Telephone Directory. Washington: Carroll Publishing Co. Useful guide to who's who and how to reach them.

The United States Government Manual (General Services Administration, published annually, $12.00). The official guide to who is in charge of what in the U.S. government.

The Washington Information Directory 1984-85. Washington: Congressional Quarterly, Inc. Provides more than 5000 information sources in Congress, the Executive Branch, and nonprofit associations.

Gerald Sheehan's *Career Opportunities in the International Field* (p. 9) provides the most thorough description of all federal agencies hiring international affairs graduates; we have relied heavily on it for the listings on pp. 160-66 of this chapter.

In the federal government, as elsewhere, it is essential to develop personal contacts. Let the net out as far as you can. Tell lots of people that you are looking for a position. Once you have done your basic homework, follow up with information interviews with people who can give you a clearer picture of your possibilities, further leads, and names of key people that you should meet.

Knowing the right people is no substitute for qualifications: OPM and the agency personnel offices guard against that. A Department of Agriculture official told us, "You have to apply both ways at once. Just taking the exam won't get you anywhere. You've got to knock on doors. But, on the other hand, no agency can hire you if you don't have your formal papers in order."

Political appointment is also a way into the U.S. government.

Political appointees get their jobs by working for the winning candidate, or on the recommendation of key people among the winning candidate's followers. Political appointees hold fairly senior positions, sometimes despite less experience than some of the civil servants who work for them. Political appointees don't enjoy the job security that civil servants do, however.

Frequent overseas employment, particularly in agencies or departments that require a change of appointments every few years (such as the Department of State), presents problems for couples in which the husband and wife are equally committed to careers (pp. 207-9). Appointments of a husband and wife, both in government service, to the same overseas post is rare, although less so now than it was, say, five years ago. On the other hand, the spouses of U.S. employees are normally given priority consideration for positions filled locally.

Economic-assistance agencies

This section is about the U.S. government agencies that provide assistance for Third World development or for U.S. commerce with the developing countries. Opinion polls show that most people in this country think foreign-aid programs are wasteful and ineffective. In fact, U.S. programs of development assistance have achieved economic and social improvements in the developing countries, sometimes pioneering in areas of special need—housing, for example, or population. The United States' bilateral assistance programs also directly serve U.S. foreign policy goals, providing support for friendly governments in the "hot spots" of our world. Along with government programs of credit and insurance, they also strengthen U.S. business internationally.

Some critics are concerned that the programs described in this section too often serve the diplomatic and commercial interests of the United States at the expense of Third World development. Multilateral programs (Chapter 7) are more single-mindedly focused on development; the conditions attached to multilateral financing are designed to assure that the investment results in economic and social benefit for the developing country. The Reagan Administration, on the other hand, has tended to favor an expansion of bilateral aid at the expense of multilateral aid, precisely because the United States retains complete control over bilateral programs and can use them to further its foreign-policy goals.

The *Agency for International Development* (AID), an arm of the U.S. Department of State, administers nearly all the government's bilateral development assistance funds. AID provides economic assistance in the form of grants and loans to developing countries. AID maintains a high profile in countries in which the United States has a critical foreign-policy interest (such as Israel, Egypt, and El Salvador). Agricultural development constitutes a large share of AID's projects. AID's current priorities are to maintain fragile democracies through economic support; to encourage private sector development; and to control population growth, improve health, and upgrade education. Its Office of U.S. Foreign Disaster Assistance coordinates the nation's public and private overseas relief efforts.

One of AID's functions is administration of the Food for Peace program (Public Law 480). Under Title I of this law (for which the Department of Agriculture has primary responsibility), U.S. agricultural produce is sold on concessional terms to other governments. Title II allows food to be donated to other governments for disaster relief, food-for-work projects, child-nutrition programs, and long-term development efforts. Title III allows poor countries to keep repayments due on Title I sales to support development programs. AID channels more than half of Title II food aid through private development agencies such as CARE and Catholic Relief Services (p. 34) and also gives cash grants to private development agencies for programs that require the flexibility that characterizes some private agencies.

AID's main office is in Washington, but it is more decentralized than most U.S. government or multilateral agencies. AID maintains field missions or representatives in 71 countries of Africa, Asia, the Middle East, and Latin America. Initial appointment overseas is normally for a tour of 24 months (including orientation in Washington and travel). AID employees can usually take their families to their overseas posts. Overseas salaries are supplemented by standard Foreign Service allowances (p. 156).

AID is currently reducing the size of its staff, so it's a difficult time to join the Agency. AID personnel include agriculturalists, engineers, public-health and nutrition specialists, economists, financial managers, education advisors, population planners, accountants, auditors, loan officers, M.B.A.'s, architects, scientists, foresters, ecologists, demographers, and political scientists. AID also uses consultants to meet needs that cannot be filled by its permanent staff. AID seldom recruits secretaries or other support staff for immediate overseas service.

AID's International Development Intern Program has, in the past, provided opportunities for younger, less experienced professionals, but this program has been suspended indefinitely due to budget cuts.

For further information on applying to AID, write: Office of Recruitment, Rm. 1430, State Annex 1, Agency for International Development, Washington, DC 20523.

The government program that has given many U.S. citizens their first experience in development work is the *Peace Corps*. The Peace Corps is the only U.S. agency that places its people in the communities of developing nations to work and live among those they assist. Each year the Peace Corps receives about 5000 requests from Third World governments for volunteers, and there are about 5000 volunteers serving in over 60 countries around the world.

The Peace Corps recruits a wide variety of people: foresters, fishery specialists, agriculturalists, and agronomists; architects, engineers, and planners; science professionals; construction workers, carpenters, masons, electricians, plumbers, welders, and energy technicians; liberal arts graduates; accountants and M.B.A.'s; nurses, medical assistants, and other health professionals; home economists and homemakers; and teachers, especially math and science teachers. Knowledge of a foreign language can be very helpful but is not always required, since all volunteers undergo intensive language training. The Peace Corps is looking for technical ability in its recruits, but also dedication and flexibility—a willingness to live modestly, adapt to local customs, and work well under the supervision of local people.

The Peace Corps was founded to assist with economic development and to promote mutual understanding between the United States and other nations. The program's most significant impact, however, may have been the education of the volunteers themselves. There have been more than 100,000 Peace Corps volunteers since President

Kennedy established the program in 1961, excluding those who serve today. Many of the professionals now working in institutions such as AID, The World Bank, and the U.S. Foreign Service got their first and most intimate exposure to the Third World as Peace Corps volunteers. Nearly all former volunteers highly value the worldwide perspective and, in some cases, spiritual direction which the opportunity to share in the life of another society gave them.

Peace Corps applicants must be at least 18 years old. Civil service ratings are not required. Volunteers normally serve two-year terms, beginning with 8 to 12 weeks of language and cross-cultural training (usually in the host country). They are given an allowance averaging $300 a month for food, lodging, incidentals, and medical care. Upon return to the United States, they receive a readjustment allowance of $175 per month of service. They are also provided a listing of employment opportunities of special interest through the Peace Corps Hotline. The Peace Corps is part of the Agency for Voluntary Service (ACTION). More information about the Peace Corps is available from ACTION recruiting offices or from ACTION, 806 Connecticut Ave. N.W., Washington, DC 20525. For an official history, see *Twenty Years of Peace Corps* by G.T. Rice (Government Printing Office, 1982). For a critical view of the Peace Corps, see *Keeping Kennedy's Promise* by Kevin Lowther and C. Payne Lucas (Boulder, Colo.: Westview Press, 1978).

The third development-aid agency of the U.S. government, smaller and less well-known than AID and the Peace Corps, is the *Inter-American Foundation* (1515 Wilson Boulevard, Rosslyn, VA 22209). The Foundation does not design, operate, or provide technical assistance for development projects, but rather funds self-help projects benefiting poor people that are proposed by local, nongovernmental groups in Latin America and the Caribbean. The emphasis is on social change rather than economic development—nonformal education, cooperatives and peasant associations, self-help housing, agricultural extension, legal-aid societies, and the like. The Foundation has a small staff; professionals (in social work fields, often with experience as Peace Corps volunteers or missionaries) and support personnel together number 67. Foreign-language ability is required for professionals, most of whom travel extensively. Most positions are in the competitive civil service.

The fledgling *African Development Foundation* was modeled after the Inter-American Foundation. The African Development Foundation has been plagued by political squabbles and other start-up delays, but managed to commit $1 million to 11 grass-roots projects in Africa during fiscal year 1984, its first year of operations. The African Development Foundation has a staff of 20. For more information, write: African Development Foundation, 1724 Massachusetts Ave. N.W., Suite 200, Washington, DC 20036.

Two relatively independent, self-sustaining financial institutions within the U.S. government assist U.S. business abroad. The *Overseas Private Investment Corporation* (OPIC) offers U.S. companies: (a) insurance against expropriation, inconvertibility of funds, war and revolution; and (b) loans, loan guarantees, and preinvestment survey assistance.

Most of the investments that OPIC supports are in developing countries, but some critics charge that OPIC mainly benefits big U.S. corporations. OPIC has a staff of about 130, half of whom are experienced professionals with backgrounds in economics, finance, and law. For more information about OPIC and possible employment, write: Overseas Private Investment Corporation, 1129 20th St. N.W., Washington, DC 20527.

The *Export-Import Bank* (Eximbank) participates in financing more than 10% of U.S. exports, and 70% of Eximbank's business involves exports to Asia, Africa, Latin America, and Oceania. Eximbank has a staff of 400 people and recruits 20 to 30 professionals each year. Staff are based in Washington, but international travel is required of most professionals. More information about Eximbank careers can be obtained from: Personnel Officer, Export-Import Bank, 811 Vermont Ave. N.W., Washington, DC 20571.

Diplomacy

The two major agencies representing the United States diplomatically are the *State Department* and the *United States Information Agency* (USIA). The State Department assists the president and secretary of state in planning, conducting, and conveying U.S. foreign policy. It also performs consular services for U.S. citizens and foreigners, including protection of U.S. private interests abroad. USIA handles "public diplomacy," which has become increasingly important with the development of mass communications. USIA maintains information offices, libraries, or cultural centers in 120 countries, sponsors exchange programs (education, cultural, athletic), and publicizes what the United States is and what we stand for through Voice of America broadcasting and other media.

The elite corps of the two organizations are the Foreign Service Officers and Foreign Service Information Officers. Each year about 15,000 hopefuls take a special written examination. Of these, about 2000 qualify for interviews, of which perhaps 200 are eventually appointed Foreign Service or Foreign Service Information Officers. Those appointed can expect a series of assignments of two to four years in Washington and in any of more than 130 countries, most of them in the Third World. Since veteran officers tend to preempt European assignments, less-experienced officers are likely to serve in developing countries. Officers spend an average of 60% of their careers abroad, and they are required to be available for service worldwide.

Applicants must be U.S. citizens in good health, at least 20 years old, but young enough to serve a trial period and two tours of duty before retirement. There are no formal educational requirements, but most successful applicants have B.A. degrees, and about 65% of them have advanced degrees in law, economics, international relations, or other fields. Foreign-language ability is important for promotion; although foreign-language ability is not a requirement for appointment, 45% of recently appointed Junior Officer Career Candidates knew at least one foreign language. Foreign Service Officers initially specialize in one of four fields: administrative, consular, economic/commercial, or political affairs. Since the need for administrative and economic/commercial officers has been expanding in recent years, backgrounds in economics, commerce, and technical fields have become more attractive to recruiters. USIA personnel administer public affairs offices, with responsibility for cultural affairs and information or press departments.

Since U.S. diplomats should be representative of the entire nation, the State Department and USIA are making special efforts to recruit women, racial minorities, and people from underrepresented regions of the country. New officers are normally appointed at the level of

Class 6, 5, or 4 (salaries ranging from $19,460 to $39,451), but new officers with exceptional qualifications or experience may be appointed Class 3, 2, or 1 ($33,154 to $65,642). None of these salary figures includes the medical benefits or housing, cost-of-living, hardship, and educational allowances that Foreign Service and Foreign Service Information Officers receive in particular posts.

In addition to Foreign Service Officers, the State Department and USIA also recruit secretaries to serve in Washington and abroad. For service abroad with the State Department an applicant must be: a U.S. citizen, at least 21 years old, a high-school graduate or equivalent, in good health, available for assignment anywhere in the world (including Washington), and able to pass a performance test. Candidates are appointed at FSS-10, FSS-9, and FSS-8 levels. All these levels require dictation speed of 80 words per minute and typing speed of 40 words per minute. The FSS-10 level implies two years of experience or education beyond high school, the FSS-9 level four years, and the FSS-8 six years. USIA's minimum requirements are slightly different; they require three years of experience or two years of business school or college, and typing speed of 50 words per minute.

The State Department also recruits:

Linguists: There are a very limited number of positions and short-term contracts for interpreters and translators, and available work is nearly all in the United States.

Doctors, nurses, and medical technologists: Foreign service medical personnel care for the health of U.S. government staff and their dependents abroad. Physicians (with at least three years of clinical experience) usually oversee the health care operations of a number of posts. Individual posts are normally served by nurses (graduates with at least five years of experience). Assignments are 18 months to three years.

Electronic communications technicians and assistants: Staff are needed to maintain and operate communications equipment. Applicants must be U.S. citizens, at least 21 years old, high school graduates or the equivalent, in good health, and ready for assignment anywhere. Communications Technicians must have good radio background training, including at least three years of installation/maintenance experience with HF, UHF, and VHF radio equipment; training or experience installing, maintaining, and repairing 1A2 Key Secretarial and EPABX telephone systems; and both training and experience with at least two types of cryptographic equipment. Communications technicians travel extensively within the region of their assignments. The equipment is routinely operated by Communications and Records Assistants, who put messages in tape format for transmission and prepare messages received on teletypewriter for distribution. These assistants also operate cryptographic equipment, prepare diplomatic pouches, deliver mail, and file.

The State Department and USIA sponsor a special program of internships in Washington and at U.S. embassies overseas for college juniors and seniors and graduate students. Remuneration is sometimes given to interns (depending on the bureau), and academic credit can frequently be arranged. Interns often replace foreign service officers who are on home leave and may be given substantial responsibility—doing research, drafting correspondence, writing media reports, or related work. Specific duties vary greatly, depending on supervisors, timing, and the activities under way. Irrespective of the position held, interns come away with an understanding of the intricacy and sensitivity of State Department work.

During the summer between her years of graduate school, Linda Powers interned at the U.S. embassy in San José, Costa Rica. Given the title and responsibilities of Acting Cultural Affairs Officer, she handled the day-to-day official business of the cultural section, conducted an independent research project on a new Costa Rican newspaper, served as liaison with some of the local universities' student federations, and represented the embassy at many public functions.

Detailed information and application forms for Foreign Service and USIA employment are available from:

Employment Division
U.S. Department of State
Washington, DC 20520

U.S. Information Agency
Special Recruitment Section, Office of Personnel
Room 524, 400 C St. S.W.
Washington, DC 20547

Other agencies with staff in the Third World

The *Department of Agriculture* has been expanding its own foreign service rapidly in recent years, annually recruiting about 25 new professionals into the Foreign Agricultural Service (FAS). Shipments of agricultural produce have come to represent one-fifth of U.S. exports, and FAS administers programs related to agriculture and foreign policy. It gathers agricultural intelligence, analyzes data, and disseminates information among U.S. agricultural interests to promote agricultural exports. FAS maintains 100 professional agriculturalists in more than 70 foreign posts and a home office staff of 350 professionals. They are mostly recruited from within the Department of Agriculture. Candidates from outside the Department are screened through the Professional and Administrative Career Examination (PACE) for FAS's Junior Professional Development Program or through Standard Form 171 for midlevel professionals. Information on FAS may be obtained from: Personnel Division, Foreign Agricultural Service, Rm. 5627, South Agriculture Building, U.S. Department of Agriculture, 14th and Independence Ave. S.W., Washington, DC 20250.

The following agencies also have some staff living in developing countries.

The *Federal Highway Administration* (under the Department of Transportation) provides technical assistance to foreign governments in the planning, design, construction, and maintenance of highways and bridges. Experienced candidates can contact:

Office of Personnel and Training
Federal Highway Administration
Washington, DC 20590

The *National Oceanic and Atmospheric Administration* (under the Department of Commerce) requires people with meteorological or electronics backgrounds to staff weather stations in Alaska, Puerto Rico, Hawaii, Wake Island, Guam, Johnson Island, American Samoa, and the Trust Territories.

Personnel Office
National Oceanic and Atmospheric Administration
Washington, DC 20852

The *Panama Canal Commission* has about 8300 employees, of which about 1600 are U.S. citizens. The Panama Canal Treaty of 1977 provided for increasing Panamanian participation at all levels of the work force, so recruitment from outside the Republic of Panama has been virtually eliminated.

Panama Canal Commission
Office of Personnel Administration
APO Miami, FL 34011

The *United States Travel and Tourism Administration* (USTTA), also under the Department of Commerce, is the national government tourist office of the United States. Its mission is to develop travel to the United States from foreign countries. USTTA has a staff of approximately 80 employees, including seven employees in each of six regional offices (London, Toronto, Frankfurt, Paris, Tokyo, and Mexico City). Competition is extremely keen for the infrequent vacancies that occur. Positions occasionally exist for persons with appropriate international sales, promotional sales, and promotional work experience.

Personnel Officer
Operations Division
Office of the Secretary
U.S. Department of Commerce
Washington, DC 20230

The *Central Intelligence Agency* (CIA) is one of the largest U.S. government bodies concerned with Third World affairs. It assigns personnel, occasionally and covertly, to U.S. embassies in the Third World, and other CIA personnel sometimes travel in developing countries. The CIA is mainly involved in collecting and evaluating information about political, military, economic, and scientific activities in foreign countries for U.S. policymakers. Covert activities abroad are a relatively small part of CIA operations, and most CIA employees never get involved. But many people looking for a career related to the Third World have serious qualms about working for the CIA because of controversy over the morality of some of its Third World activities. If you are considering intelligence work, you should certainly read books such as:

Rositzke, Harry. *The CIA's Secret Operations.* New York: Reader's Digest Press, 1976. Generally pro-CIA.

Snepp, Frank. *Decent Interval.* New York, Random, 1977. Generally anti-CIA.

The CIA recruits a wide variety of staff: international-affairs specialists, economists, cartographers, scientists, computer programmers, systems analysts, transport specialists, contract negotiators, engineers, accountants, general administrators, secretaries, printers, and security officers. The CIA has developed its own procedures for employment and career development separate from those of the Office of Personnel Management. For recruitment information, write: Director of Personnel, Central Intelligence Agency, Washington, DC 20505.

Students can sample CIA work through its Student Trainee Program and Summer Intern Program. Students of engineering, computer science, mathematics, and physics in the Student Trainee Program are allowed to alternate periods of study at school with periods of work with the Agency. For further information, contact the Coordinator for Student Trainee Programs, Department of State, Room 4N20C, P.O. Box 1925, Washington, DC 20013.

Washington offices with Third World responsibilities

Most U.S. government departments and agencies have some staff specialized in international aspects of their work, and a few of these people travel to the Third World from time to time. The people who represent the department or agency abroad must be experienced in its work, so they are recruited from within. Thus, people who want to live and work in the Third World would not normally choose a career in the Department of the Interior, for example, even though quite a few Interior offices have international responsibilities. Someone already within the Department, however, who developed an interest in the Third World, or perhaps someone outside the Department with experience in a related field (mining, geology, fisheries, or the like) might seek a position in one of the Department's internationally oriented offices.

In the following list of departments and agencies with Third World-related functions, each description is followed by addresses you might use (the department's central personnel office or the particular offices within the department that handle its Third World-related functions). After the Executive Office of the President, we have listed departments (in alphabetical order) and then agencies (in alphabetical order).

The *Executive Office of the President* has far-reaching influence on developing countries. Most involved are the White House itself, the Office of Management and Budget, and the Office of the United States Trade Representative.

The White House
1600 Pennsylvania Ave. N.W.
Washington, DC 20500

Office of Management and Budget
Executive Office Building
Washington, DC 20503

Office of the United States Trade Representative
600 Seventh St. N.W.
Washington, DC 20506

Within the *Department of Commerce* (in addition to the two administrations that have staff living overseas, noted on pp. 158-9), the Bureau of the Census sends consultants to assist foreign governments with census work. The Office of International Fisheries, National Marine Fisheries Service, is concerned with fisheries development overseas.

Employment Information Center
U.S. Department of Commerce
14th St. between Constitution Ave. and E St. N.W.
Washington, DC 20230

Bureau of the Census
Personnel Division
Building 3, Rm. 3250
Suitland, MD 20233

National Marine Fisheries Service
National Oceanic and Atmospheric Administration
Washington, DC 20852

Within the *Department of Education,* the International Activities Office, National Institute of Handicapped Research, works on research and demonstration programs concerned with the rehabilitation of disabled persons from developing countries.

International Activities Office
National Institute of Handicapped Research

U.S. Department of Education
Room 3520, 330 C St. S.W.
Washington, DC 20202

The *Department of Energy's* Office of International Affairs and Energy Emergencies has only two overseas positions, and they are not currently recruiting applicants for those positions.

Within the *Department of Health and Human Services,* the Public Health Service (PHS) is most widely involved in international activities, including exchange of experts. Offices at PHS headquarters in Rockville, Maryland, that are concerned with international affairs include: Office of International Health; International Health Affairs, Health Resources and Services Administration; International Affairs Staff, Office of Health Affairs, Food and Drug Administration; and International Affairs, Alcohol, Drug Abuse, and Mental Health Administration. The Fogarty International Center and the Center for Disease Control are also under PHS, but at different locations. Outside the Public Health Service, there are also international activities in the Office of Human Development Services, and the Social Security Administration is engaged in international comparative studies of social security systems.

Office of International Affairs
Department of Health and Human Services
200 Independence Ave. S.W.
Room 655-G
Washington, DC 20201

Public Health Service
5600 Fishers Lane
Rockville, MD 20857

Fogarty International Center
National Institute of Health
9000 Rockville Pike
Room 605-A, Building 38-A
Bethesda, MD 20014

Center for Disease Control
1600 Clifton Road, N.E.
Room 2122, Building I
Atlanta, GA 30333

International Activities
Office of Human Development Services
200 Independence Ave. S.W.
Room 736-E
Washington, DC 20201

Within the *Department of Interior*, there are international affairs offices in the Office of the Secretary, Bureau of Land Management, Bureau of Mines, Bureau of Reclamation, National Park Service, Office of Territorial Affairs, Fish and Wildlife Service, and Geological Survey.

U.S. Department of the Interior
Office of Organization and Personnel Management
Between Eighteenth and Nineteenth Sts. N.W.
Washington, DC 20240

Within the *Justice Department*, the Immigration and Naturalization Service administers federal laws concerning immigration. About 85% of its employees are outside Washington, some in Hong Kong, Mexico City, and Rome. The Drug Enforcement Administration cooperates with other governments and assists in related efforts internationally.

U.S. Department of Justice
Office of Personnel
425 I St. N.W.
Washington, DC 20536

Within the *Department of Labor*, the Bureau of International Labor Affairs (365 employees) helps provide direction to U.S. labor attachés at embassies abroad, carries out overseas technical-assistance projects, and arranges trade-union exchanges and other programs for foreign visitors to the United States. The Bureau also represents the United States in various U.N. organizations and in the Manpower and Social Affairs Committee of the Organization for Economic Cooperation and Development (OECD).

U.S. Department of Labor
Office of Personnel Management
Rm. N5456
200 Constitution Ave. N.W.
Washington, DC 20210

U.S. Department of Labor
Bureau of International Labor Affairs
Office of Management, Administration, and Planning

Rm. S5303
200 Constitution Ave. N.W.
Washington, DC 20210

Within the *Department of Transportation,* the Office of International Programs coordinates international cooperative research, technical assistance to developing countries, and U.S. government participation in international conferences. The Office of International Aviation Affairs and the Technical Assistance Division in the Federal Aviation Administration carry out technical cooperation/research programs and participate in the U.N. Civil Aviation Organization. The Civil Aeronautics Board used to deal with international conferences and agreements and process applications from air carriers for international service, but the Civil Aeronautics Board has been abolished and its remaining functions transferred to the Department of Transportation. The Federal Highway Administration has some staff resident in developing countries (as described on p. 158).

> U.S. Department of Transportation
> Central Employment Information Office
> Office of Personnel and Training
> 400 Seventh St. S.W.
> Washington, DC 20590
>
> Federal Aviation Administration
> Employment Office
> 800 Independence Ave. S.W.
> Washington, DC 20591

Within the *Department of the Treasury,* the Office of the Assistant Secretary for International Affairs advises the Secretary of Treasury on international economic policy, coordinating U.S. participation in international lending institutions and monitoring money markets, balance of payments data, and international capital flows.

> U.S. Department of the Treasury
> Office of the Secretary
> Main Treasury Building, Rm. 5116
> Fifteenth St. and Pennsylvania Ave. N.W.
> Washington, DC 20220

Within the *Environmental Protection Agency,* the Office of International Activities works with other countries, often through the United Nations, its specialized agencies, and OECD, on environmental and ecological problems. It administers programs of data collection, technology transfer, exchange of information and personnel, and international research. The office has 16 professional positions.

Office of International Activities
U.S. Environmental Protection Agency
401 M St. S.W.
Washington, DC 20460

Office of Personnel Management
U.S. Environmental Protection Agency
401 M St. S.W.
Washington, DC 20460

Foreign banking analysts assist the *Federal Reserve Board of Governors* in supervising international banking activities of member banks and in analyzing international financial questions.

Board of Governors
Federal Reserve System
Twentieth St. and Constitution Ave. N.W.
Division of Personnel
Rm. M-1438
Washington, DC 20551

The *International Trade Commission* is an advisory and fact-finding agency on .tariffs and import quotas, commercial policy, and trade law. It investigates foreign competition with U.S. industry, East-West trade, unfair trade practices, and workers' adjustment assistance. Professional staff numbers 400, none of whom is currently working on projects related to developing countries.

Office of Personnel and Management Systems
U.S. International Trade Commission
701 E St. N.W.
Washington, DC 20436

The Commission on International Relations of the *National Academy of Sciences,* with a staff of 40 (mostly scientists and engineers), conducts the Academy's relations with foreign scientific institutions, provides consultative services to federal agencies engaged in international endeavors, and helps formulate government policies in scientific and technical fields. The Academy is a private scientific organization chartered by Congress to advise the government.

Commission on International Relations
National Academy of Sciences
2101 Constitution Ave. N.W.
Washington, DC 20418

The Office of International Activities of the *Smithsonian Institution* is responsible for the international liaison functions of the Smithsonian museums. The Office of Fellowships and Grants administers a program for the use of excess foreign currencies by U.S. scholars, and the Office of Museum Programs designs individualized internships for professionals sent by other museums or governments. Other offices of the Smithsonian with international responsibilities include the Woodrow Wilson International Center for Scholars, the International Exchange Service, the Office of Smithsonian Symposia and Seminars, and the Office for Exhibitions Abroad of the National Collection of Fine Arts.

Smithsonian Institution
1000 Jefferson Drive S.W.
Washington, DC 20560

The *U.S. Congress* deals extensively with the Third World, of course. Each senator or representative has a staff. Senior congressional staff occasionally travel with senators and representatives in the Third World and, in any case, are certainly influential on issues of importance to people in developing countries. Senators and representatives especially involved in international affairs may have specialized advisers in that area. Senate and House committees, too, employ their own staffs to do research in international matters. More than 80 people serve as staff for the House Foreign Affairs Committee, and another 70 serve the Senate Foreign Relations Committee. About 20 other congressional committees sometimes deal with international matters. To apply for a staff position, contact senators and representatives you would like to serve, the chairpersons of relevant committees, or senior staff or staff directors. Congressional staff positions do not fall under the civil service system.

Congress is also served by its own Budget Office, General Accounting Office, and the Library of Congress, each with international divisions. There are 19 professionals in the National Security and International Affairs Division of the Congressional Budget Office, more than 400 in the National and Security Affairs Division of the General Accounting Office, and more than 200 in the Foreign Policy and National Defense Division of the Library of Congress. Although these people, too, can have a significant impact on U.S. policy toward the Third World, they are even less likely to travel in the Third World than the staff of senators, representatives, and their committees.

The U.S. military

One quarter of all U.S. military personnel are stationed outside the United States, and one-third of U.S. military personnel overseas are stationed in Asia, Africa, or Latin America. The largest army bases are in Korea, Panama, and Okinawa. The Navy has nearly 60,000 men on ships and bases scattered throughout the developing world, with large bases in Okinawa, the Philippines, Guam, Diego Garcia, Puerto Rico, Bermuda, and Cuba (Guantanamo). The Marines have contingents in Okinawa and other Pacific islands and also provide guard units for all U.S. embassies.

In addition, thousands of military personnel stationed in the United States, many of them in Washington, do work related to—and sometimes travel to—developing countries. They support military personnel stationed abroad and also administer large programs of military sales and assistance. In fiscal year 1983, the U.S. Department of Defense channeled $9 billion in military sales, $16 billion in military assistance, and $36 billion worth of military training into Asia, Africa, and Latin America.

Finally, the U.S. military also employs one million civilian personnel (compared to two million active military personnel). A relatively small, but still significant number of these civilian jobs also involve residence or travel in developing countries.

The U.S. defense budget has been growing more rapidly than almost any other sector of the U.S. economy in recent years. The military budget increased 10% a year (in real terms) for the five years 1981 to 1985, swelling from 5% to 7% of U.S. GNP. The number of people in uniform has not increased significantly, but they are paid and equipped better than they were. Partly as a result of better pay, 91% of U.S. military personnel were high-school graduates as of 1983, compared to 68% in 1980.

Military service raises obvious ethical issues for Christians. Warfare is in tension with the gospel ethic, and U.S. military presence in some developing countries helps to protect the privileged from the oppressed. On the other hand, U.S. military presence abroad is necessary and welcome in some situations, and many Christians support the current U.S. military buildup in the name of both world peace and national security. For discussion of these life-and-death ethical issues, see:

Feinberg, Richard E. *The Intemperate Zone: The Third World Challenge to U.S. Foreign Policy.* New York and London: W.W. Norton and Company, 1983. Argues that both superpowers are increasingly limited in what they can achieve through military intervention in the developing countries, and that measures to maintain the vitality of the global economy are more important to U.S. security.

LaFeber, Walter. *Inevitable Revolutions: The United States in Central America.* New York and London, W.W. Norton and Company, 1983. Argues that the United States has repeatedly intervened in Central America to block needed social change and, in the process, made the situation more and more oppressive and violent.

McSorly, Richard, S.J. *Kill for Peace.* Center for Peace Studies, Georgetown University (Washington, DC 20057). $5. A plea for Christian pacifism.

National Conference of Catholic Bishops. *The Challenge of Peace: A Pastoral Letter on War and Peace.* 1983. The bishops applied traditional Catholic teaching on war and peace to the unprecedented problems of our nuclear age. Excellent, genuinely enlightening. Available from: National Conference of Catholic Bishops, 1312 Massachusetts Ave. N.W., Washington, DC 20005.

Podhoretz, Norman. *The Present Danger.* New York: Simon and Schuster, 1980. Argues for a resurgence of U.S. will to contain Communism.

Tucker, Robert W. "America in Decline," *Foreign Affairs,* vol. 58, no. 3, 1980. Argues that U.S. power declined precipitously and unnecessarily under the Nixon and Carter administrations. Calls for a rebuilding of the U.S. military.

A new recruit into the Air Force, Army, Navy, or Marines can volunteer to go overseas, or for a particular sort of duty overseas, but there is no guarantee of where he or she might be stationed. The military services are trying to take individual preferences seriously, but personnel requirements still come first. Those who complete a tour of duty abroad can request an extension at the same place. Since most people in the military prefer not to serve in Third World posts, the preference to stay would be more likely to be honored than would more popular requests. The place to get information about military careers is your local recruiting office.

Civilians who work in the military establishment have more control over where they work. High-level Pentagon offices employ civilians in work related to developing countries, some of it involving occasional travel. About half of the high-level international jobs are in the Department of Defense and the other half in the Departments of the Army, Navy, and Air Force. In addition, the services employ a wide variety of civilians (accountants, auditors, budget and program officers, management analysts, procurement officers, shorthand reporters, equipment specialists, supply officers, communication officers, computer specialists, engineers, social workers, housing officers, medical officers, psychiatrists, alcohol and drug specialists, and historians) for support work on bases overseas.

Lower-level civilian jobs on military bases overseas (GS-10 and below, including secretarial, trades, crafts, and general labor) generally go to dependents of military personnel stationed there, citizens of the host country, or to U.S. companies contracted to perform these functions on particular bases. The three services together recruit less than a thousand people in the United States for overseas positions each year, and very strong preference for these openings (and, of course, for high-level positions in the Pentagon) is given to people who are already employees of the military or other federal agencies. In general, the military establishment recruits outsiders for positions that involve residence or travel abroad only in the relatively few cases when they cannot fill an opening locally or from among career employees.

Moreover, the procedures for recruiting civilian personnel are quite complicated. The Department of Defense and the Departments of the Army, Navy, and Air Force each recruit civilian personnel separately, and even within each department some offices recruit separately.

The personnel office for the Washington headquarters of the Department of Defense is: Directorate for Personnel and Security, Washington Headquarters Services, Rm. 3B 347, The Pentagon, Washington, DC 20301. They handle recruitment for the most important Department of Defense offices that have international dealings. These include the Office of the Secretary of Defense, the Office of the Assistant Secretary of Defense for International Security Affairs (country and area desks similar to those in the Department of State), the Office of the Undersecretary of Defense for Research and Engineering (which exercises export control responsibilities), and the Defense Security Assistance Agency (military grants and sales). There is no file of past applicants, so job-seekers must continually inquire or check the *Federal Times* regarding current job openings. As in any large bureaucracy, job seekers should make contact directly with the offices that might employ them, as well as with the relevant personnel office. To do that within the Department of Defense, you might find it helpful to get the *Department of Defense Key Personnel Locator* (an organization chart with room and telephone numbers) from OSD Public Affairs, Rm. 2E777, Pentagon, Washington, DC 20301.

The central recruitment offices for overseas civilian positions in the military services are:

Director of Civilian Personnel
Deputy Chief of Staff for Personnel
Department of the Army
Washington, DC 20310.

Naval Civilian Personnel Command Headquarters
Department of the Navy
800 North Quincy St.
Arlington, VA 22203

Director of Civilian Personnel
Deputy Chief of Staff
Manpower and Personnel
Department of the Air Force
Washington, DC 20330

These offices maintain lists of openings abroad that cannot be filled locally. The information for each service is made available to civilians who are working stateside for the service, and much of it is reprinted in the *Federal Times*.

There is a centralized information system for overseas vacancies that serves the Department of Defense and all three services. It is called the Department of Defense Overseas Employment Program. Once a year the Department of Defense and all the services list their anticipated vacancies, and the combined list is sent to the Civilian Personnel Office of every Department of Defense installation within the United States. Your point of contact is the Civilian Personnel Office at the installation nearest you. If you are a federal employee or have civil-service status, you can register with the system through your Civilian Personnel Office. If one of the services is having difficulty filling a position, they may ask the Overseas Employment Program for a printout of registered applicants with the necessary qualifications.

The *Defense Intelligence Agency* provides military intelligence to the Department of Defense and the Joint Chiefs of Staff. It studies military capabilities, geography, military targets, and transportation systems in other countries. Its intelligence research specialists do economic, political, photographic imagery, scientific, and technical analysis. DIA is not part of the normal civil service system. It compensates its staff at a higher level than most government agencies and recruits separately. It recruits graduating college seniors who have specialized in pertinent fields; they enter a two-year training program, including rotational assignments and a variety of educational opportunities. There are also opportunities for experienced professionals, especially for people with military intelligence experience. Write:

Defense Intelligence Agency
Civilian Personnel Operations Division
Recruitment Office
Washington, DC 20301

The *National Security Agency* was established to protect U.S. communications, to produce foreign intelligence information, and to provide computer security for the Department of Defense. Eighty percent of NSA's employees are civilians; with the exception of a handful on "field assignments," they all live in Washington, Baltimore, and the suburbs in between. Most NSA jobs are in three broad areas: cryptography, computers, and communications. NSA, too, is excepted from the normal civil service; they advertise that their salary structure is highly competitive, even in comparison to private industry. They hire a large number of college graduates each year in electronic engineering, computer science, mathematics, and Slavic, Near Eastern, and Asian languages. Graduates with degrees in other areas can also be considered if they pass the Agency's Professional Qualification Test. At times, NSA offers student programs (summer employment, cooperative education, and high-school work-study arrangements) to assist its campus recruitment efforts. NSA also seeks out experienced professionals in industry, from technology schools, and from among former military personnel. Clerks, secretaries, and craft employees are drawn mostly from local Maryland high schools. Write:

> The National Security Agency
> Attn: M322
> Fort George Meade, MD 20755

The military service exchanges ("PX stores") serve military personnel, also abroad, but are private organizations. The service exchanges fill their overseas openings by hiring local citizens, dependents of U.S. official personnel already in the country, or their own managers with experience at service exchanges in the United States.

The American National Red Cross (National Headquarters, Washington, DC 20006) is a private organization, but officially chartered by the federal government. Except for cooperation with the international League of Red Cross Societies (p. 144), its only involvement in developing countries is to provide services to U.S. military personnel abroad. New recruits for this work must have a college degree or the equivalent. The first assignment is normally in the United States, with transfers to U.S. military bases and hospitals abroad as the need arises. In recent years, the Red Cross has been cutting costs and reducing staff for its program of service to U.S. military personnel.

Opportunities for teachers in Department of Defense schools abroad are described on p. 117.

Seminarians or clergy interested in becoming military chaplains might contact their denomination's chaplaincy office and should also contact the chief of chaplains' offices of the three services:

Army Chief of Chaplains
Washington, DC 20310

Navy Chief of Chaplains
Washington, DC 20350

Air Force Chief of Chaplains
Washington, DC 20330

Business

American firms employ the great majority of U.S. citizens who work overseas. As many U.S. firms watched their overseas income grow as a share of total company profits in recent decades, they carved out more management positions dedicated to international operations.

Business employment related to the Third World has expanded especially rapidly. The developing countries have been the fastest-growing market for U.S. firms abroad, and they now buy two-fifths of U.S. exports. On the imports side, the United States depends on developing countries for four-fifths of its fuel imports, a quarter of its imports of capital goods and industrial supplies, and half its imports of consumer items.

The developing countries have also been attractive to U.S. investors. Commercial-bank lending to developing countries grew 22% a year from 1970 to 1980 (in current dollars). Direct investment—that is, investment by a corporation in a foreign subsidiary—grew 19% a year. U.S. direct foreign investment in developing countries is concentrated in manufacturing, mainly in Latin America, and in energy and mining throughout the developing world. Some 5000 U.S. companies now have subsidiaries abroad, and some *Fortune* 500 companies earn more than half their income overseas.

Current trends and issues

These trends toward increased U.S. business in the Third World were interrupted in the early 1980s. The global recession stalled business expansion generally. The overvalued U.S. dollar has made U.S. exports less competitive, forcing many firms to retrench in their international operations. Falling oil prices ended the boom in the oil-exporting developing countries; and falling export revenues during the global recession, coupled with the international debt crisis of 1982 and 1983, forced many developing countries to slash imports. The debt crisis also frightened many foreign investors. The developing countries are now paying more principal and interest on medium- and long-term loans back to the banks than they are getting in new loans, and direct investment has also slumped somewhat.

Over the longer term, however, international commerce is likely to continue expanding. All nations have a common interest in cooperating to avoid another severe recession and to encourage renewed expansion of international trade. If Congress and the president can succeed in reducing the U.S. budget deficit, that would tend to lower interest rates, reduce the value of the dollar, and make U.S. exports more competitive again.

It also seems likely that much of the Third World will be a dynamic element within the global economy again in the future. The under-utilized resources of the developing countries, their past record of economic dynamism, and their intense aspirations for development almost guarantee it. With over $600 billion in loans outstanding to the developing countries as of 1984, the commercial banks will necessarily remain deeply involved in the Third World, and more hospitable policies in some developing countries should elicit an expansion of foreign direct investment. The average rate of return on investment in the developing countries is much higher than in the industrial countries (partly because capital is scarce relative to labor and natural resources in developing countries), so the resumption of growth in international investment is in the interests of both the industrial and developing countries.

Good sources of general information on international business include:

Business International (Business International Corporation, One Dag Hammarskjold Plaza, New York, NY 10017). A weekly newsletter serving international management.

Development Business (Division for Economic and Social Information, Department of Public Information, United Nations, P.O. Box 5850, Grand Central Station, New York NY 10163). Currently $250 per year. Trends for international business in developing countries, plus specific procurement information from The World Bank and regional development banks. Subscribers are mostly business firms and libraries.

Walter, Ingo, and Murray, Tracy. *Handbook of International Business.* New York: New York University, 1982. A comprehensive reference for people in international business. Treats the international business environment; international trade and finance; and legal, marketing, and management aspects of international operations.

Wattles, Charles W. *A Resource Guide to Corporate Involvement in Development in the Third World.* A.T. International (1724 Massachussetts Ave. N.W., Washington, DC 20036), 1983. Brings together examples, resources, and publications on this subject.

Some Christians are suspicious of business in general, and especially of the role of international business vis-a-vis developing countries. Latin America's liberation theologians, for example, tend to favor state-directed economic development and domestic production for domestic needs. Other Christians are convinced that the discipline of markets generally forces business to earn its keep, providing value-for-money to consumers and creating jobs. Some point to the mounting body of evidence that the more market- and trade-oriented developing countries have generally achieved more rapid economic growth and, in the process, made impressive strides in reducing poverty.

For a readable introduction to liberation theology, see Robert McAfee Brown's *Gustavo Gutierrez* (Atlanta: John Knox Press, 1980). For a theological defense of U.S. capitalism, see Michael Novak's *The Spirit of Democratic Capitalism* (New York: American Enterprise Institute/Simon and Schuster, 1982).

One of the most controversial aspects of international business has been the role of large multinational corporations in developing countries. Defenders of the multinationals argue that they provide investment, jobs, managerial skill, and technical know-how. Critics charge that they distort developing economies, catering to the desires of high-income countries and local elites at the expense of the poor majority.

There are both positive and negative instances of the involvement of multinational corporations in Third World development. In Kenya, for example, two multinationals strengthened the research-and-development capabilities of the local tea industry. As a result, the Kenya Tea Development Authority is now the biggest single supplier of tea to the world market, and tea smallholders in Kenya earn much higher incomes. In the case of the soap industry in Kenya, however, multinational firms undercut local firms by aggressively marketing fancy, brand-name soap. They fostered frivolous tastes, and their use of capital-intensive technology reduced the number of jobs provided by the soap industry.

The controversy about multinational corporations in Third World countries has been less heated in recent years—partly because the developing countries have learned to use regulation and bargaining more effectively in their dealings with foreign companies, and partly because the debt crisis has made countries more eager for whatever foreign investment they can get.

The debt crisis has also, however, sparked new controversy about the role of commercial banks in developing countries. Critics charge that the big banks and developing-country governments were careless in their lending and borrowing in the 1970s. But most informed observers attribute the debt crisis mainly to the unexpectedly long recession of the early 1980s—the most severe recession in over 40 years. About 53,000 U.S. companies were forced into bankruptcy in 1982, the same year that many developing countries found themselves unable to keep up their debt-service payments.

For further reading on the pros and cons of multinationals in Third World development, see:

Enterprise and Development (U.S. Council for International Business, 1212 Avenue of the Americas, New York, NY 10036). Monthly newsletter. An excellent ongoing source of information on corporate involvement in the social and economic development of the Third World.

Gladwin, Thomas and Ingo Walter. *Multinationals Under Fire*. New York: John Wiley, 1980.

McCormack, Arthur. *Multinational Investment: Boon or Burden for the Developing Countries?* W.R. Grace & Co. (Publications Department, 1114 Avenue of the Americas, New York, NY 10036), 1981. Discusses how multinational companies can aid development and reduce poverty in Third World countries.

Moskowitz, Milton, ed. *Everybody's Business: The Irreverent Guide to Corporate America*. San Francisco: Harper and Row, 1980 (with 1982 update). A profile of the largest U.S. multinational corporations.

Transnational Corporations in World Development. United Nations Centre on Transnational Corporations (United Nations, New York, NY 10017), 1983.

Vernon, Raymond. *Storm over the Multinationals*. Cambridge: Harvard University Press, 1977.

For analysis of developing-country problems with debt, see:

Clausen, A.W. *Third World Debt and Global Recovery*. Washington: The World Bank, 1983. Argues that the debt crisis was only one result of what turned out to be the most severe recession since the Great Depression of the 1930s.

Gwin, Catherine. *Beyond Debt Crisis Management*. Washington: Carnegie Endowment for International Peace, 1984. Includes recommendations for reform at the International Monetary Fund and World Bank.

The World Bank. *World Development Report 1985*. Washington, 1985. A detailed analysis of the origins of the debt crisis and of steps toward revival of capital flows to the developing countries.

Lernoux, Penny. *In Banks We Trust*. New York: Doubleday, 1984. A left-wing populist critique of the big banks, especially their role in developing countries.

The Investor Responsibility Research Council (1319 F St. N.W., Suite 900, Washington, DC 20004) investigates the social impact of specific corporations for subscribing church and university investors. IRRC was founded in 1972 as an independent, nonprofit corporation to conduct research and publish impartial reports on contemporary social and public policy issues and the impact of those issues on major corporations and institutional investors; they are willing to answer inquiries from job seekers too. The Interfaith Center on Corporate Responsibility (475 Riverside Drive, Room 566, New York, NY 10115) publishes a monthly newsletter, *The Corporate Examiner* (annual subscription: $25), on the social performance of major U.S. corporations.

Who's getting the jobs?

Competition for overseas positions has never been more fierce. One factor has been the downturn in international business over the last few years. But even in good times, firms are finding a larger pool of candidates with solid international experience, including foreign-country nationals who possess technical skills and U.S.-style business know-how as well as foreign-language fluency and a built-in understanding of another culture.

Most companies doing business internationally rely mainly on personnel from host countries. U.S. companies do use a higher proportion of U.S. staff in developing countries than in other industrialized countries because technically trained local personnel are not as plentiful as in Europe or Japan. But many developing countries now require foreign firms to rely on local citizens for 80% or more of the company's work force, and, in any case, hiring locally, if possible, is certainly much cheaper than paying U.S. wages and resettling U.S. employees abroad.

The openings for U.S. citizens are mostly executive or other high-level positions. There is seldom any shortage of personnel desiring to go overseas for extended periods of time, so although companies don't always spare their very best people for overseas work, most choose employees who have already served the company for years within the United States. A new recruit with an international background and interests is often put to work in a domestic department at first, with the expectation that he will be given special consideration for international work later. If a company does place a new recruit in its international department, he will normally be based at the company's U.S. headquarters and perhaps travel overseas on occasion for negotiations or conferences.

There are some exceptions to this pattern, mainly among big banks, construction contractors, the travel industry, and consulting firms. This chapter includes sections on these areas of business.

What qualities are firms looking for in persons they send overseas?

- *Work Experience:* A survey conducted by the U.S. Chamber of Commerce reveals that virtually all companies attach prime importance to an individual's previous work experience. They want people who have proven their ability to work in challenging environments. Among recent graduates, a company looks for internship experience that attests to the candidate's interest and ability in a particular business area.

- *Education:* Any candidate for an international assignment must possess top-notch oral and written communication skills. He should also have some educational background in accounting, finance, marketing, management, or engineering. Liberal-arts students interested in business after graduation should take some courses in business.

- *Adaptability:* Firms look for evidence of flexibility and adaptability to alien cultures. They scout out candidates who have an open mind, tolerance for different ways of life, and demonstrated sensitivity to a foreign environment.

- *Language Ability:* Different companies place different degrees of emphasis on foreign-language proficiency, depending partly on how much contact a firm has with local customers. Some companies surveyed, like Eastman Kodak, report that foreign-language proficiency is beneficial, but not among the most critical factors considered in hiring. Lockheed calls foreign-language proficiency "unimportant," while certain commercial banks in New York describe it as "essential" for assignments in some parts of the world.

Where are the jobs?

For lists of corporations involved in international business (and for further discussion of overseas business employment) we highly recommend the chapters on business in Kocher's *International Jobs* and Sheehan's *Careers in International Affairs* (p. 9).

The World Trade Academy Press (50 East 42nd St., New York, NY 10017) specializes in books about firms in international business. These include:

Directory of American Firms Operating in Foreign Countries. 1984. Lists 3200 U.S. corporations and their 21,000 subsidiaries and affiliates in 121 countries. It costs over $100, but many libraries have a copy. Country-by-country listings are also available from World Trade Academy Press.

The Multinational Marketing and Employment Directory. 1982. $90. Describes more than 7500 U.S. corporations. Divided into three sections: the first lists corporations alphabetically; the second arranges them in 40 groups to form a marketing register; the third is a guide for selling skills according to profession and occupation.

The following references also list companies of various types that hire people for international work:

American Register of Exporters and Importers. New York: American Register of Exporters and Importers Corporation, annual. Information on 30,000 manufacturers and export-import firms, organized according to product class.

Cument, E.E. *Exporters' Encyclopedia.* New York: Dun and Bradstreet International, annual. World marketing guide.

Dunning, John H. and John M. Stopford, eds. *World Directory of Multinational Enterprises,* 2nd ed. Detroit: Gale Research Company, 1983. Profiles 500 multinational enterprises with important foreign investments.

Corporations occasionally advertise publicly for international positions. Such advertisements are placed in trade and professional journals, in newspapers such as the *New York Times, Washington Post, Wall Street Journal,* and *International Herald Tribune,* and in regional magazines such as the *Far Eastern Economic Review* and the *Middle East Economic Digest.* Check the classified ads, or place an ad of your own.

The following types of firms offer the bulk of the business employment opportunities in developing countries:

● *Commercial Banks.* See pp. 183-87.

- *Construction Contractors.* See pp. 188-89.

- *Travel and Transportation.* See pp. 189-90.

- *Consulting.* See pp. 190-94.

- *Extractive Industries.* Petroleum companies and mining firms need many on-site managers and technicians for long periods of time. Company policies for hiring overseas personnel vary. Mobil told us that their overseas offices do their own hiring. Exxon, on the other hand, does all its overseas hiring through its New York branch.

- *Manufacturing Firms.* Marketing personnel are most likely to travel extensively in developing countries. Some firms have relocated relatively simple, labor-intensive processes to advanced developing countries, so production people are increasingly involved in overseas travel too.

- *Export-Import Firms.* These companies abound in areas of the country heavily involved in foreign trade. They tend to be small and have little turnover. Three out of every five U.S. exporters have fewer than 100 employees.

Small businesses are more important in international commerce than most people realize. Over 65% of overseas business is performed by companies that are not among the *Fortune* 500. Business International, an organization that analyzes the overseas business environment, predicts that the large multinationals will increasingly find it economical to rely on smaller, more specialized companies rather than trying to manage an entire production process (from raw materials to final product) in-house. This would imply an increasing share of the jobs in international business among small- and medium-sized firms.

You might even be able to go into international business for yourself. Someone with an established domestic business might try exporting to developing countries; someone with experience and contacts in a developing country or region might try importing. David Beckmann's wife, Janet, managed for some years to supplement her teacher's salary by importing and wholesaling jute handicrafts from Bangladesh. In the process, she helped provide employment for several hundred Bangladeshi women (mostly widows in cooperatives).

The Small Business Administration conducts courses and conferences to inform and motivate exporters and potential exporters; provides counseling on whether to expand overseas activities; and offers financial assistance to defray costs of testing, developing, and penetrating international markets. Contact field offices in major U.S. cities or the headquarters at 1441 L St. N.W., Washington, DC 20416.

Another way to find business employment in a developing country might be to search in the country itself, rather than to look in the United States for a job that might eventually take you abroad. If you are traveling abroad and happen to knock on the right door at the right time, you just might stumble onto a position at a U.S. firm's overseas office. But you will probably get a temporary or support-staff position at local wages.

There are 51 U.S. Chambers of Commerce abroad, and you could write or visit one of them for help in finding a job in a particular country or region; see *American Chambers Abroad,* available from the Chamber of Commerce of the United States (1615 H St. N.W., Washington, DC 20062). You could also contact the Department of State commercial officer in a U.S. embassy or consulate abroad; it's part of his or her job to provide U.S. business people with on-the-spot advice, introductions, and marketing assistance.

Commercial banking

Paging through the annual report of any one of the largest commercial banks in the country—referred to as money-center banks—you can see that the international division comprises a sizeable percentage of the bank's total business. New lending to developing countries has been cut drastically since the international debt crisis, however, and the future of international lending by the commercial banks is uncertain. The debt crisis is part of the story, but, in addition, deregulation has introduced a new element of uncertainty into all aspects of U.S. banking. As explained on pp. 174-75, we're relatively bullish about the long-term future of international lending, but if you are considering working for a bank, you will want to scrutinize its intentions for its international division as carefully as you can.

The big international banks hire people (including some relatively young people just coming out of graduate school) specifically for work that involves travel or residence abroad. They say that they look for "the best person, not necessarily the candidate with the top business background." Their philosophy is that they can teach accounting and finance to graduates with an international-affairs background easier than they can teach international relations to business majors. Citibank, for example, will hire someone who has never taken even one business course. But most of its hirees come with some finance background and have already demonstrated an interest and ability for business. Candidates for Citibank's international division are also expected to have some foreign-language proficiency and previous living or working experience overseas.

The larger banks all offer extensive training programs (6 to 20 months) to orient new staff to the bank and teach them the analytical skills required of bankers. These programs consist of intensive coursework (in accounting, finance, and credit analysis) mixed with on-the-job training. Normally, there are separate training tracks for recruits with business degrees and for those with liberal-arts backgrounds. After completing the training program, you may be sent abroad right away to one of the bank's foreign branches, subsidiaries, or representative offices. Or you may be expected to work for several years at U.S. headquarters, while traveling from time to time to overseas offices, before receiving your first assignment abroad.

Regional banks that have international operations usually have more limited training programs, so they favor applicants with business degrees or at least substantial coursework in finance and accounting. The international staff of a regional bank is usually based at the bank's headquarters in the United States.

Listed below are the 20 largest U.S. commercial banks in terms of assets (in billions of dollars):

Citibank NA, New York	120.1
Bank of America NT&SA, San Francisco	104.1
Chase Manhatten NA, New York	80.4

Morgan Guaranty Trust Co., New York	63.5
Manufacturers Hanover Trust Co., New York	62.4
Chemical Bank, New York	51.2
Bankers Trust Co., New York	44.1
Security Pacific National Bank, Los Angeles	40.1
First National Bank of Chicago	35.0
Continental Illinois NB&T Co., Chicago	30.0
Mellon Bank NA, Pittsburgh	24.5
Wells Fargo Bank NA, San Francisco	24.0
Crocker National Bank, San Francisco	22.0
Marine Midland Bank NA, Buffalo	21.7
First Interstate Bank of California, Los Angeles	20.0
First National Bank of Boston	18.4
Irving Trust Co., New York	16.5
Bank of New York	14.7
Republic Bank Dallas NA	14.4
Texas Commerce Bank NA, Houston	12.1

Since the top 10 banks all have substantial overseas activities, we describe these banks (in alphabetical order) below:

Bank of America (Professional Recruitment, Bank of America, P.O. Box 37000, San Francisco, CA 94137). Bank of America is one of the world's largest privately owned banks. The World Banking Division offers the best opportunities for international placement. This division is organized into four geographic units: Asia; Europe, Middle East, and Africa; Latin America; and North America. The bank prefers candidates with previous background in finance, accounting, or economics.

Banker's Trust (College and University Relations, Banker's Trust Company, 280 Park Ave., New York, NY 10015). Banker's Trust concentrates its efforts and resources on wholesale financial services, providing the market capabilities and career opportunities of commercial banks as well as traditional investment banks. The bank has a network of branches, subsidiaries, representative offices, and affiliates in almost 40 countries worldwide. International loans amount to over half of the bank's total loans. The hiree is not generally guaranteed entry into the international department. Instead, placement decisions are made after the conclusion of the formal training program. This program lasts four months for M.B.A.'s and seven months for non-M.B.A.'s.

Chase Manhattan Bank (Professional Recruitment, The Chase Manhattan Corporation, One Chase Manhattan Plaza—27th floor, New York, NY

10081). Chase has one of the most extensive global networks, with offices in more than 100 countries. Its international earnings in recent years have represented over half the bank's total earnings. The entry-level training program at Chase, which can last from 10 to 14 months, is reputed to be one of the most complete and rigorous in the banking world.

Chemical Bank (College Recruitment Department, Chemical Bank, 277 Park Ave., New York, NY 10172). Chemical's International Division represents an increasingly important segment of the bank's operations and earnings. International loans make up over 40% of the bank's total loans. Latin America is perhaps the area of Chemical's deepest market penetration, while Asia is slated as the primary future growth area. If hired into an international division, you normally spend two to four years in New York before going overseas.

Citibank (Manager, External Recruiting, Mezzanine, Citicorp, 399 Park Ave., New York, NY 10043). Citicorp, the holding company for Citibank, has 1603 offices in 94 countries. Referred to as "the bank for all," Citicorp is the largest financial-services organization in the United States and the largest international bank in the world. The Institutional Banking group is responsible for worldwide business, providing a full range of services to corporations, governments, nonprofit organizations, and financial institutions outside the United States. This group is subdivided into five groups, four serving geographic areas: the North American Banking Group; the Asia/Pacific Banking Group; the Caribbean, Central and South American Banking Group (Citibank is the largest international bank in this part of the world); and the Europe, Middle East and Africa Banking Group.

Continental Bank (Manager, College Relations, Continental Illinois Corporation, 231 South LaSalle St., Chicago, IL 60693). Continental maintains an overseas network of subsidiaries, branches, and offices in 39 countries. The International Banking Department, however, had to cut back expansion of its operations due to the bank's recent management difficulties. Candidates interested in the international area are hired into the General Banking Services Department, where they participate in a seven-month training program. Decisions for first assignments are made in the final weeks of training. Those recruits placed with the International Department normally spend several years at U.S. headquarters before being sent abroad.

First Chicago (College Recruitment Manager, The First National Bank of Chicago, One First National Plaza, Suite 0001, Chicago, IL 60670). First Chicago recently established a threefold strategic goal: to be a world class money-center bank with national and international reach, to be the premier bank in the Midwest, and to be the leader in bringing banking services to the Chicago community. Foreign loans make up over a third of the bank's loan portfolio. With some 46 banking locations overseas, First Chicago hires 10-15 people a year into the international division. The Relationship Manager Development Program can last anywhere from 7 to 13 months. International hirees are generally sent abroad soon after completion of the training program.

Manufacturers Hanover (College Relations Staff, Manufacturers Hanover Trust Company, 350 Park Ave., New York, NY 10022). With a worldwide organization that connects over 100 facilities in more than 40 countries, Manufacturers Hanover is committed to being the premier operating bank for business, banks, and central governments around the world. In recent years, the Corporation's average loan portfolio has had one of the leading performances among major banking corporations in the United States. Overseas deposits alone are greater in size than the total deposits of the tenth largest bank in the United States. Candidates must demonstrate an interest in international business and be fluent in a foreign language. A knowledge of accounting, finance, and political science is helpful.

Morgan Guaranty (Corporate Recruiting, Morgan Guaranty Trust Company, 23 Wall St., New York, NY 10015). J.P. Morgan and Company is the bank holding company whose principal subsidiary is Morgan Guaranty Trust Company. Since the bank's customers are predominantly corporations and institutions, Morgan is referred to as "the corporate bank." The best opportunities for international assignment lie with the Banking Division, which is organized into four groups along primarily geographic lines. After completion of the 8- to 10-month Commercial Bank Management Program, you generally serve a first assignment in the United States before becoming eligible for overseas positions.

Security Pacific (College Relations Director, Employment Division, Security Pacific National Bank, 333 South Hope St., Los Angeles, CA 90051). Security Pacific has a record of substantial involvement in international banking. The International Department now recruits five to six people annually. The bank prefers recruits with a business and international studies background. The World Banking System Training Program consists of training modules, self-instructional and workshop resources, on-the-job work, and performance evaluations. Trainees are assigned to line units from date of hire. The M.B.A. trainee will be expected to complete the program within 12 months; the undergraduate trainee will probably finish the program in 15 to 20 months.

Construction contracting

Construction contracts call for the sudden recruitment of small armies of engineers, supervisors, and workers for relatively short periods of time. Most of the opportunities are in Pacific Asia and the Middle East. It's simply a matter of economics: international contracting thrives where there is money. The Pacific Asia region is enjoying rapid economic growth again, and although the Middle East is no longer awash with liquidity, petrodollars still bring contracting work to the area. There are few new projects in those parts of the developing world, notably Africa and Latin America, that are still hobbled with economic and financial difficulties.

Virtually all the employment opportunities for U.S. citizens are at the management/professional level. Engineers and health-care professionals are most in demand. A spokesman for Bechtel, the largest international contractor, told us that there are relatively few opportunities abroad for laborers from the United States. It is much less expensive to employ "third-country nationals" (for example, migrants from Pakistan for a U.S.-managed project in Saudi Arabia).

Contractors don't usually hire anyone until they have been awarded a contract. They keep an inventory of people and draw on that first when they are in a position to hire. They also advertise positions in technical or trade journals. *Engineering News Record* (P.O. Box 430, Hightstown, NJ 08520) is the major weekly of the heavy construction business, and contractors often use it to advertise openings for engineers. They often advertise health care positions in the magazine *Hospitals*.

The Construction Men's Association (P.O. Box 691, Canal Street Station, New York, NY 10013) provides job information on overseas construction projects. You might also read:

The Construction Employment Guide in the National and International Field. New York: World Trade Academy Press (50 East 42nd St., New York, NY 10017), 1979 (with new edition under preparation). $15. Lists U.S. contractors with projects overseas by country, describing compensation, fringe benefits, and other features of overseas employment.

Foreign Projects Newsletter (Richards Lawrence & Co., P.O. Box 2311, Van Nuys, California 91404). Biweekly. Offers information on contracts awarded to U.S. and foreign firms abroad.

Summary of Future Construction Projects Abroad (International Liaison and Trade Opportunities, U.S. Department of Commerce, Office of Business Services, Washington, D.C. 20230).

Travel and transportation companies

Many people are attracted to travel businesses by the opportunities they offer for employee travel. Most opportunities are with the airlines, shiplines, and tourism.

Airlines: The international airlines employ pilots and copilots (with previous flying experience in the military), flight attendants, agents, and ground crew. The chances of spending much time abroad are better for the flight crews, of course, and even they tend to be in one place for only a day or two at a time. Deregulation has led to bankruptcy for at least one international airline, but a few of the more competitive airlines are doing well.

Shiplines: There are about 39,000 people working on U.S. ocean-going ships, and many more serve on ships registered under foreign flags. They spend most of their work time at sea, and their contacts with people in the port cities tend to be somewhat cursory. They do, however, perform an essential service for the developing countries and the rest of the world.

There is some opportunity for casual or short-term labor as a seaman. You must get your seaman's papers from the Coast Guard, join the union, and wait at the union hall to be shipped out by one of the steamship companies. There are some tanker companies, such as Atlantic Richfield, Getty, and Mobil, that don't require you to be a labor-union member. The best way to become an officer is through the Merchant Marine Academy in Kings Point, New York, where admission is by congressional nomination, or through one of six state maritime academies for engineer officers.

For more information about working in the Merchant Marine, write: Office of Maritime Labor and Training, Maritime Administration, U.S. Department of Transportation, 400 Seventh St. S.W., Room 7302, Washington, DC 20590. Ask for a pamphlet called *Information Concerning Employment and Training Opportunities in the U.S. Merchant Marine.*

Tourism: Travel agents are often offered free or inexpensive trips and tours on a promotional basis, and they can sometimes lead tours abroad themselves. These opportunities are limited to experienced agents, and deregulation of the airlines has also introduced more uncertainty into the travel-agency business. But the possibility of cheap travel still attracts enough hopeful beginners to keep wages for starting agents low.

The same dynamic has made it almost impossible to make one's living as a travel writer. Plenty of people are glad to write about faraway places for almost nothing.

U.S.-owned hotels abroad often have a few of their experienced staff from the United States in managerial positions.

For more information on travel businesses, see Robert Scott Milne's *Opportunities in Travel* (V.G.M. Career Horizons, 8259 Niles Center Road, Skokie, IL 60076).

Consulting

Consulting is business, but an unusual kind of business. Consultants sell themselves—their advice and management skills.

Consultants come in all stripes. Some work as individuals, some in small firms, and some in giant firms of more than 1000 professionals. Some consultants serve under two- or three-year contracts, but some are hired for only two or three days. Many consultants work for private firms, either multinationals or local firms, while others work for public agencies. Consulting contracts in the developing countries are often financed by international agencies like AID and The World Bank, but some consulting contracts are financed by private companies or by developing-country governments with purely domestic funds.

Although each consulting contract is relatively short-term, thousands of people have made careers accepting one contract after another. A sanitation engineer might work for three years under contract with the government of Zaire, assisting on a specific project, then accept a two-month assignment with The World Bank in Botswana, then go without work for several months until offered a one-year contract by an engineering firm in Nigeria.

The types of expertise sought among consultants are also extremely varied. Most construction projects are designed and supervised by engineering consulting firms, and the largest accounting firms also have worldwide operations on both an accountacy and management consultancy basis. Companies or agencies usually look to consultants to provide very specialized skills that aren't required often enough to justify a permanent staff position. Thus, general administrators are less in demand as consultants than engineers, financial analysts, architects, economists, or specialists in industry or agriculture. There are also niches in the consulting field for pollution experts, geologists who specialize in predicting earthquakes, specialists in improved pit-latrine technologies—people in all sorts of relatively esoteric fields.

In general, consultants are paid more than their equals in more secure positions. Payment varies depending on experience, length of contract, and the source of the contract, but official agencies often pay $200 to $300 per day for short-term assignments. When budgets shrink, however, or a consultant's ability to produce decreases due to illness or age, no one feels at all obliged to employ him or her. Consultants must always be selling themselves, and, of course, they have less authority to actually act on their recommendations than the business executives or civil servants who hire them.

The supply of consultants far exceeds the demand, and nobody wants to hire an inexperienced consultant. Normally, consultants have graduate degrees and years of relevant experience. Experience in the country or region where the work is to be done, or at least somewhere in the Third World, is valuable. But if, let's say, the government of Indonesia wanted a U.S. real-estate development company to send an experienced employee to advise them about a planned shopping center in Jakarta, someone with relevant technical experience who had never been outside the United States might well be acceptable.

Consulting can, with some luck, be an avenue into development work abroad for bright, young professionals. A visit to the offices of the company, public agency, or international funding source that might be hiring may help a would-be consultant break into the ranks of experienced and proven consultants. Also, consulting firms tend to grow and shrink as contracts come and go, and on the upswing some firms might hire a relatively inexperienced person to supplement a team of senior consultants. The person might, for example, assist in a nine-month feasibility study for a rural-development project in East Africa. If he proves himself, he would probably be rehired by the same firm and would also be more attractive to other firms.

Large contracts with consulting firms are usually awarded on the basis of competitive procedures designed to assure openness and impartiality, and some individual consultants are hired on the strength of their written applications alone. But individual consulting positions are more often offered through networks of people who have come to know each other's work through previous jobs. Of the 3500 individual consulting appointments The World Bank makes each year, for instance, perhaps three-quarters go to consultants who have either consulted for the Bank before or are personally known by Bank staff. Since most World Bank consultants work for only a few weeks per contract, usually overseas and under pressure, the responsible staff are naturally hesitant to depend on anyone inexperienced or unknown. Successful performance in a short assignment is likely to lead to another assignment.

Many consultants affiliate themselves more or less permanently with a consulting firm because a firm can provide them some security. The firm gets a share of what its associates earn, but also helps them find work and sometimes provides them some salary during the months between contracts.

A firm called PADCO might be taken as an example of the many consulting firms that work entirely on Third World development. PADCO is small and highly respected. It specializes in urban and regional planning in developing countries. PADCO includes 30 people, 24 of them professionals (of which 11 are permanent staff and 13 hired for specific projects). Eighteen of PADCO's staff members presently live in developing countries, and U.S.-based staff normally travel in developing countries between 90 and 120 days a year. In hiring, PADCO requires at least two years of overseas work experience; a graduate degree in planning, economics, or a technical field; and the ability to speak a foreign language. Since PADCO is moving toward less traditional urban planning and project-related work and toward more policy and institutional analysis, they are also shifting their skill mix more toward finance and economics. PADCO seldom hires inexperienced people, even as interns.

A firm called Development Associates is, in some ways, representative of the larger group of consulting firms that work both in the United States and abroad. Development Associates has 100 staff (75 of them professionals), plus a roster of more than 250 specialists they can contact when need arises. About half of Development Associates' work is in developing countries, mostly in areas such as community development, education, health, private-sector development, and administration. Only five of their staff are living in developing countries, but U.S.-based staff normally go abroad on short-term assignments about once a month. In hiring, Development Associates requires at least a college degree, one foreign language, and overseas experience of five years. They use interns or relatively inexperienced staff, but infrequently.

There are thousands of consulting firms, so individuals will want to focus on a few firms in their field of interest. Information about firms can be garnered by word of mouth, from trade journals, or in the following references:

Federal Register. Frequently lists the consulting contracts awarded by U.S. government agencies. Check for a copy at your local library.

International Engineering Directory. American Consulting Engineers Council (Suite 802, 1015 Fifteenth St. N.W., Washington, DC 20005). $15. Lists about 70 firms, with information on services offered, branch offices, personnel, and selected projects.

Wasserman, Paul and Janine McLean. *Consultants and Consulting Organizations Directory.* Detroit: Gale Research Company, 1985. Lists more than 8500 firms, individuals, and organizations active in 116 fields. Organized alphabetically, geographically, and by activity.

Gerard Sheehan's book (p. 9) also includes a good list of some of the larger consulting firms.

Many Third World governments urge international consulting firms to work together with local consulting firms, and training of local staff is often included as an explicit part of the consultants' responsibility. As countries have gradually developed a larger pool of technically qualified local people, they have become less dependent on foreign firms for relatively conventional work (like standard engineering design). But the use of foreign consultants by developing countries has continued to increase, with highly specialized and sophisticated knowledge increasingly in demand.

The typical consulting contract in developing countries over most of the past generation would have called for an engineering firm to plan and estimate costs for a civil-works project, perhaps a road or dam, and then supervise the construction companies actually executing the plan. But as development projects have evolved, so has the role of consultants. In the 1970s, development-assistance agencies and many developing countries intensified direct efforts to include low-income groups in the process of development. There was continuing demand for engineering consultants to design roads and turbines, but a larger share of consulting business went to people who could give helpful advice on ways to assist small farmers, devise low-cost improvements to local technologies, design projects adapted to particular sociocultural realities, and contribute to the evolution of more effective national institutions.

The general crisis in Third World development in the early 1980s provoked another shift in priorities. The developing countries and institutions that assist them, like The World Bank, might well begin seeking more financial analysts to help with debt management and economists to help plan programs of policy reform (changes in trade policy, for example) to revive economic growth.

Another relatively recent development is increasing demand by multinational corporations for political risk analysis. Political risk analysis involves investigation of how political and economic factors in a country might affect a particular firm's manufacturing or marketing activities. Some firms are hiring more people with graduate degrees in political science, economics, or international relations to do political risk analysis in-house. Other firms are relying on consultants to do this kind of work for them, especially since there is disagreement within the business community as to whether political risk analysis is a passing fad or here to stay. For further information on this subject, you might read Theodore Moran's *International Political Risk Assessment: The State of the Art* (Washington: Landegger Papers, School of Foreign Service, Georgetown University, 1981) or contact the Society for Risk Analysis (1340 Old Chain Bridge Road, Suite 300, McLean, VA 22101).

Networks of contacts

The U.S. Department of Commerce helps business people make contacts and get current information on overseas markets. They sponsor trade missions to other countries, international trade fairs, and trade seminars and export conferences in major industrial centers throughout the United States. They also publish *Commerce Today* and *Business America,* both weekly magazines about international trade, and a long series of related publications, including background studies on particular countries and commodities. For advice or publications, contact Commerce field offices in major U.S. cities or: Bureau of International Commerce, The Department of Commerce, 14th and Constitution Ave. N.W., Washington, DC 20230.

The National Governors' Association also sponsors international business opportunities conferences, mainly for small- to medium-sized manufacturers, and most states have development agencies that provide some international business assistance.

Chambers of commerce can give you helpful information too. Most local chambers of commerce have foreign-trade departments. Big city chambers are well-equipped to provide information and help their members make contacts abroad. The Chamber of Commerce of the United States (1615 H St. N.W., Washington, DC 20062) publishes a useful pamphlet called *Employment Abroad: Facts and Fallacies.* Other publications available from the U.S. Chamber include *Foreign Commerce Handbook* and *Guide to Foreign Information Services.*

An increasingly important resource is the nationwide network of world-trade clubs. New trade clubs have sprouted up across the country as business has become more aware of the importance of exports. At last count, there were trade clubs in 32 states. Several large cities have more than one club, with the different groups overlapping to some extent, but tending to represent different parts of the international trade constituency. Some clubs have full-time staff. By attending the functions of trade clubs, you can familiarize yourself with the opportunities available in your area for overseas business involvement. Most trade clubs also have publications that might prove helpful.

You can find out about other trade clubs in your area from the Department of Commerce district office, but some of them are listed here:

Alabama

Birmingham Area Chamber of
Commerce
P.O. Box 10127
Birmingham, AL 35202

Center for International Trade and
Commerce
University of South Alabama
Mobile, AL 36688

Arizona

Arizona World Trade Association
34 West Monroe, Suite 900
Phoenix, AZ 85003

Arkansas

Arkansas Exporters Round Table
1650 Union National Bank Building
Little Rock, AR 72201

California

International Business Association
of Long Beach
c/o Long Beach Area Chamber
of Commerce
50 Oceangate Plaza
Long Beach, CA 90802

Los Angeles Area of Chamber of
Commerce
International Commerce Executive
Committee
404 S. Bixel St.
Los Angeles, CA 90051

Foreign Trade Association of
Southern California
333 S. Flower St., Suite 226
Los Angeles, CA 90071

Export Managers Association of
California
10919 Vanowen St.
North Hollywood, CA 91605

Fresno County and City Chamber
of Commerce
P.O. Box 1469
Fresno, CA 93716

World Trade Association of San
Diego
110 W. "C" St., Suite 1600
San Diego, CA 92101

Colorado

Denver Chamber of Commerce
International Trade Committee
1301 Welton St.
Denver, CO 80204

Connecticut

Connecticut International Trade
Association
c/o Colt Industries
Huyshope Ave.
Hartford, CT 06114

Connecticut Foreign Trade
Association
c/o Manufacturers Association of
South Connecticut
608 Ferry Boulevard
Stratford, CT 06497

Florida

International Center of Florida
Suite 280, Gables One Tower
1320 South Dixie Highway
Coral Gables, FL 33146

Space Coast World Trade Council
1005 East Strawbridge Lane
Melbourne, FL 32901

Florida Exporters-Importers
Association
P.O. Box 450648
Miami, FL 33145

Orlando International Trade Center
4805 Sandlake Road
Orlando, FL 32809

World Trade Council of Palm Beach
County
3601 Broadway
Riviera Beach, FL 33404

Sun Coast Export Council
c/o Petersburg Area Chamber of
Commerce
225 Fourth St., South
St. Petersburg, FL 33701

Georgia

Georgia Chamber of Commerce
1200 Commerce Building
Atlanta, GA 30335

Hawaii

Hawaii World Trade Association
735 Bishop St., Suite 220
Honolulu, HI 96813

Idaho

Idaho World Trade Association
Box 660
Twin Falls, ID 83301

Illinois

International Business Council
  Midamerica
401 North Wacker Drive
Chicago, IL 60611

International Business Council
  Trade Club
401 North Wabash Ave.
Suite 538
Chicago, IL 60611

Indiana

World Trade Club of Indiana
928 Chamber of Commerce
  Building
320 North Meridian St.
Indianapolis, IN 46204

Michiana World Trade Club
230 West Jefferson Boulevard
P.O. Box 1677
South Bend, IN 46634

Louisiana

World Trade Club of Greater New Orleans
Suite 1132, International Trade Mart
2 Canal St.
New Orleans, LA 70130

Maryland

Export Club of Baltimore
326 Charles St.
Baltimore, MD 21201

Maryland International Trade
  Association
210 East Lombard St.
Baltimore, MD 21202

Suburban Maryland International Trade Association
200A Monroe St., Suite 225
Rockville, MD 20850

Massachusetts

International Business Center of New England, Inc.
22 Batterymarch
Boston, MA 02109

Michigan

Western Michigan World Trade
Club
7373 Fulton - Building 342A
Ada, MI 48355

World Trade Club of Detroit
150 Michigan Ave.
Detroit, MI 48226

Minnesota

Minnesota World Trade Association
5235 Xerxes Ave. S.
Minneapolis, MN 55410

Minnesota Association of
Commerce and Industry
480 Cedar St.
St. Paul, MN 55101

Mississippi

International Trade Club of Mississippi, Inc.
P.O. Box 16673
Jackson, MS 39236

Missouri

World Trade Club of St. Louis, Inc.
7730 Carondelet Ave., Suite 106
St. Louis, MO 63105

Montana

Montana International Trade Commission
Suite 415, Power Block
Helena, MT 59601

Nevada

Nevada World Trade and International Tourism Association
P.O. Box 7534
Las Vegas, NV 89101

New York

Buffalo World Trade Association
146 Canterbury Square
Williamsville, NY 14221

American Association of Exporters
and Importers
11 West 42nd St.
New York, NY 10036

National Association of Export
Management Companies, Inc.
200 Madison Ave.
New York, NY 10016

North Carolina

North Carolina World Trade Association
P.O. Box 10387
Raleigh, NC 27605

Ohio

The International Business and
Trade Association
Akron Regional Development
Board
8th Floor, One Cascade Plaza
Akron, OH 44308

Greater Cleveland Growth
Association
Cleveland World Trade Association
690 Union Commerce Building
Cleveland, OH 44115

Dayton Area Chamber of
Commerce
World Trade Council
Suite 1980
Winters Bank Tower
Dayton, OH 45423

Greater Cincinnati Chamber of
Commerce
World Trade Club
120 West 5th St.
Cincinnati, OH 45202

Columbus Area Chamber of
Commerce
World Trade Club
37 North High St.
Columbus, OH 43216

Toledo Area International Trade
Association
218 Huron St.
Toledo, OH 43604

Oregon

Pacific Northwest International Trade Association
200 S.W. Market St., Suite 220
Portland, OR 97201

Pennsylvania

World Trade Association of
Philadelphia, Inc.
717 Land Title Building
Philadelphia, PA 19110

World Affairs Council of Pittsburgh
One Oliver Plaza, Suite 310
Pittsburgh, PA 15222

Tennessee

World Trade Council of
Chattanooga
1001 Market St.
Chattanooga, TN 37402

Memphis World Trade Club
P.O. Box 3577
Memphis, TN 38103

World Trade Council of
   Middle Tennessee
P.O. Box 17367
Nashville, TN 37217

Texas

International Trade Association of
   Dallas, Inc.
P.O. Box 672
Dallas, TX 75221

World Trade Association
1520 Texas Ave.
Houston, TX 77002

Export-Import Club of Fort Worth
P.O. Box 27372
Fort Worth, TX 76102

Utah

World Trade Association of Utah
P.O. Box 26774
Salt Lake City, UT 84126

Virginia

Piedmont Foreign Trade Council
P.O. Box 1374
Lynchburg, VA 24505

Hampton Roads Foreign Commerce
   Club
P.O. Box 1263
Norfolk, VA 23501

Northern Virginia International
   Trade Association
c/o Virginia National Bank
6830 Old Dominion Drive
McLean, VA 22101

Virginia World Trade Committee
Virginia State Chamber of
   Commerce
611 E. Franklin St.
Richmond, VA 23219

Washington, D.C.

International Trade Association
1800 M St. N.W., Suite 1030N
Washington, DC 20036

West Virginia

West Virginia Small Business Development Center
The University of Charleston
2300 MacCorkle Ave. SE
Charleston, WV 25304

Wisconsin

Madison International Trade
  Association
P.O. Box 90
Madison, WI 53701

Milwaukee World Trade
  Association
756 N. Milwaukee St.
Milwaukee, WI 53202

Western Wisconsin World Trade
  Association
First Wisconsin—Eau Claire
Box 7
Eau Claire, WI 54702

Some Practical Matters

U.S. citizens living and working abroad enjoy substantial tax advantages. The first section of this chapter discusses these advantages and also gives advice on how to save money on airfares.

The second section is about the delights and problems of living in a foreign environment, and the third section is more specifically about living in an environment that includes many poor people. Living in the Third World is not like trying *sushi;* it demands a major adjustment in life-style, and you can't drop it for something different the next day if it doesn't meet your tastes. So if you are thinking about going abroad, it helps to know what you are getting into. If your expectations are unrealistic, you are likely to become dissatisfied and do less well at the task for which you go to the Third World.

Taxes and discount travel

The Tax Reform Act of 1981 made working abroad much more attractive financially. Proponents of favorable tax treatment for U.S. citizens living and working overseas argue that many other countries give tax advantages to their citizens and companies doing business abroad, and that U.S. companies had been losing business because U.S. tax law used to make it too expensive for them to send their personnel abroad.

But as of 1985, a U.S. citizen can exclude the first $95,000 of income earned abroad from his taxable income. If his annual housing costs exceed about $7000, he can exclude those additional housing costs. If his employer provides him or his family meals and lodging (on business premises and for reasons of business convenience), that income can be excluded from taxable income too.

To qualify for the full amount of these exclusions, you must be a bona fide resident of another country for an entire tax year, or be physically absent from the United States for 330 days of any 12-month period. If you are a resident of another country or physically absent from the United States for a shorter period of time, you can still claim a prorated share of the exclusions. If you are not covered by these exclusions but pay tax to another government on income earned abroad, you can subtract that tax amount from your U.S. tax bill. Income that the U.S. government itself pays its employees cannot be excluded from their taxable income.

For full details, read Internal Revenue Service Publication 54, *Tax Guide for U.S. Citizens and Residents Abroad*. This publication offers the following illustrated example of what these tax advantages can mean. The example is so striking that we quote from pp. 11-12 of IRS Publication 54 at length:

Jim and Judy Adams are married, with two dependent children. Jim is a petroleum engineer. He works primarily in the Persian Gulf region. His salary amounted to $82,000. In addition, his employer provided him an annual housing allowance of $18,000, which he used to maintain a rented apartment at his tax home in Country X. At various times during the year, Jim worked at remote oil drilling sites in nearby countries. While he worked at these remote sites, his employer provided him lodging and meals at nearby camps. Jim determines that the fair market value of the lodging and meals in these camps was $3000.

Because of adverse conditions in Country X, Judy and the children lived in Paris, France, while Jim worked in the Middle East. Judy had a job as an executive secretary with a U.S. company in Paris. Her earnings from this job were $25,000. These earnings were subject to French income tax. The Adams family rented an apartment in Paris during 1983 for Judy and the children. They paid $750 a month rent, including utilities, or $9000 for the year. The Adamses choose to treat the expenses for the Paris apartment as those for a qualifed second foreign household, because conditions at Jim's tax home in Country X are considered to be adverse.

The Adamses also had U.S. interest income of $7500. Including that and Jim's $18,000 housing allowance, their total income was

$132,000. IRS Publication 54 explains how this family is able to claim exclusions and deductions of $125,000, so that their adjusted gross income is only the $7,500 of interest income! IRS Publication 54 concludes:

> After subtracting $1000 for each of their four exemptions, Jim and Judy arrive at taxable income of $3500. The tax on this amount, from the Tax Table, is $14.

You can also save money (although not on such a lavish scale) on international travel. Most important, you need to be familiar with the rules and regulations regarding international airfares.

The main factor that determines a normal, economy-class international fare is the airline you choose to cross the Atlantic or Pacific. Different airlines charge significantly different amounts, and the rest of your fare will also be constructed according to the rules of your transoceanic carrier.

You should know, too, that an international ticket from Point A to Point B normally allows you to make intermediate stops along the way at no extra cost, as long as your total mileage does not exceed a permitted maximum. If your mileage does exceed the maximum by 5, 10, 15, 20, or 25 percent, your fare goes up by the same percentage. A businessman on a tight schedule would probably need to fly directly from Point A to Point B, but if you have time and curiosity to wander, check various combinations of intermediate stops.

There are several ways to calculate a given international itinerary. An apparently simple question like, "How much more would it cost me to go to Calcutta too?" may require your travel agent to do more than a little research and recalculation. He or she may get impatient about exploring options sooner than you do. Try to get your travel agent to answer your questions, but then you may also want to check with another agent or with the airlines themselves.

You could also investigate special fares, charter flights, and student discounts.

Council Travel Services (205 E. 42nd St., New York, NY 10017), a bureau of the Council on International Educational Exchange, provides discount fares for air travel to Europe, Latin America, the

Near East, Africa, and the Orient. They also arrange tours, some of them designed for the 18-35 age group. Biking in China or trekking in Nepal are just two of the hundreds of tours organized by Council Travel. For more information, contact any of the Council offices.

Two other sources of travel information that go way beyond the standard commercial fare are:

Departure, self-billed as the "professional Christian traveler's journal." Offers a wide range of helpful information on domestic and international travel. The subscription price for four issues is $12.97. Write *Departure*, P.O. Box 15360, Richmond, VA 23227. The publisher, Fellowship Travel (8824 Old Mountain Road, Glen Allen, VA 23060), also offers discount fares for groups and individuals. Telephone 800-446-7667.

Transitions Magazine. Another useful guide to travel and study abroad. Four issues a year for $9.50. Order from: 18 Hulst Road, Amherst, MA 01002.

If you want to travel abroad, money shouldn't be an insuperable obstacle. One airline now offers a round-the-world economy class ticket for $2000. Add 50 days' expenses at about $50 a day (an economy budget), and the total, $4,500, is still less than the cost of many used cars. Few Americans need to forego travel because they can't afford it.

A new environment

It is difficult to generalize across the wide variety of Third World situations in which U.S. citizens abroad find themselves. Life in a Latin American city is only faintly comparable to conditions in an African village. A commercial banker and a volunteer schoolteacher will have very different experiences, even in the same country. There are, however, a number of problems and some particular pleasures and conveniences that people from richer countries almost always experience when they move to poorer countries.

Most find great excitement and satisfaction in being exposed to a new environment. They are stimulated by the change in climate, exotic arts, foreign cuisine, and unexpected ways of doing things. At first, everything is remarkable. The mind and senses race. Many

Americans who go to the Third World stay two years or less, so some of the thrill of newness lasts until the end, especially if they take short vacations in neighboring countries or make stopovers on their route back home.

Beyond the excitement of novelty are the deeper, more gradual satisfactions of adjustment. The host culture is in some ways better, more truthful, or more beautiful than U.S. culture. In time Americans come to imitate manners that at first appeared odd and to accept ideas that once seemed bizarre.

Living abroad is also virtually the only way to thoroughly learn another language. Living in Ecuador will turn your school Spanish into a living, practical language. If you know a little French, aim for French-speaking Africa. And if you try to learn an Asian, African, or American Indian language, you will be crossing a barrier that relatively few Europeans and North Americans have crossed. You will find yourself greatly enriched by serious involvement with a non-Western culture.

You can learn a lot in another country, especially during a short visit, without knowing the language. But even in those countries of Asia and Africa where English is the official language, you will be limited to the small and relatively privileged circle of people who speak English. Your contacts with ordinary people will necessarily be limited and superficial. Staying in another country for any length of time without continually trying to learn the language is likely to lead to self-isolation and discontent.

On the other hand, just making the effort to learn the language (especially if it is an African or Asian language that few foreigners have bothered to learn) usually inspires enthusiastic hospitality. The frustration of trying to express more sophisticated ideas with a child's vocabulary in a foreign tongue is often met with incredible patience on the part of the listener. Language learning itself can be a first topic for conversation, giving foreigners and their hosts opportunities to be together, eat together, and cordially study each other in some detail. Only foreigners who finally achieve fluency come close to understanding or feeling at home in another country.

The difficulty of learning a foreign language is part of the broader problem of cultural adjustment. Symbols and social expectations of another culture are like a foreign language. It is tedious, patient work to learn about another culture. The way other people do things may seem unintelligible—like jibberish—at first. As a foreigner, you are almost sure to draw attention to yourself, despite all attempts to blend in with the locals. Linda Powers found that her blond hair was a source of some wonderment in rural Mexico; not a few children sneaked opportunities to touch her hair to see if it was real. Such attention can be fun for a while, but most people experience days when they would rather not be the object of such interest.

The normal cycle for people living in another culture is to be elated at first, but when the initial excitement wears off, to experience frustration, depression, and a sense of superiority and alienation, leading to loneliness. It is only later, at least for those able to weather the period of culture shock, that foreigners obtain a more balanced view, including lasting appreciation for some aspects of the host culture. Their world is enlarged.

A helpful little handbook on cultural adjustment is L. Robert Kohls' *Survival Kit for Overseas Living* (Intercultural Press, Inc., P.O. Box 768, Yarmouth, ME 04096). Kohls is Director of Training and Development for the U.S. International Communication Agency. We also recommend Henri J. Nouwen's *Gracias! A Latin American Journal* (New York: Harper and Row, 1983), reflections of a U.S. Christian living in the slums of Lima, Peru.

It is often difficult for both husband and wife to find employment in another country. Foreigners cannot normally take jobs without work permits, and the host country normally doesn't issue a work permit to the spouse; the United States, for example, doesn't allow the spouses of foreign diplomats to enter the job market in our country. Even if there is no work-permit problem, the spouse may be frustrated by local certification requirements in certain fields or by the more obvious difficulties of looking for a job in a faraway place. If the husband is in the Foreign Service, for example, and is required to move repeatedly—from Khartoum, to Washington, to Caracas, to Washington, to Bonn, and so on—it's hard to imagine many careers that the wife could successfully pursue. Employers can sometimes be persuaded to provide employment at one overseas post for both husband and wife, or at least to give the unemployed spouse some help in finding a job, but that's still the exception rather than the rule.

Foreigners can also expect special regulations on their financial affairs (laws pertaining to business organization, land ownership, and profit expatriation), and they are, of course, excluded from full participation in the political processes of their host countries.

The authorities of some developing countries punish certain legal infractions, drug abuse for example, more severely than the United States does. In some countries, especially if the political situation of a country is tense, you may need to remember that local friends have to be careful about expressing political opinions.

Finally, Christians who are drawn to serve in countries torn by violence subject themselves to special risks. As Paul McCleary, then director of Church World Service, reported to his board of directors:

The continued fighting in the Middle East and Central America has not by-passed the church but engulfed it. In the past, the biblical passage most frequently associated with the service ministries of compassion of the church has probably been the story of the good Samaritan. Let me suggest that it may sometimes be more appropriate to focus our understanding on the story of Stephen, the first Christian martyr.

Surrounded by poverty

Living in the Third World means not only adjustment to a new environment, but to a society in which the majority are poor. The ill effects of poverty cannot be entirely avoided even by relatively rich foreigners in a poor country.

Most seriously, it may be more difficult to stay healthy than in the United States. Change itself—changed climate, water, personal hygiene—may upset health, and people who go to poor countries, especially people who mingle with the poor, take extra risks. Inoculations and rudimentary caution reduce the risk, but water and some food contain bacterias to which our systems have not built up immunities. A certain amount of diarrhea must be expected, and there is a chance of contracting a serious disease. In some parts of the Third World, medical facilities are inadequate and inaccessible. In case of serious illness, Americans can usually afford to fly to medical facilities in the capital city or another country, but poor local facilities do increase the danger of medical emergencies.

Crime rates are lower in many developing countries than in the United States. But as a foreigner, you'll probably stand out in a crowd, and thieves expect that a traveling American will have something valuable to steal. In some Third World countries, women, especially foreign women, are sometimes the target of off-color remarks from passersby, and a young American woman might face a higher risk of physical attack than she would in the United States.

People from developed countries also sometimes have difficulty finding the schools they want for their children. Children usually adjust easily and learn much in a foreign culture, but parents may be concerned that local schools are not of the same quality as U.S. schools, or that local curriculum and pedagogy will not prepare their children for a later return to U.S. schools. The U.S. government provides dependents' schools in most places where it has stationed large numbers of its military or civilian personnel, and other foreigners are served by the "international schools" in many Third World cities. Parents working in remote areas may need to tutor small children themselves and send older children to boarding schools within the region.

Luxury goods may not be available in countries where few people can afford them. Don't expect up-to-date movies, a wide selection in retail shops, fine libraries, or the other stimulations of urbane affluence in Bangladesh or Burundi.

Americans, in particular, tend to be frustrated by widespread inefficiencies in most Third World countries. An hour at the post office or a day at the car repair shop can be agony for the American who can't slow down and can't tolerate everyone else's apparent lack of concern about time.

Selfishly speaking, there are also some advantages to living among people who are relatively poor.

Wealth implies status, so relatively rich foreigners are often accorded respect they would not receive at home. They are placed in seats of honor at feasts. They are sometimes sold tickets out of turn, even if there is no room on the bus for "ordinary people."

As long as the U.S. dollar remains strong, a U.S.-dollar salary will buy more in most foreign countries than it would in the United States. More generally, labor-intensive goods and services, very expensive in the United States, are affordable where wages are lower. Almost any U.S. citizen in the Third World can afford at least one servant. "Rich" foreigners will be sought after by many people eager to do their cooking, washing, driving, or cleaning for very low wages. Shoe repair, stitchery, handicrafts, jazz bands, ditch digging, carpentry, haircuts, door-to-door sales—anything that is labor intensive—will be relatively inexpensive.

Some people who have never been to Third World countries may overestimate the difficulties of living there. They have seen photographs of poverty abroad, and photographers tend to focus on whatever is interesting and unconventional; they take pictures of peasants in native dress or of urban slums, not of shopping centers or affluent neighborhoods.

A few U.S. citizens abroad live directly among the poor—in huts, eating simple food, in remote areas. Even in the starkest situations, however, they are never really poor. They have the choice of being there or not, knowledge of the wider world, high status, and access to money. They are knowledgeable about hygiene and disease. From time to time they go on leave and splurge on movies, air-conditioning, and good food. More people from the United States in Third World countries live in modest affluence—in a properly built house with screens or maybe air-conditioning, with adequate furniture and appliances, without some of the comforts of home, but perhaps with a cook or maid. Finally, some U.S. citizens enjoy a much higher standard of living in the Third World than they would at home. Their employer may ship all their furniture, maybe even U.S. foods and entertainment, and pay them extra salary for living abroad.

It is not for those who are even more comfortably distant from the poor to criticize U.S. citizens abroad who spend flagrantly, surround themselves with servants, and remain remote from the life experiences of most of the people around them. People looking for their own niche abroad, however, may want to steer a more careful course between hardship and palatial isolation. And whatever their relative standard of living materially, Christians will want to treat people who have much less with sensitivity and respect.

ELEVEN

A Christian Rationale

Why might Christians be especially eager for opportunities to live and work in developing countries? Because developing countries are the scene of some of God's most dynamic activities in the contemporary world.

First, economic development among the poor peoples of the world is surely a blessing from God. It is not God's intention for people to have too little to eat, the condition of nearly a billion people around the world. It is not God's intention for people to be ignorant— unable to calculate their own best advantage, protect themselves from the powerful, or understand the wider world. Nor is it God's intention that some people should wear browned and tattered clothes, house their families in shacks, and eat monotonous diets, while a privileged minority luxuriates in fashion and waste.

Some people, mostly people who are quite rich and remote from the poor, imagine that the poor are somehow better off in their "traditional" state and that development should not be "imposed" on them. The argument may be valid for a few isolated tribes, but most of the world's poor are scrambling to better their lives. There is no question about their preference for a more balanced diet or for proper clothes and housing. They are almost universally eager to send their children to school. If U.S. Christians in the Third World can, in some small way, assist poor people in reaching such basic aspirations, they are doing God's work. It is especially urgent work in the 1980s, since economic circumstances in many developing countries are now exceptionally harsh.

Second, God is surely present in the magnificent sharing of culture that is under way. We know that God, Father of all the nations, has been involved in the development of each people. We know that Babel, the confusion of tongues, is the result of human arrogance, and that God's intention is for all nations to be united in Christ. The model of the New Creation is the church, a spectacular mix of people from all nations invited together by God's free grace in Christ. We are not compelled to conform to any human custom in order to be united with God and one another.

The modern mix of cultures began in an entirely different spirit— with European imperialism. The conquered peoples of the world were allowed "in" only if they rejected their own traditions, learned a European language, and conformed to European culture and manners. Even then, they were expected to accept the superiority of people with white skin. Others who hadn't had a chance to learn the conquerors' ways were considered uncivilized and crude. The highly literate cultures of China and India were at least somewhat respected, and from about the 1930s anthropologists began to convince the West of the dignity and rationality of the cultures of illiterate peoples. Racism and cultural imperiousness thrived, however, until submerged peoples overthrew the colonial order.

Political independence was accompanied by a revival of cultural self-confidence in the Third World. Racism remained official, explicit policy only in southern Africa. Europeans and North Americans in the Third World had to be less arrogant and more polite if they wanted to stay. As a result, the situation in the Third World is now more conducive to genuine sharing among cultures, rather than to imposing one culture on another.

The industrialized, predominantly white nations have already absorbed more of poor people's cultures than they usually admit. For example, Pentecostalism, a movement that has been rapidly expanding its influence within the churches of North America and Europe, is partly rooted in African religious practice. The music we like, our artistic sensibilities, and even the way we walk and carry our bodies have been influenced by Africa. Hinduism and Buddhism have modified Western religious sensibilities through philosophers such as Schopenhauer and groups such as Christian Science, as well as through explicitly Asian missionary organizations such as Hari Krishna and Transcendental Meditation.

Until recently, however, the spread of non-Western cultural influences always had to overcome the assumption of Western superiority. It is not long since non-Western cultures began to receive the appreciation they deserve. Thus, a prime purpose of a U.S. Christian in a developing country ought to be to listen. Real conversation among cultures, real sharing among peoples, requires Europeans and North Americans to carefully cultivate—make our own—the best in other cultures.

Third, God is present in the developing countries, as elsewhere, in the spread of his Word. Parts of the Third World are readier to receive the Word than Europe and the Americas. In countries that have been nominally Christian for centuries, many people who have virtually no understanding of Christian teaching assume that they learned "all that" as children. It may be that more people in Asia and Africa can really listen to what Christianity has to say. That may be one reason why the church is growing fastest in Africa and Indonesia, while it is losing members in Europe and seems almost stagnant in the Americas. Or perhaps, just perhaps, Europe and the Americas have already had their chance. There may be a limit to God's patience among peoples who have long heard the Word but not kept it.

The Word of God reverberates throughout the Third World, also in distorted forms. The ideologies of modernization—Communism, nationalism, and a host of local varieties—try to reshape traditional cultures to be more rational, progressive, and egalitarian. They convey the ideals of industrialization, the Enlightenment, and the French Revolution, and those ideals are rooted partly in the biblical revelation of God. For example, the ancient people of Israel learned that history had a purpose and was not cyclic (as most ancient peoples thought) because their God moved them forward, unpredictably and irreversibly, toward his great intentions for the world. Today's revolutions and nationalism may be violent and sometimes petty, but they are proclaiming the progressive view of history to many peoples still captured in rigid custom and fatalism.

Similarly, modern egalitarianism is rooted in Old Testament law, which forbade extravagant concentrations of wealth. Greek tyrants and Roman consuls paid their dues of bread and circuses to the plebs, but our sense that egalitarianism is somehow a divine norm is rooted in the Bible. Although the medieval church accommodated itself to feudalism, peasants still knew that in the final judgment serf and lord would stand side by side. When, in modern times, Christendom began to reform itself so that social practice would conform to spiritual insights, biblical egalitarianism was available to justify the political claims of the rising bourgeousie, then of the proletariat, now of the Third World poor.

The church has tended to lag behind in this revolutionary period of world history. Secular reformers have often applied God's Word to social structures more uncompromisingly than have most Christians. One result has been the church's declining credibility. Another result is the violence, one-sidedness, and idolatry of secular ideologies.

Christians in the Third World (including U.S. Christians among them) may have opportunities to share their faith and to demonstrate its radical implications for social reform.

Economic development, sharing of culture, and proclamation of the Word of God—these are noble goals, and U.S. Christians in developing countries have opportunity to serve them. But some forms of U.S. involvement in the developing countries run counter to these goals. In whatever aspect of the U.S. presence abroad they are involved, Christians need to be prayerful and ethically awake.

Given the great potential for the misuse of U.S. power in the developing countries, hesitance in wielding power—humility—may be the best counsel:

- If U.S. citizens want to contribute to economic development, they will be most helpful if they support programs that local people really want or already have underway. Initiatives that foreigners start on their own often fail to respond to local realities and evaporate when foreign financing comes to an end. Foreigners are most effective when they train local people to carry on without foreign help.

- If U.S. citizens want to participate in the sharing of culture, they will be most effective when they listen most of the time—when they learn the local language; enjoy local art, music, and dance; and work to appreciate local morality, religion, and philosophy.

• And if foreigners want to assist with evangelism in developing countries, they will be most effective if they work with and through the local church (pp. 72-74). U.S. Christians in developing countries who are not church professionals could assist local churches in their mission, but, unfortunately, many U.S. Christians in developing countries fail to take part in local church life. Some may not feel comfortable with local practices (a U.S. Catholic, for example, might find some aspects of Catholic church life in Latin America abrasive). More often, U.S. Christians abroad simply "take a vacation" from going to church.

People who have once lived in a developing country are usually never the same again. They are more keenly aware of international interdependence. For them world hunger can never again be a faceless abstraction. So the opportunities for service don't stop when your tour abroad is over. On the contrary.

Back in the United States, you can give money and other support to private agencies that are doing good work in developing countries. You might be able to stay involved in some area of international business that contributes to higher living standards for Third World people. Most important, you can involve yourself in shaping U.S. public opinion and public policy on foreign aid, international trade, and other issues of importance to the developing countries. U.S. government policy on international economic issues makes a big difference to the prospects of poor people around the world.

Some groups are already doing fine work on public policy issues (pp. 63-68), and we urge you to join their efforts. We are convinced that the U.S. churches must become a much, much more effective constituency for poor people in order to be faithful to our Lord during these last years of the 20th century. Christians who have served in developing countries can also serve by becoming lifelong, vigorous advocates for poor people in developing countries.

The possibilities for service in developing countries are real and, potentially, of world historic significance. The challenge is not only to get there (even though that's tough enough), but to be of service. And beyond that, to work—through politics and other means—to make the entire U.S. presence in developing countries more supportive of God's purposes.

Index

Index to activities

Accountancy, 37, 39, 49, 76, 94, 135-38, 140-41, 152, 160, 162, 169, 180, 183-87, 189-91; see also Economics

Administration, 35, 37, 39, 55, 85, 90, 117-18, 128, 133, 138, 140-44, 152, 156, 160, 162; see also Managerial and technical assistance

Agriculture, 28-30, 36-41, 44-48, 50, 57, 59, 70, 76, 79-80, 83, 87, 93-95, 100, 112, 128, 132, 137-38, 140-43, 147, 151, 153, 158, 191, 194; agricultural economics, 46, 49; agronomy, 46, 134, 152; food production, 29, 40, 42, 46-47, 95; research and agricultural education, 45-46, 50, 58, 89, 100, 153; rural development, 29, 42, 44, 46, 50, 59, 132; see also Animal husbandry; Environmental sciences; Managerial and technical assistance

Animal husbandry, 28, 45

Archaeology, 30, 112

Architecture, 59, 112, 134, 151-52, 191

Art, 30, 112, 135, 141, 166

Aviation, 79, 81, 85, 138, 164, 189

Banking, 133, 137, 140-41, 165, 183-87; see also Managerial and technical assistance

Business, 174-202; see also Accountancy; Banking; Construction; Consulting; Economics; Engineering; Extractive industries; Managerial and technical assistance; Secretarial services; Trade; Transportation; Travel services

Cartography, 160

Communication, 35, 39-40, 43, 50, 59, 70, 79-81, 83, 85, 88, 94, 128, 136, 139, 156, 162, 169, 172, 193

Community development. See Socioeconomic development

Computer programming, 43, 59, 128-29, 137, 147, 160, 169, 172

Construction, 30, 37, 39-40, 42, 80-81, 83, 86-87, 89-90, 94-95, 147, 152, 188-89; skilled tradesmen, 37, 59, 76, 82, 147, 152, 162, 188; see also Housing

Consulting, 33, 53, 129, 152, 160, 190-94

Cryptography, 157, 172

Cultural assistance. See Exchange programs and cultural assistance

Demography, 57, 71, 128, 137, 152, 161; see also Family planning

Dentistry, 28, 31, 41, 51-52, 54, 62

Economics, 33, 111, 128, 133-37, 140-42, 147, 151, 154-55, 160, 164-65, 171, 180, 183-87, 191, 193-94; financial analysis and economic planning, 39, 43, 128, 133, 137, 140-43, 151, 154, 164-65, 180, 183-87, 189, 191, 193-94

Editing, 128

Education, 28, 31, 35-42, 44-48, 50, 52, 58-60, 69-71, 76, 79-85, 87-88, 92-95, 99, 101, 112-13, 115-25, 128, 133-35, 137, 140-41, 147, 151-53, 193; blind, education of, 47, 53; development education, 37, 41, 43-44, 50, 59-60; handicapped/rehabilitation education, 36, 45, 52, 54-55, 119, 161; literacy programs, 36, 40, 50, 135; literature/preparation of literacy materials, 40, 50, 79-83, 87-88; peace education, 28, 57, 64, 84; religious education, 48, 80, 82, 88, 94-95; teacher training, 39; university-level teaching, 121-22; see also Public policy; Vocational training; Youth group leadership

Electronics, 59, 158, 160, 169

Energy, 132, 161, 182; see also Extractive industries

Engineering, 28, 59, 80, 95, 112, 128, 134, 137-38, 140-41, 147, 152, 157-58, 160, 165, 169, 172, 180, 188-94

Environmental sciences
ecology, 29, 112, 132, 139, 152, 161, 163-64; environmental sanitation, 42, 45; fisheries, 44, 132, 152, 161, 163; forestation, 38, 41, 45, 132, 152; irrigation/water resource development and management, 38, 41-42, 44-46, 134, 137; land reclamation and regeneration, 38, 41, 163; resource conservation, 42, 45

Evangelism, 31, 72-94; church planting, 80-81, 83-84, 86-89; interchurch aid, 37; ministry to military, 81, 173; pastoral ministry, 92-94

Exchange programs and cultural assistance, 35, 45, 60, 71, 98, 100-102, 104, 111, 135, 143, 155, 166

Extractive industries, 182

Index to nations and territories

Index to organizations